The Anglican Psalter

*The Psalms of David
pointed and edited for chanting
by John Scott*

CANTERBURY
PRESS

The Dean and Chapter of St Paul's
Chapter Office, St Paul's Churchyard, London   EC4M 8AD

© 1997 The Dean and Chapter of St Paul's
First published as *The New St Paul's Cathedral Psalter* 1997
Second impression, with revisions, 2000
Second edition as *The Anglican Psalter*, 2009

ISBN 978-1-85311-988-0

The Anglican Psalter is published by
Canterbury Press Norwich
an imprint of Hymns Ancient & Modern Ltd
13-17 Long Lane, London EC1A 9PN.
Details of grants for bulk purchase by cathedrals, churches,
and similar establishments may be obtained from the distributor.

Music engraving, typesetting and design by Andrew Parker
Printed and bound in Great Britain by
CPI Antony Rowe Chippenham SN14 6LH

PREFACE TO THE SECOND EDITION

The *New St Paul's Cathedral Psalter* first appeared in print in 1997. I am grateful to Canterbury Press for their willingness to produce a second edition, now with a new title, *The Anglican Psalter,* which reflects its wide use in parish churches as well as in cathedrals. The opportunity has been taken to correct a small number of errors which appeared in the original, and the biography of composers has been updated. In all other respects, the Psalter remains true to the original edition, and the basic principle behind the manner of pointing is unaltered, namely, the matching of primary verbal stress to the music. The chant is the vehicle which gives flight to the words, though it remains firmly the servant of the text.

A specific feature of *The Anglican Psalter* is the editing of the chant, where necessary, to enable the words to be sung in a flowing manner without the encumbrance of unnecessary melismas. In performing what Dr Bernard Rose termed 'chant surgery', the editor recognises that his pointing is perhaps more complex than that found in previously published Psalters but has striven, nonetheless, to illuminate the sense and underlying ethos of the text.

I am greatly indebted to Father Andrew Mead, Rector of St Thomas Church, New York, and the Gentlemen and Boys of the St Thomas Choir for so willingly adopting this version of the Psalter as their own.

"A Psalm is the voice of the church. It gladdens Feast Days, it creates the grief which is in accord with God's will, for a psalm brings a tear even from a heart of stone."

St Basil of Caesarea (c.330–378)

John Scott
January 2009
St Thomas Church Fifth Avenue, New York.

No. 132.

FLINTOFT.

Edward Rimbault: *Cathedral Chants, 1844*. Chant by Flintoft. (See Preface example 2 for discussion.)

Preface to the 1997 edition

THE PSALMS have been sung to the glory of the all holy, transcendent God in Temple, Synagogue and Christian Church for century upon century. Though piously described as *The Psalms of David* in the *Book of Common Prayer*, we can doubt personal Davidic authorship without questioning that many psalms date back to the early years of the Israelite monarchy and in their original form were used in the worship of the First Temple at Jerusalem built by King Solomon just over 900 years before the birth of Jesus Christ.

From the beginning most of the Psalms were probably composed for choral use with instrumental accompaniment. The Greek ψαλμοι means 'songs accompanied by string instruments'. Vestigial choral and orchestral directions are still to be found in the Psalter as printed in the Bible. The 'rubrics' preceding Psalms 75 and 76, for example, are addressed to the choirmaster and tell him which tune to use or that the psalm should be accompanied with strings!

The worship of the Christian Church grew out of the Synagogue and Second Temple in which the Psalter remained central. Peter and John, we hear in the Acts of the Apostles, went 'up to the Temple at the hour of prayer, the ninth hour' (3:1). It was the normal practice of Paul to attend the Synagogue on his missionary journeys (17:1-12). Jesus himself regularly shared in the worship of the Synagogue (e.g. Luke 4). Our Lord and his Apostles therefore used the Psalms as an essential part of their regular corporate worship of God. St Mark notes that Jesus and the Disciples sang a hymn after the Last Supper (14:26): this would have been the *Hallel*; Psalms 113-118 sung as a whole at the great Jewish festivals, but particularly appropriate to the Passover because of Psalm 114, *When Israel came out of Egypt*. The Psalms were also part of their personal vocabulary of prayer. Jesus echoes Psalms 22 and 31 in his words from the Cross: 'My God, My God, why hast thou forsaken me' and 'Into thy hands I commend my spirit'. The Passion narratives as a whole contain frequent references to the Psalms.

In using the Psalter in the services of the Church we are therefore at one with those who have worshipped the one true God for almost three thousand years. And we are at one with the Lord of the Church, Jesus Christ, for whom the Jewish Psalter was a treasury of familiar liturgical hymns and a vehicle of prayer at the deepest moments of suffering.

Over the centuries Christians have indeed seen the Psalms as the prayer of Christ and our use of them as uniting us to him. St Augustine of Hippo (d. 430) tells us that the Psalms are the voice of the whole Christ, head and body. In the Psalms, he tells us, Christ 'prays for us and in us and we make our prayer to him. He prays for us as priest, he prays for us as head and we pray to him as our God' *(Enarrationes in psalmos 85, i)*. For all the Fathers of the Church, Christ was mysteriously present in and through the recitation or singing of the Psalms.

For this reason the whole Church has always made the Psalter a major part of its official prayer, most especially the offices of Morning and Evening Prayer, by whatever name they have been known, and in whatever language they have been said or sung. For this reason, through singing the Psalms we are not only joined to Christ but also with Christians throughout history and throughout the world today as each morning and evening the Church offers its one sacrifice of praise.

Admittedly, some psalms do not seem particularly edifying as instruments of prayer. The blessing of those who beat the brains of a Babylonian baby against the stones seems less than Christian (Psalm 137:9). One solution is to omit such verses, as do the modern Roman *Divine Office*, and the *Alternative Service Book* of the Church of England. At St Paul's Cathedral my predecessor as Precentor, Canon John Collins, edited the Psalter in this way, in part following the excisions of the *Proposed Prayer Book of 1928*. Another solution was advocated by C S Lewis, who not only argued that we must see the Psalms in their historical and often primitive setting but also that the same feelings of resentment and revenge are also found in *our* hearts. It is best that the *whole* of us is brought to God, not only in praise and thanksgiving, but also even in frustration, anger and eventual penitence, rather than trying to hide our true self from God, our neighbour, or ourselves.

Lewis says: 'we are, after all, blood brothers to these ferocious, self-pitying, barbaric men' *(Reflections on the Psalms* p. 26). The *New St Paul's Cathedral Psalter* allows either excision or use of these 'imprecatory psalms'.

Another apparent problem for moderns is the fact that the God of the psalms is very much a God of nature and a God of battles: 'Let God arise, and let his enemies be scattered ... magnify him that rideth upon the heavens' (Psalm 68: 1 & 4). We, on the other hand, have largely lost the sense of God's transcendence; that is to say, God's otherness, his lordship over all creation and our total dependence upon him for the whole of our existence. Modern western man has come to regard God as subjective rather than objective; at best a fulfilment of religious emotion and aspiration. Or God is recognised only in the horizontal, human plane of our interpersonal relations. Note the songs and choruses of recent decades which point to God-in-our-neighbour. True as this is, it is not the whole truth. For the Hebrew mind God is always the author of all that is and everything that happens. If, on the contrary, we permit the idea of God to be reduced to our emotions or even to the service of others we devalue ourselves and our neighbour. Only a transcendent Creator can give transcendent worth to his creatures. If we are really all that is, man has neither meaning, purpose nor destiny. The Psalmist's science may be primitive; his sense of God in history somewhat interventionist: but his emphasis on the involvement of God in the natural processes and in human history redeems us from the bleak alternative of nihilism.

But how do we use the Psalms liturgically? When Archbishop Thomas Cranmer translated and adapted the Medieval Service Books he subdivided the Psalter over a month rather than a week. The Roman *Divine Office* followed suit after the Second Vatican Council. The *Alternative Service Book* meagrely offers us the whole Psalter only five times a year. At other times in Christian history other permutations have been devised. In some monastic communities the whole Psalter was said or sung in one day! Only recently however have scholars come to ask radical questions about the principle of using the whole Psalter in its biblical order, *recitatio continua*. In fact this was not how the psalms were used in the earliest daily choral office. This so-called 'Cathedral Office' used a selection of psalms based on the liturgical season, the time of day (morning or evening), or a daily call to praise by the use of psalms 148-150 which went back to the Synagogue itself. The developing monastic communities in East and West subsequently invented the continuous recitation of the Psalter and this eventually displaced the earlier thematic system almost everywhere. A recent office book has been published with the encouragement of the Liturgical Commission of the Church of England which reintroduces the principle of thematic psalmody (*Celebrating Common Prayer*, Mowbray, 1992). The sensitive extension of thematic psalmody, even if it does not replace continuous psalmody entirely, would be a great enrichment of liturgical provision for cathedrals and parish churches. The present St Paul's usage entails the recitation of the Psalter twice a quarter, once at Matins and once at Evensong. Provision for the Greater Festivals has, of course, always been thematic.

The *St Paul's Psalter* makes no apology for the continued use of the Prayer Book version of the Psalms, itself almost identical with that of the Psalter in the Great Bible of 1539 translated by Miles Coverdale. Modern versions are of great value in discovering the meaning of the Hebrew Psalms, where the old may be obscure, but they cannot compare with the euphony and poetic beauty of Coverdale. Anglican use of newer translations for the choral recitation of the Psalter is very rare indeed and it is surely appropriate to use the texts for which most of the chants were actually composed. Moreover, Coverdale translated his Psalter from the Latin rather than the Hebrew. At first sight this may seem a disadvantage. But this traditional Latin text was based upon the Greek version of the Psalter, and consequently reflects a much earlier (and in some places more authentic) Hebrew text than that now extant. Conservatism in translations of the Psalter is notorious. When St Jerome translated the Hebrew Psalter for the Vulgate it was never fully accepted for liturgical use because the earlier Latin version, based on the Greek Septuagint, was already treasured *and memorised*.

The Psalms have always been *sung*. When Jesus read the prophecy of Isaiah in the Synagogue (Luke 4) he probably used a 'cantillation' which a modern Jewish Cantor would still recognise today. Contemporary Jewish free-rhythm chants are clearly related to the 'modes' found in Byzantine and Western chant. All derive from a common stock. Anglican chant, itself originally a harmonised variant of Western plainsong, can thus be seen to be intimately related to the wider tradition of the singing of the Psalms by Jew and Christian. Though it should be remembered that such harmonisation of plainsong is not exclusive to England or Anglicans!

The whole of the *New St Paul's Cathedral Psalter* is in the process of being recorded on tape and CD on the Hyperion label. It will thus be available not only for aesthetic listening, but also for devotional use. Individuals or small groups of priests or lay people can say the offices of Morning and Evening Prayer together and listen meditatively to the Psalms as sung in St Paul's.

In commending the *New St Paul's Cathedral Psalter* I can do no more than say that the day by day experience of Evensong, sung by the Choristers and Vicars Choral of St Paul's using this Psalter as it has evolved experimentally over the years, has not only deeply enhanced my appreciation of the Psalms within the context of the 'common prayer' of the Church but also convinced me that, done well, there is nothing to match the beauty of the best of Anglican Chant. Anglicans possess here a unique blend of objectivity and emotion. I believe the *New St Paul's Cathedral Psalter* will be a valuable instrument for the performance of Anglican Chant and also a means by which the Church will more truly know that Christ 'prays for us and in us and we make our prayer to him'.

Christopher Hill, Bishop of Stafford
Canon Residentiary and Precentor of St Paul's 1989–1996

25th January 1997: The Conversion of St Paul

PREFACE TO THE MUSIC

In the Anglican choral offices of Mattins and Evensong, the singing of the allocated portions of the Psalter on a daily basis to Anglican chant provides for many people the spiritual backbone of this continuum of worship. The Book of Psalms encompasses the whole gamut of human emotion: not only joy, praise, love, hope and faith; but also sorrow, despair, fear, penitence, aggression and revenge. When heard at its finest, sung in the ambience of a great cathedral or college chapel, and combined with the visual bonus of magnificent architecture, Anglican chant can assume a significance and inspiration which readily identifies it as an essential ingredient of worship, in addition to being an art-form in itself.

The 1549 Prayer Book adopted Miles Coverdale's incomparable translation of 1531, and it is this version which was maintained in the 1662 and 1928 Prayer Books in preference to the translation found in the Authorised Version of 1611. While it is accepted that Coverdale's work may be faulted in terms of accuracy, there can be no doubt that the beauty and the resonance of the language has established itself firmly in the hearts of those within the Anglican Communion.

In his English prose, Coverdale understood and retained the principle of one of the chief structural features of Hebrew poetry identified by Bishop Louth in the 18th century and known as 'parallelism', implying a symmetry of form and sense. This can take the form of *similarity*, as in Psalm 103, v.10:

He hath not dealt with us after our sins : nor rewarded us according to our wickednesses.

of *contrast*, as in Psalm 37, v.21:

The ungodly borroweth, and payeth not again : but the righteous is merciful and liberal.

or of *logical expansion*, as in Psalm 123, v.4:

Our soul is filled with the scornful reproof of the wealthy : and with the despitefulness of the proud.

The emergence of printed Psalters

Because of its fixed design, Anglican chant requires the text to be marked (pointed) so that certain syllables may be sung to particular notes of the text. Before the emergence of the Oxford Movement in the first half of the 19th century, the pointing of the psalms for use with Anglican chant was a rare practice other than in cathedrals. Indeed, one of the many upheavals effected by the Oxford Movement was that of the fully choral service which became widespread, especially in the larger parish churches.

Some method of indicating to choirs the portion of the verse to be recited and the portion to be inflected became necessary. J.C. Beckwith, Organist of Norwich Cathedral, wrote in 1808, *'Suppose the organist and choir were to meet every morning and afternoon for one month, and agree on the proper place in each verse of the psalms, where the reciting should end in both the first and last parts of the chant, and under that particular word or syllable place a conspicuous red mark; if one book were thus marked, the others might be rendered similar to it. The benefit would be, all the members of the choir might recite as one person, and all come together to that word which they are previously sure is the most proper to end the recital.'* (i.e. the recitation)

The first such attempt to present in printed form a method of pointing appeared in 1837, edited by Robert Janes, Organist of Ely Cathedral. Since that period, numerous pointed versions of the Psalms and Canticles have appeared, with a considerable variety of methods of indicating the allocation of the syllables to the notes. Of these, *The Cathedral Psalter* (1875), edited by Stainer, Barnby and others, long held the most prominent position. It is interesting to note, however, that Stainer, during his tenure of office as Organist of St Paul's (1872-1888), did not use the *Cathedral Psalter* chants at St Paul's, despite having introduced the *Cathedral Psalter* soon after its appearance, but instead produced his own compilation of chants which later formed the nucleus of *The St Paul's Cathedral Chant Book* (1878).

A radical change in the approach to pointing took place on the publication of a pamphlet written by Robert Bridges in 1912. Its contents were to be of profound influence in that the author sought to emphasise the supremacy of the words around which the chant must be fitted. It was his decree that the verbal accents correspond with the musical ones. As a result of this, new psalters began to appear in profusion, all paying allegiance to the 'speech rhythm' method of pointing, as it became known. The most significant and enduring of these proved to be *The Oxford Psalter* (1929) edited by Ley, Roper and Hylton Stewart and *The Parish Psalter* (1932) edited by Nicholson.

In recent years language has loomed large in liturgical revision and the psalter has by no means remained exempt from this. *The Revised Psalter*, published in 1966, was the first real attempt to update Coverdale. A distinguished team, under the chairmanship of Bishop Coggan (later Archbishop), included such literary figures as T.S. Eliot and C. Day Lewis. This was followed in 1977 by *The Psalms - a new translation for worship*, under the chairmanship of Andrew Macintosh, Dean of St John's College, Cambridge, and the version now incorporated into ASB. Although the language differs, often considerably, from Coverdale, these two psalters still retain the familiar framework of each verse divided into two halves, thus lending themselves to antiphonal treatment for use with Anglican chant.

Anglican chant

Anglican chant grew out of the traditional plainsong or Gregorian tones, being derived from the harmonised plainchant (fauxbourdon) which was very common throughout Europe during the sixteenth and seventeenth centuries. Since the end of the seventeenth century there has been a constant flow of chant composition, which has resulted in an abundance of original examples, some good, others less distinguished.

It is said that Dvorak, on first visiting England and hearing a psalm sung in St Paul's Cathedral, asked, *'Why do they sing such a bad tune over and over again?'* Not every chant can be said to be remarkable, many being drab or banal in the extreme. Despite some excellent twentieth-century additions to the chant repertoire, the Anglican chant is probably seen at its best in a surprisingly large number of eighteenth- and nineteenth-century examples in which basic, coherent harmonies support concise melodic lines.

The Anglican chant is in essence a miniature, and a challenge for any composer to imprint a characteristic stamp on the form. As well as being musically satisfying, a chant must be more than capable of enduring constant repetition during the course of a single psalm. These qualities are the more necessary when the chant is reflected against the background of its particular function, that of being a vehicle for the psalm text. The feebleness of a poor chant becomes increasingly irksome the more it is heard repeated.

In compiling *The New St Paul's Cathedral Psalter*, the editor has drawn not only upon material from the various chant collections to have been used previously in the Cathedral, but the opportunity has also been taken to include chants from other sources, in addition to more recently composed examples. Although the volume is intended primarily for practical use in St Paul's, it is hoped that this publication may become a useful resource in other *'Quires and Places where they sing'*.

The chants represent here, as far as possible, the acceptably 'correct' versions, based on historical research, and the editor is indebted to Andrew Parker for much invaluable and far-reaching work in this field. Many sources have been consulted in the editing of the chants in this collection, of which the principal ones, upon which the versions here are based, are shown in the table on page xv.

Until the earlier part of this century, the predominant style of performance of psalms to Anglican chant dictated that, within each quarter of the chant, the portion following the recitation was rendered in strict metre. Many chants still in current usage, and among them some of the finest examples of the genre, thus date from an age when composers expected the major part of each chant melody and its harmonies to be heard slowly and distinctly, and they therefore felt at liberty to provide numerous additional decorations and passing notes in any of the four parts. With the adoption of the 'speech rhythm' chanting, pioneered by

Sir Sydney Nicholson from the late 1920s, the strict adherence to all of these extra notes can hold up the flow of a chant in the performance of a particular psalm verse, while they may remain essential to the chant harmony as conceived.

In the case of a number of eighteenth- and nineteenth-century chants, it is impossible to arrive at an *Urtext* version, particularly with regard to the inner voices, for these were often represented only by means of a figured bass in the organ score. In assembling the collection, the editor is responsible for arriving at a synthesis of various versions of a chant, which represent, in the editor's view, the most satisfactory and 'workable' version of each chant, where alternatives exist. Similarly, a somewhat selective attitude has been taken towards the vexed issue of 'passing notes', eliminating those (especially at cadences) where the natural flow of the words and pointing would be impeded.

Thomas Attwood

A good illustration of how a chant has 'evolved' is that by Flintoft *(Example 2)*, while the difficulty in establishing an *Urtext* can be seen in Example 3. Even where an original existed in four parts, this has still been subjected to regional variation, partly dictated, no doubt, by changing fashions *(Example 4).*

Example 2, attributed to Luke Flintoft

Bennett and Marshall (1829), 55 "1760"

Walmisley (1845)

Example 3, Thomas Norris

Bennett and Marshall (1829)

Wesley (1843)

Walmisley (1845)

Westminster Abbey (1855)

York (1859)

St Paul's (1878)

Example 4, Richard Woodward

Woodward, Cathedral Music (1771) (in B♭)

Bennett and Marshall (1829) (in B♭)

Dublin (1867) (in B♭)

St Paul's (1878) (in B♭)

Parish Psalter (1932) (in G)

Notes on performance

A fundamental principle of the *New St Paul's Cathedral Psalter* is the allocation of primary verbal stresses to musical ones. Thus, the method of pointing has been governed by the underlying sense of the words, and by the rhythms of well-modulated speech. The words should flow naturally and at the pace of corporate, deliberate speech, with unanimity of emphasis.

The art of good chanting is good singing, embodying all the integral elements of choral technique. Thus, blend, ensemble, intonation, dynamic gradation, diction and attack are all vital components in providing a musical medium for the clear and expressive singing of the psalter. The text comes to life with its meaning enriched and enhanced by the addition of music, and this includes the many possibilities presented by the mood, drama and atmosphere of the words, although both singers and accompanists should beware of the dangers of over-interpretation.

Care should be taken to avoid hurrying the text of the recitation (i.e. that which is sung before the first bar-line), and then slowing down to accommodate the obstacles in the remainder of the verse where words and music inevitably move more quickly (eg. Psalm 68 vv.4, 30). Similarly, cadences should neither slow down nor speed up, creating a false metrical effect. The established speed of the recitation should remain the same throughout the verse.

As in normal speech, certain words or syllables need emphasis to clarify meaning and to give variety. There are many instances in the text where, by leaning on a particular word or syllable and making it longer than others, the meaning is amplified. However, care should be taken to avoid singing the text with irregular, contrived dotted rhythms.

By contrast, a manner of singing in which equal weight is given to every syllable will, inevitably, result in a dull and lifeless performance. This allows for no light and shade, nor does it allow for unaccented words to be sung lightly.

Unimportant words or syllables at the beginning of lines should be treated as anacrusic, moving towards the first primary accent. In general, emphasis is achieved by a slight lengthening of the crucial word or syllable (agogic accent) rather than by an abrupt dynamic stress.

The overall pace of the psalm must be geared towards the pervading mood of the words: faster for joyful psalms; slower for penitential and reflective ones. The tempo is also regulated by such factors as the number of singers and the size and reverberation of the acoustic in which they are singing.

A particular feature of the *New St Paul's Cathedral Psalter* is the truncation of certain portions of the chant in order to allow the text to flow more freely, unencumbered by vocal melismas (i.e. more than one note to a syllable). In this manner the chant truly becomes the servant of the words. In many instances such melismas are difficult to avoid (e.g. Psalm 35, v.11; Psalm 70, v.3), and in some cases desirable (e.g. Psalm 115, v.18; Psalm 130, v.8), but the editor has attempted, as much as possible, to preserve musical and grammatical integrity within the chant at such places where 'surgery' has occurred.

The organ is the usual instrument for the accompaniment of Anglican chant. In order that complete concentration can be given to the words and the pointing, the accompanist should aim to memorise the chant. The creative accompanist will enhance the interpretation of the text by providing an imaginative, though never intrusive background palette to the choir's singing. Reeds and other colourful stops may add dramatic importance in certain verses, and the judicious application of descants and counter-melodies, when sensitively executed, can further adorn the overall effect. In addition, it is desirable for the organist to vary the texture of the accompaniment; the pedals need not be used for every verse and, where appropriate, it is effective to hear certain verses sung unaccompanied.

Symbols

† is used to signify a verse where there is no break at the double bar, between the two quarters of the chant.

* indicates a break (usually a breath).

‡ refers to verses where a portion of the chant has been omitted. A bracket above and below the section of the chant indicates those chords which are excised and a dash in the text corresponds to each chord which is deleted.

•• implies that more than one chord is sung to one syllable, such as in the Gloria.

All dynamic indications are intended as a guide only, and may be adjusted according to personal taste.

The first two verses and the Gloria of each psalm are usually sung Full (as indicated), the intervening verses being sung antiphonally, Decani singing verse 3 and Cantoris singing verse 4, and so on.

Acknowledgements

The process of revision and compilation was initiated in 1986 and in the ensuing years successive choristers, vicars choral and organists at St Paul's have sung from various prototypes of the finished product. I am grateful to them all for their patience and much perceptive, informed and relevant comment.

The end product would not have been realised without much practical assistance, in the initial stages, from the Revd Michael Beck and the Revd Stephen Waine, Succentors of St Paul's. I am particularly indebted both to Maurice Bevan for providing the biography of composers and to Geoffrey Shaw for undertaking the laborious task of reading proofs, and for many helpful and ingenious pointing suggestions. I remain grateful to Ted Perry of Hyperion Records for his enthusiastic willingness to undertake the project of recording the Psalter, and Mark Brown, Antony Howell and Julian Millard have been the most amiable and patient of colleagues in this process. Mention must also be made of Stephen Ridgley-Whitehouse who typeset the Psalter to its first proof, but sadly did not live to see the finished fruits of his labour. John Upton rescued the project at that difficult time and Canon Christopher Hill gave every encouragement to the venture during his Precentorship. I am greatly indebted to Andrew Parker who has guided this project through its final stages, and, in addition to meticulously researching the chant collection, incorporated a revised page layout. Lionel Steuart Fothringham has provided invaluable assistance in the realm of copyright clearance. Financial support was generously provided by the Dean and Chapter, the Friends of St Paul's and the St Paul's Musical and Historical Presentation Committee. By happy coincidence, this volume appears during the year in which we celebrate the Tercentenary of the opening of Wren's Quire for worship in 1697.

Finally, there is bound to be a degree of personal choice in both the selection of chants and pointing of the text. Good pointing will always mirror the meaning of the words; it will never distort it. Any shortcomings in this area must inevitably be mine, but I am indebted to a number of people for past inspiration, vision and insight, namely Jonathan Bielby, George Guest, David Willcocks, Harry Bramma, Barry Rose and Christopher Dearnley.

> *Benedicam Dominum in omni tempore :*
> *semper laus eius in ore meo.*
>> (Psalm 34, v.1)

John Scott

25th January 1997: The Conversion of St Paul

A set of 12 CDs of recordings of the *New St Paul's Cathedral Psalter*, with the St Paul's Cathedral Choir under the direction of John Scott, has been made by Hyperion Records Limited, www.hyperion-records.co.uk.

THE SOURCES OF THE CHANTS

As mentioned in John Scott's Preface, the most fruitful period in the development and collecting of Anglican Chants was from the start of the nineteenth century until the end of the 1930s. The principal sources consulted fall, therefore, within that period, although a few were examined from earlier periods, where necessary. In the eighteenth century, where chants are published they are included as "fillers" to subscription editions of canticle settings and anthems by single composers, and even in Boyce's anthology *Cathedral Music* they have that lesser position.

The sources here listed are mostly to be found in the Cambridge University Library. The collections there are particularly fine, not only because, since the 1820s, as a copyright library, it was obliged to take a copy of all books published in Great Britain, but because, through the deposits from the private libraries of such indefatigable collectors as Dr A.H. Mann (1850-1929), formerly Organist of King's College, the genres of chant books, hymn books and books of words of anthems sung in particular choral establishments have been considerably enriched. I therefore include, where appropriate, the class-mark by which a particular book is identified in that library. I am grateful to Richard Andrewes and the staff of the Music Department of the University Library for much patient help during my work in Cambridge.

For reasons of space, this list is presented as a handlist, rather than as a full bibliographical reference.

Andrew Parker

January 1997

A CHRONOLOGICAL HANDLIST OF THE PRINCIPAL SOURCES CONSULTED

Boyce, W.: Cathedral Music Vol.1, 1760	MR220.bb.75.8
Boyce, W.: Cathedral Music Vol.2, 1768	MR220.bb.75.9
Woodward, R.: Cathedral Music, 1771	*private collection*
[An Oxford Collection by William Cross, c.1815]	Mus.62.57^2
Cathedral Chants, ed. Bennett & Marshall, 1829	Mus.10.42^1
Cathedral Chants, ed. Bennett & Marshall, second edition	MR240.b.80.10
Hawes, W.: [serial-published collection c.1830 - c.1836]	Mus.10.42^2
Attwood, T.: Cathedral Music, ed. Walmisley	*private collection*
The Psalter, ed. Wesley, S.S., 1843	*private collection*
Cambridge Collection of Chants, ed. Walmisley, [1845]	Mus.36.49
Anglican Chant Book ed. Monk, 1853	M250.d.85.52^{14}
Westminster Abbey Chants, ed. Turle, 1855	M250.d.85.40
York collection, ed. Monk, 1859	M250.d.85.45
Salisbury collection, ed. Richardson, 1859	Mus.36.25^{10}
Revd B.StJ.B. Joule's collection, 1861	Mus.62.52
Parr, H.: Church of England Psalmody, 1863	M250.b.85.25
Havergal, W.H.: A Century of Chants, 1871	M250.c.85.25
Parr, H.: Church of England Psalmody, third edition, 1872	M250.b.85.23
Wesley, S.S.: The European Psalmist, 1872	M250.b.85.26
St Paul's Cathedral Chants, 1878	*private collection*
Westminster Abbey Chants, ed. Turle & Bridge, 1878	M240.d.85.48
Cathedral Psalter Chants, 1878	MR240.d.85.1
Anglican Chant Book, 1879	M240.c.85.10
King's College Cambridge, ed. Boyle & Mann, 1884	MR240.b.85.1
Gauntlett, H.J.: Encyclopædia of Anglican Chant, 1885	Mus.36.78

Church Choir Chant Book, 1899	M240.c.85.4
Parish Church Chant Book, second edition, 1902	M240.d.90.1[2]
New Cathedral Psalter Chants, 1909, Cathedral Use (81)	M240.c.90.33[1]
New Cathedral Psalter Chants, 1909, Parish Church Use (82)	M240.c.90.33[2]
New Cathedral Psalter Chants, 1909, Village Church Use (83)	M240.c.90.33[3]
Choir Chant Book, ed. Mann, 1910	M240.d.90.11
Church Music Society Chant Book, 1912	M240.d.90.10
St Audries Chant Book, 1920	M240.d.90.1[4]
St Nicolas Chant Book, ed. Nicholson, 1930	M240.c.90.6
Worcester Cathedral Chant Book ed. Atkins, 1930	M240.b.90.2
Stewart, C Hylton: A Collection of Chants, 1930	M240.a.90.1
Oxford Chant Book No.1, 1933	M240.c.90.8
Oxford Chant Book No.2, 1934	M240.c.90.9
Durham Cathedral Chant Book, ed. Eden, 1939	M240.b.90.7
The Broadcast Psalter, 1948	M240.c.90.30
Anglican Chant Book, 1955	M240.c.95.5
King's College Cambridge, ed. Langdon & Willcocks, 1968	*private collection*
100 20th-Century Chants, Œcumuse, 1976	
RSCM Chant Book, 1981	

COPYRIGHT ACKNOWLEDGEMENTS

The publishers are grateful to the following composers who have given permission for their copyright chants to appear in this Psalter:

Malcolm Archer (TD Set 6, Ben 7); Robert Ashfield (Ps 2); John Barnard (TD Set 7, Mag 7), copyright 1996, Œcumuse; John Bertalot (Ps 141, Jub 5); Maurice Bevan (Ps 71, TD Set 8, BenOm Set 2, Jub 9); Jonathan Bielby (Ps 136); Christopher Brown (BenOm Set 3); Andrew Carter (Ps 6); Lionel Dakers (Nunc 8), copyright © The Royal School of Church Music; Stephen Darlington (Jub 2); Christopher Dearnley (Ps 117); Paul Edwards (Mag 8); Gerre Hancock (Jub 6); Alan Hemmings (Ps 119 vv.145-52); Martin How (Ben 8); Peter Hurford (Ps 108); Francis Jackson (TD Set 6); John Joubert (TD Set 6); Donald Mossman (Ps 133); Noel Rawsthorne (Ps 150); Barry Rose (Ps 121); John Scott (Ps 30, Easter Anthems); Martindale Sidwell (Jub 10, Easter Anthems); Peter Melville Smith (Easter Anthems); Stanley Vann (Ps 113), from *Peterborough Chants*, by permission of Anglo-American Music Publishers; David Willcocks (Pss 81, 83, 148).

Thanks are also acknowledged to the following for copyright permission:

Miss Helen Armstrong (Thomas Armstrong: BenOm Set 1); E. Wulstan Atkins (Ivor Atkins: Pss 39, 66, 78); Banks Music Publications (Thomas Hanforth: Ps 145); Mark Bridges (Mary Monica Bridges: Ben 6); S.G.B. Brown (Edward Bairstow: Pss 107,114); The Syndics of Cambridge University Library (Peter Tranchell: Pss 102, 103); Miss Anna-Magdalena Hesford (Bryan Hesford: Nunc 7); Tim Hewitt-Jones (Tony Hewitt-Jones: TD Set 7); Novello & Co Ltd (Ivor Atkins: Ps 80, Edward Bairstow: Ps 51, C.S. Lang: Ps 137), used by permission of Novello & Co Ltd, 8/9 Frith St, London; Oxford University Press (Henry Ley: Pss 29, 105, Stanley Marchant: Ps 119 vv.97-104, Gordon Slater: Nunc 5), from the *Oxford Chant Book No.2* by permission of Oxford University Press, (Henry Ley: TD Set 3), by permission of the Oxford University Press for the Dohnavur Fellowship; The Royal School of Church Music (Gerald Knight: Ps 115, Sidney Nicholson: Pss 76, 101), copyright © The Royal School of Church Music; John Thalben-Ball (George Thalben-Ball: Pss 50, 56, 119 vv.33-40, Mag 2).

Copyright is acknowledged in the following chants. While the publishers have made every effort, without success, to trace or to contact the current copyright owner, they hereby apologise for any unintentional breach of copyright, and will be glad to make due acknowledgement in any subsequent edition of this Psalter.

H. Walford Davies (Pss 5, 91, 212, Ven 8); William Harris (TD Set 4); Herbert Howells (Ps 37); Ivor Keys (Nunc 2); Wilfred Mothersole (Ps 119 vv.65-72); Herbert Murrill (Ben 3); T.T. Noble (Ps 74); Clement Palmer (Ps 123); Elizabeth Poston (Jub 3); Gerald Scaife (Ps 52); Gordon Slater (Nunc 5); H.C. Stewart (Jub 4).

(Abbreviations: Ben: Benedictus; BenOm: Benedicite Omnia Opera; Jub: Jubilate; Mag: Magnificat; Nunc: Nunc Dimittis; TD: Te Deum)

PSALM 1

E. Elgar

Beatus vir, qui non abiit

Full	*mp*	1	Blessed is the man that hath not walked in the counsel of the ungodly * nor stood in the │ way of │ sinners : and hath not │ sat in • the │ seat • of the │ scornful.
Full		2	But his delight is in the │ law • of the │ Lord : and in his law will he │ exercise • him│self • day and │ night.
		3	And he shall be like a tree │ planted • by the │ water-side : that will │ bring forth • his │ fruit • in due │ season.
		4	His leaf│ also • shall not │ wither : and look * whatso│ever • he │ doeth • it shall │ prosper.
	mf	5	As for the ungodly it is not │ so with │ them : but they are like the chaff which the wind scattereth a│way • from the │ face • of the │ earth.
		6	Therefore the ungodly shall not be able to │ stand in • the │ judgement : neither the sinners in the congre│gation │ of the │ righteous.
		7	But the Lord knoweth the │ way • of the │ righteous : and the │ way of • the un│godly • shall │ perish.
Full			Glory be to the Father │ and to • the │ Son : and │ to the │ Holy │ Ghost.
Full			As it was in the beginning is │ now and • ever │ shall be : world without │ end. A │ . . │ men.

PSALM 2

Robert Ashfield

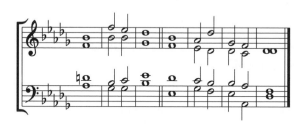

Quare fremuerunt gentes?

Full *f*	1	Why do the heathen so │ furiously • rage to│gether :
		and why do the │ people • i│magine a • vain │ thing?
Full	2	The kings of the earth stand up * and the rulers take │ counsel • to│gether :
		against the │ Lord • and a│gainst • his A│nointed.
Full	3	Let us break their │ bonds a│sunder :
		and │ cast away • their │ cords │ from us.
Dec.	4	He that dwelleth in heaven shall │ laugh them • to │ scorn :
		the │ Lord shall │ have them • in de│rision.
Can.	5	Then shall he │ speak unto them • in his │ wrath :
		and │ vex them • in his │ sore dis│pleasure.
Dec.	6 †	Yet have I │ set my │ King up‖on my │ holy │ hill of │ Sion.
Can. *mf*	7	I will preach the law whereof the │ Lord hath │ said unto me :
		Thou art my Son * this │ day have │ I be│gotten thee.
Dec.	8	Desire of me * and I shall give thee the │ heathen for • thine in│heritance :
		and the utmost parts of the │ earth for │ thy pos│session.
Can.	9	Thou shalt bruise them with a │ rod of │ iron :
		and break them in │ pieces • like a │ potter's │ vessel.
Dec. *mp*	10	Be wise now │ therefore • O ye │ kings :
		be learned │ ye that • are │ judges • of the │ earth.

Psalm 2, continued

Robert Ashfield

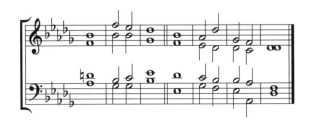

Can. p   11   Serve the | Lord in | fear :
                          and re|joice • unto | him with | reverence.

Dec. mf   12   Kiss the Son lest he be angry * and so ye | perish • from the | right way :
                          if his wrath be kindled (yea but a little) * |
                          blessed are • all | they that • put their | trust in him.

Robert Ashfield

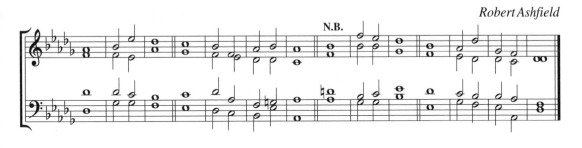

Full f   Glory be to the Father | and to • the | Son :
                          and | to the | Holy | Ghost.

Full   As it was in the beginning is | now and • ever | shall be :
                          world without | end. A | . . | men.

PSALM 3

E. J. Hopkins

Domine, quid multiplicati sunt?

Full	**p**	1	Lord how are they in|creased that | trouble me :
			many are | they that | rise a|gainst me.
Full	**mp**	2	Many one there be that | say of · my | soul :
			There is no | help for · him | in his | God.
	mf	3	But thou O | Lord art · my de|fender :
			thou art my worship and the | lifter | up of · my | head.
		4	I did call upon the | Lord · with my | voice :
			and he heard me | out of · his | holy | hill.
	p cresc.	5 ‡	I laid me down and slept * and | rose up · a|gain :
			– | – for the | Lord sus|tained me.
	mf	6 †	I will not be afraid for ten | thousands · of the | people ‖
			that have | set themselves · a|gainst me · round a|bout.

7 §   Up Lord and \| help me · O my \| God :
for thou smitest all mine enemies upon the cheekbone *
thou hast \| broken · the \| teeth of · the un\|godly.

	dim.	8	**2nd part** Salvation be|longeth · unto the | Lord :
			and thy | blessing · is up|on thy | people.
Full	**p**		Glory be to the Father | and to · the | Son :
			and | to the | Holy | Ghost.
Full			As it was in the beginning is | now and · ever | shall be :
			world without | end. A | . . | men.

§ Omitted in the St Paul's Cathedral use

PSALM 4

G. J. Elvey

v. 5, Gloria

Cum invocarem

Full *mp*   1   Hear me when I call O | God of • my | righteousness :
         thou hast set me at liberty when I was in trouble *
         have mercy upon me and | hearken | unto • my | prayer.

Full   2   O ye sons of men * how long will ye blas|pheme mine | honour :
         and have such pleasure in | vanity • and | seek • after | leasing?

    p   3   Know this also * that the Lord hath chosen to himself the | man • that is | godly :
         when I | call upon • the | Lord • he will | hear me.

            4   Stand in | awe and | sin not :
         commune with your own heart and in your | chamber | and be | still.

   mp   5   Offer the | sacrifice • of | righteousness :
         and | put your | trust • in the | Lord.

          6 †   There be | many • that | say ‖ Who will | shew us | any | good?

          7 †   Lord | lift thou | up the ‖ light of • thy | counte|nance up|on us.

   mf   8   Thou hast put | gladness • in my | heart :
         since the time that their corn and | wine and | oil in|creased.

  dim.   9   **2nd part** I will lay me down in | peace and • take my | rest :
         for it is thou Lord only that | makest • me | dwell in | safety.

Full *p*   Glory be to the Father | and to • the | Son :
         and | to the | Holy | Ghost.

Full   As it was in the beginning is | now and • ever | shall be :
         world without | end. A | . . | men.

PSALM 5

v. 3

H. Walford Davies

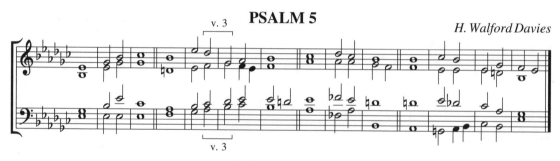

v. 3

Verba mea auribus

Full *mp* 1 Ponder my | words O | Lord :
con|sider • my | medi|tation.

Full 2 O hearken thou unto the voice of my calling my | King • and my | God :
for unto | thee • will I | make my | prayer.

3 ‡ My voice shalt thou hear be|times O | Lord :
early in the morning will I direct my prayer unto thee * |
and will – | – look | up.

4 For thou art the God that hast no | pleasure • in | wicked•ness :
neither shall | any | evil | dwell with • thee.

mf 5 Such as be foolish shall not | stand in • thy | sight :
for thou | hatest • all | them that • work | vani•ty.

6 Thou shalt destroy | them that • speak | leasing :
the Lord will abhor both the | blood-thirsty • and de|ceitful | man.

mp 7 But as for me I will come into thine house *
even upon the | multitude • of thy | mercy :
and in thy fear will I | worship to•ward thy | holy | temple.

8 Lead me O Lord in thy righteousness be|cause of • mine | ene•mies :
make thy way | plain be|fore my | face.

mf 9 For there is no | faithfulness • in his | mouth :
their inward | parts are | very | wicked•ness.

10 § Their throat is an | open | sepul•chre :
they | flatter | with their | tongue.

11 § Destroy thou them O God * let them perish through their |
own i•magi|nations :
cast them out in the multitude of their ungodliness * |
for they • have re|belled a|gainst thee.

§ Omitted in the St Paul's Cathedral use

Psalm 5, *continued*

H. *Walford Davies*

12   And let all them that put their | trust in thee · re|joice :
　　　　they shall ever be giving of thanks because thou defendest them *
　　　　they that love thy | Name · shall be | joyful · in | thee;

mf　　13　　2nd part   For thou Lord wilt give thy | blessing · unto the | righteous :
dim.　　　　　　　　and with thy favourable kindness wilt thou de|fend him |
　　　　　　　　as · with a | shield.

Full　*mp*　　Glory be to the Father | and to · the | Son :
　　　　　　and | to the | Holy | Ghost.

Full　　　As it was in the beginning is | now and · ever | shall be :
　　　　　world without | end. A | . . | men.

Day 1: Evening

PSALM 6

Andrew Carter

Domine, ne in furore

Full *p*　　1　O Lord rebuke me not in thine | indig|nation :
　　　　　　　　　　neither | chasten me · in | thy dis|pleasure.

Full　　　　2　Have mercy upon me O | Lord for · I am | weak :
　　　　　　　　　　O Lord | heal me · for my | bones are | vexed.

　　　mp　　3　My soul | also is · sore | troubled :
　　　　　　　　　　but | Lord how | long · wilt thou | punish me?

　　　　　　4　Turn thee O Lord and de|liver · my | soul :
　　　　　　　　　　O | save me · for thy | mercy's | sake.

　　　p　　5　For in death | no man · re|membereth thee :
　　　　　　　　　　and who will | give thee | thanks · in the | pit?

　　　　　　6　I am weary of my groaning * every night | wash I · my | bed :
　　　　　　　　　　and | water · my | couch · with my | tears.

　　　　　　7　[2nd part] My beauty is | gone for · very | trouble :
　　　　　　　　　　　　and worn a|way be|cause of · all mine | enemies.

change chant (Decani)

Andrew Carter

Dec. *f*　　8　Away from me all | ye that · work | vanity :
　　　　　　　　　　for the Lord hath | heard the | voice of · my | weeping.

　　　　　　9　The Lord hath | heard · my pe|tition :
　　　　　　　　　　the | Lord · will re|ceive my | prayer.

Psalm 6, continued

Andrew Carter

10   **2nd part**   All mine enemies shall be con|founded and · sore | vexed :
                 they shall be turned | back and | put to · shame | suddenly.

Full   Glory be to the Father | and to · the | Son :
                  and | to the | Holy | Ghost.

Full   As it was in the beginning is | now and · ever | shall be :
                  world without | end. A | . . | men.

PSALM 7

R. Cooke

Domine, Deus meus

Full   *mp*   1   O Lord my God * in thee have I | put my | trust :
                         save me from all them that | perse·cute me | and de|liver me;

Full   *mf*   2 ‡   Lest he devour my soul like a lion and | tear it · in | pieces :
                         – | while there · is | none to | help.

       p   3   O Lord my God * if I have done | any · such | thing :
                         or if there be any | wicked·ness | in my | hands;

              4   If I have rewarded evil unto | him that · dealt | friendly with me :
                         yea I have delivered him that with|out · any | cause · is mine | enemy;

Psalm 7, continued

R. Cooke

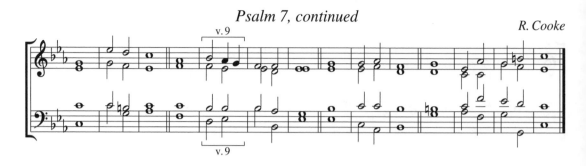

mp	5	Then let mine enemy | persecute my · soul and | take me :
		yea let him tread my life down upon the earth *
		and lay mine | honour | in the | dust.
mf	6	Stand up O Lord in thy wrath and lift up thyself *
		because of the indig|nation · of mine | enemies :
		arise up for me in the | judgement · that | thou · hast com|manded.
	7	And so shall the congregation of the | people · come a|bout thee :
		for their sakes therefore | lift up · thy|self a|gain.
	8	The Lord shall judge the people; * give | sentence with · me O | Lord :
		according to my righteousness *
		and according to the | innocen·cy | that is | in me.
	9 ‡	O let the wickedness of the ungodly | come · to an | end :
		but | – – | guide thou · the | just.
	10 †	For the | righteous | God ‖ trieth the | very | hearts and | reins.
mp	11	My help | cometh · of | God :
		who preserveth | them · that are | true of | heart.
	12	God is a righteous | Judge · strong and | patient :
		and | God · is pro|voked · every | day.
	13	If a man will not turn he will | whet his | sword :
		he hath bent his | bow and | made it | ready.
	14	He hath prepared for him the | instruments · of | death :
		he ordaineth his | arrows · a|gainst the | persecutors.
p	15	Behold he | travaileth · with | mischief :
		he hath conceived | sorrow · and | brought forth · un|godliness.
	16	He hath graven and | digged up · a | pit :
		and is fallen himself into the de|struction · that he | made for | other.

Psalm 7, continued

R. Cooke

mf	17	For his travail shall come up|on his • own | head :
		and his wickedness shall | fall • on his | own | pate.
f	18	I will give thanks unto the Lord ac|cording • to his | righteousness :
		and I will praise the | Name • of the | Lord most | High.
Full		Glory be to the Father | and to • the | Son :
		and | to the | Holy | Ghost.
Full		As it was in the beginning is | now and • ever | shall be :
		world without | end. A | . . | men.

PSALM 8

J. Corfe (from H. Lawes)

Domine, Dominus noster

Full f	1	O Lord our Governor * how excellent is thy | Name in • all the | world :
		thou that hast set thy | glory • a|bove the | heavens!
Full	2	Out of the mouth of very babes and sucklings hast thou ordained strength
		be|cause of • thine | enemies :
		that thou mightest still the | ene•my | and the • a|venger.
mf	3	For I will consider thy heavens * even the | works • of thy | fingers :
		the moon and the | stars which | thou hast • or|dained.
	4	What is man that | thou art | mindful of him :
		and the | son of • man | that thou | visitest him?

Psalm 8, continued

v. 5 & Gloria

J. Corfe (from H. Lawes)

5   Thou madest him │ lower • than the │ angels :
to │ crown him • with │ glory • and │ worship.

6   Thou makest him to have dominion of the │ works • of thy │ hands :
and thou hast put all things in sub│jection │ under • his │ feet.

7   All │ sheep and │ oxen :
yea and the │ beasts │ of the │ field;

8   The fowls of the air and the │ fishes • of the │ sea :
and whatsoever │ walketh • through the │ paths • of the │ seas.

Full *f*   9   **2nd part** O │ Lord our │ Governor :
how excellent is thy │ Name in │ all the │ world!

Full   Glory be to the Father │ and to • the │ Son :
and │ to the │ Holy │ Ghost.

Full   As it was in the beginning is │ now and • ever │ shall be :
world without │ end. A │ • • │ men.

PSALM 9

J. Stainer

Confitebor tibi

Full *f*   1   I will give thanks unto thee O Lord with my │ whole │ heart :
       I will │ speak of ∙ all thy │ marvel∙lous │ works.

Full   2   I will be │ glad ∙ and re│joice in thee :
       yea my songs will I make of thy │ Name O │ thou most │ Highest.

mf   3   While mine enemies are │ driven │ back :
       they shall │ fall and │ perish ∙ at thy │ presence.

4   For thou hast maintained my │ right ∙ and my │ cause :
       thou art set in the │ throne that │ judgest │ right.

5   Thou hast rebuked the heathen and de│stroyed the ∙ un│godly :
       thou hast put out their │ name for │ ever ∙ and │ ever.

6   O thou enemy * destructions are come to a per│petu∙al │ end :
       even as the cities which thou hast destroyed *
       their me│morial ∙ is │ perished │ with them.

f   7   But the Lord shall en│dure for │ ever :
       he hath also pre│pared his │ seat for │ judgement.

8   For he shall judge the │ world in │ righteousness :
       and minister true │ judgement │ unto ∙ the │ people.

mf   9   The Lord also will be a de│fence ∙ for the op│pressed :
       even a │ refuge ∙ in due │ time of │ trouble.

10   And they that know thy Name will │ put their │ trust in thee :
       for thou Lord hast │ never ∙ failed │ them that │ seek thee.

Psalm 9, continued

J. Stainer

11   O praise the Lord which │ dwelleth • in │ Sion :
      shew the │ people │ of his │ doings.

12   For when he maketh inquisition for │ blood • he re│membereth them :
      and for│getteth not • the com│plaint • of the │ poor.

change chant (Decani)

T. Attwood

Dec.   *mp*   13   Have mercy upon me O Lord *
      consider the trouble which I suffer of │ them that │ hate me :
        thou that liftest me │ up • from the │ gates of │ death.

14   That I may shew all thy praises within the ports of the │ daughter • of │ Sion :
      I will re│joice in │ thy sal│vation.

15   The heathen are sunk down in the │ pit • that they │ made :
      in the same net which they hid │ privi•ly │ is their • foot │ taken.

16   The Lord is known to │ exe•cute │ judgement :
      the ungodly is │ trapped in • the │ work of • his own │ hands.

17   The wicked shall be │ turned • into │ hell :
      and all the │ people │ that for•get │ God.

p   18   For the poor shall not │ alway • be for│gotten :
      the patient abiding of the │ meek • shall not │ perish • for │ ever.

change chant (Full)

Psalm 9, continued

J. Stainer

Full *f*   19   Up Lord and let not man have the │ upper │ hand :
                                let the │ heathen • be │ judged • in thy │ sight.

Full   20   Put them in │ fear O │ Lord :
                                that the heathen may │ know themselves • to │ be but │ men.

Full   Glory be to the Father │ and to • the │ Son :
                                and │ to the │ Holy │ Ghost.

Full   As it was in the beginning is │ now and • ever │ shall be :
                                world without │ end. A │ . . │ men.

PSALM 10

T. Attwood

Ut quid, Domine?

Full *p*   1   Why standest thou so far │ off O │ Lord :
                                and hidest thy │ face • in the │ needful • time of │ trouble?

Full   2   The ungodly for his own lust doth │ persecute • the │ poor :
                                let them be taken in the crafty │ wili•ness │ that they • have i│magined.

          mp   3   For the ungodly hath made boast of his │ own heart's • de│sire :
                                and speaketh good of the │ covetous • whom │ God ab│horreth.

                    4   The ungodly is so proud that he │ careth • not for │ God :
                                neither is │ God in │ all his │ thoughts.

Psalm 10, continued

T. Attwood

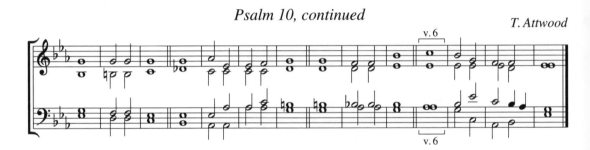

5   His ways are | alway | grievous :
       thy judgements are far above out of his sight *
       and therefore de|fieth • he | all his | enemies.

6 ‡   For he hath said in his heart * Tush I shall | never be • cast | down :
       – | there shall • no | harm • happen | unto me.

mf   7   His mouth is full of cursing de|ceit and | fraud :
       under his | tongue • is un|godliness • and | vanity.

8   He sitteth lurking in the thievish | corners • of the | streets :
       and privily in his lurking dens doth he murder the innocent *
       his | eyes are | set a•gainst the | poor.

mp   9   For he lieth waiting secretly * even as a lion | lurketh he • in his | den :
       that | he may | ravish • the | poor.

10   He doth | ravish • the | poor :
       when he | getteth • him | into • his | net.

p   11   He falleth | down and | humbleth himself :
       that the congregation of the poor may | fall • into the |
       hands • of his | captains.

12   He hath said in his heart * Tush | God • hath for|gotten :
dim.   he hideth away his | face and • he will | never | see it.

change chant (Full)

Psalm 10, *continued*

J. Stainer

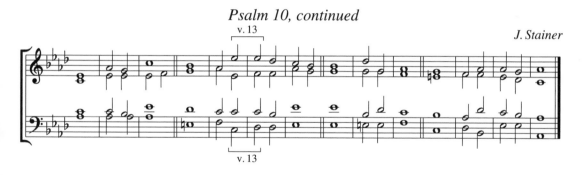

Full *f*	13 ‡	Arise O Lord God and | lift up • thine | hand :
		for|get not – | – the | poor.
Full	14	Wherefore should the | wicked blas•pheme | God :
		while he doth say in his heart * | Tush thou | God • carest | not for it.
mf	15	Surely | thou hast | seen it :
		for thou be|holdest • un|godliness • and | wrong.
	16	That thou mayest take the | matter • into thy | hand :
		the poor committeth himself unto thee; *
		for | thou art • the | helper • of the | friendless.
	17	Break thou the power of the un|godly • and ma|licious :
		take away his un|godliness • and | thou shalt • find | none.
	18	The Lord is King for | ever • and | ever :
		and the | heathen are • perished | out of • the | land.
mp	19	Lord thou hast heard the de|sire • of the |.poor :
		thou preparest their heart * and thine | ear | hearkeneth • there|to;
	20	To help the fatherless and poor | unto • their | right :
		that the man of the earth be no | more ex|alted • a|gainst them.
Full *f*		Glory be to the Father | and to • the | Son :
		and | to the | Holy | Ghost.
Full		As it was in the beginning is | now and • ever | shall be :
		world without | end. A | . . | men.

PSALM 11

S. Elvey

In Domino confido

Full	*mf*	1	In the Lord | put I • my | trust :
			how say ye then to my soul *
			that she should flee as a | bird | unto • the | hill?
Full		2	For lo the ungodly bend their bow and
			make ready their | arrows with•in the | quiver :
			that they may privily shoot at | them which • are | true of | heart.
		3	For the foundations | will be • cast | down :
			and | what • hath the | righteous | done?
	mp	4 ‡	The Lord is in his | holy | temple :
			– | – the | Lord's seat • is in | heaven.
		5	His eyes con|sider • the | poor :
			and his | eye-lids • try the | children • of | men.
		6	The Lord al|loweth • the | righteous :
			but the ungodly and him that delighteth in |
			wickedness • doth his | soul ab|hor.
	mf	7 ‡	Upon the ungodly he shall rain snares * fire and brimstone | storm and | tempest :
			– | this shall • be their | portion • to | drink.
		8	For the righteous | Lord • loveth | righteousness :
			his countenance will be|hold the | thing • that is | just.
Full	*f*		Glory be to the Father | and to • the | Son :
			and | to the | Holy | Ghost.
Full			As it was in the beginning is | now and • ever | shall be :
			world without | end. A | . . | men.

Day 2: Evening

PSALM 12

C. H. Wilton

Salvum me fac

Full *p*   1   Help me Lord * for there is not one | godly • man | left :
for the faithful are minished from a|mong the | children • of | men.

Full   2   They talk of vanity | every one • with his | neighbour :
they do but flatter with their lips * and dis|semble • in their | double | heart.

mp   3   The Lord shall root out all de|ceitful | lips :
and the | tongue that | speaketh | proud things;

4   Which have said * with our | tongue will • we pre|vail :
we are they that ought to | speak * who is | lord | over us?

5   Now for the comfortless trouble's | sake • of the | needy :
and because of the deep | sighing | of the | poor,

mf   6   I will | up • saith the | Lord :
and will help everyone from him that swelleth a|gainst him *
and will | set him • at | rest.

p   7   The words of the | Lord are | pure words :
even as the silver * which from the earth is tried and purified |
seven • times | in the | fire.

8   Thou shalt | keep them • O | Lord :
thou shalt preserve him from | this • gene|ration • for | ever.

mf   9   2nd part   The ungodly | walk on • every | side :
when they are exalted * the children of | men are |
put to • re|buke.

Full   Glory be to the Father | and to • the | Son :
and | to the | Holy | Ghost.

Full   As it was in the beginning is | now and • ever | shall be :
world without | end. A | . . | men.

PSALM 13

W. Croft

Usque quo, Domine?

Full *p*	1	How long wilt thou forget me O | Lord * for | ever : how | long · wilt thou | hide thy | face from me?
Full	2	How long shall I seek counsel in my soul * and be so | vexed · in my | heart : how | long · shall mine | enemies · triumph | over me?
mp	3	Consider and hear me O | Lord my | God : lighten mine | eyes · that I | sleep not · in | death.
	4	Lest mine enemy say I have pre|vailed a|gainst him : for if I be cast down * they that | trouble · me | will re|joice at it.

change chant (Full)

T. Tomkins

Full *mf*	5	But my | trust is in · thy | mercy : and my heart is | joyful · in | thy sal|vation.
Full	6	I will sing of the Lord * because he hath dealt so | loving·ly | with me : yea I will praise the | Name of · the | Lord most | Highest.
Full *f*		Glory be to the Father | and to · the | Son : and | to the | Holy | Ghost.
Full		As it was in the beginning is | now and · ever | shall be : world without | end. A | · · | men.

PSALM 14

T. Attwood

Dixit insipiens

Full	*f*	1 †	The | fool hath | said ‖ in his | heart * there | is no | God.
Full		2	They are corrupt * and become a|bominable · in their | doings : there is | none that · doeth | good * no not | one.
	mf	3	The Lord looked down from heaven upon the | children · of | men : to see if there were any that would under|stand and | seek · after | God.
	f	4	But they are all gone out of the way * they are alto|gether be·come a|bominable : there is | none that · doeth | good * no not | one.

> 5 §   Their throat is an open sepulchre * with their \| tongues have · they de\|ceived : <br> the poison of \| asps is \| under · their \| lips.
>
> 6 §   Their mouth is full of \| cursing · and \| bitterness : <br> their \| feet are \| swift to · shed \| blood.
>
> 7 §   **2nd part**   Destruction and unhappiness is in their ways *
 and the way of \| peace have · they not \| known : <br> there is no \| fear of \| God be·fore their \| eyes.

	mf	8	Have they no knowledge that they are all such | workers · of | mischief : eating up my people as it were bread * and | call not · up|on the | Lord?
	mp	9	There were they brought in great fear * even where | no fear | was : for God is in the gene|ration | of the | righteous.
	mf	10	As for you * ye have made a mock at the | counsel · of the | poor : because he | putteth · his | trust · in the | Lord.
		11	Who shall give salvation unto Israel out of Sion? * When the Lord turneth the cap|tivity · of his | people :
	cresc.		then shall Jacob rejoice and | Isra·el | shall be | glad.
Full	*f*		Glory be to the Father | and to · the | Son : and | to the | Holy | Ghost.
Full			As it was in the beginning is | now and · ever | shall be : world without | end. A | · · | men.

§ *Omitted in the St Paul's Cathedral use*

PSALM 15

v. 7

C. Gibbons

v. 7

Domine, quis habitabit?

Full	*mp*	1	Lord who shall │ dwell in · thy │ tabernacle : 　　　or who shall │ rest up·on thy │ holy │ hill?
Full		2	Even he that leadeth an │ uncor·rupt │ life : 　　　and doeth the thing which is right * and │ speaketh · the │ 　　　truth · from his │ heart.
		3	He that hath used no deceit in his tongue * nor done │ evil · to his │ neighbour : 　　　and │ hath not │ slandered · his │ neighbour.
		4	He that setteth not by himself * but is │ lowly · in his own │ eyes : 　　　and maketh │ much of · them that │ fear the │ Lord.
		5	He that sweareth unto his neighbour * and disap│pointeth · him │ not : 　　　though it │ were to · his │ own │ hindrance.
		6	He that hath not given his │ money · upon │ usury : 　　　nor taken re│ward a│gainst the │ innocent.
Full	*mf*	7 †‡	Whoso │ doeth │ these things ‖ – │ – shall │ never │ fall.
Full			Glory be to the Father │ and to · the │ Son : 　　　and │ to the │ Holy │ Ghost.
Full			As it was in the beginning is │ now and · ever │ shall be : 　　　world without │ end. A │ . . │ men.

PSALM 16

W. H. Havergal

Conserva me, Domine

Full	*mf*	1	Pre|serve me · O | God :
			for in | thee · have I | put my | trust.
Full		2	O my soul thou hast | said · unto the | Lord :
			Thou art my God * my | goods are | nothing · unto | thee.
		3	All my delight is upon the | saints that are · in the | earth :
			and upon | such · as ex|cel in | virtue.
		4 †	But they that run | after · a|no||ther | god shall | have great | trouble.
		5	Their drink-offerings of | blood will I · not | offer :
			neither make mention of their | names with|in my | lips.
		6 ‡	The Lord himself is the portion of mine in|heritance · and of my | cup :
			thou shalt | – main|tain my | lot.
		7	The lot is fallen unto | me in a · fair | ground :
			yea I | have a | goodly | heritage.
		8	I will thank the Lord for | giving · me | warning :
			my reins also | chasten · me | in the | night-season.
	f	9	I have set God | always · be|fore me :
			for he is on my right hand | therefore · I | shall not | fall.
		10	Wherefore my heart was glad and my | glory · re|joiced :
			my flesh | also · shall | rest in | hope.
	mf	11	For why? * thou shalt not leave my | soul in | hell :
			neither shalt thou suffer thy | Holy One · to | see cor|ruption.
		12	Thou shalt shew me the path of life *
			in thy presence is the | fulness · of | joy :
			and at thy right hand there is | pleasure · for | ever | more.
Full	*f*		Glory be to the Father | and to · the | Son :
			and | to the | Holy | Ghost.
Full			As it was in the beginning is | now and · ever | shall be :
			world without | end. A | . . | men.

PSALM 17

J. Turle

Exaudi, Domine

Full   **mp**   1   Hear the right O Lord * con|sider • my com|plaint :
                 and hearken unto my prayer that | goeth • not | out of • feigned | lips.

Full   2   Let my sentence come | forth • from thy | presence :
                 and let thine eyes | look up•on the | thing • that is | equal.

             3   Thou hast proved and visited mine heart in the night-season; *
             thou hast tried me and shalt find no | wicked•ness | in me :
                 for I am utterly | purposed • that my | mouth shall • not of|fend.

             4   Because of men's works that are done against the | words • of thy | lips :
                 I have | kept me • from the | ways of • the de|stroyer.

mf   5 ‡   O hold thou up my | goings • in thy | paths :
                 – | – that my | footsteps | slip not.

             6   I have called upon thee O | God for • thou shalt | hear me :
                 incline thine ear to me and | hearken | unto • my | words.

             7   Shew thy marvellous loving-kindness *
             thou that art the Saviour of them which | put their | trust in thee :
                 from | such as • re|sist • thy right | hand.

p   8   Keep me as the | apple • of an | eye :
                 hide me | under • the | shadow • of thy | wings,

mp   9   From the un|godly • that | trouble me :
                 mine enemies compass me round a|bout to | take a•way my | soul.

           10 ‡   They are in|closed in • their own | fat :
                 and their | – – | mouth • speaketh | proud things.

Psalm 17, continued

J. Turle

11 ‡   They lie waiting in our | way on • every | side :
           – | – turning their eyes | down • to the | ground;

12   Like as a lion that is | greedy • of his | prey :
           and as it were a lion's whelp | lurking • in | secret | places.

mf   13   Up Lord * disappoint him and | cast him | down :
           deliver my soul from the un|godly | which is • a | sword of thine;

14   From the men of thy hand O Lord *
      from the men I say and from the | evil | world :
         which have their portion in this life *
         whose | bellies thou • fillest | with thy • hid | treasure.

15   They have | children • at their de|sire :
           and leave the | rest of • their | substance • for their | babes.

16   But as for me I will behold thy | presence • in | righteousness :
           and when I awake up after thy | likeness • I shall be | satis•fied | with it.

Full   *mf*   Glory be to the Father | and to • the | Son :
           and | to the | Holy | Ghost.

Full   As it was in the beginning is | now and • ever | shall be :
           world without | end. A | . . | men.

PSALM 18

Diligam te, Domine

Full *f*	1a	I will love thee O │ Lord my │ strength : the Lord is my stony │ rock and │ my de│fence:
Full	1b	My Saviour my God and my might in │ whom • I will │ trust : my buckler * the horn also of my sal│vation │ and my │ refuge.
Full	2 ‡	**2nd part** I will call upon the Lord which is │ worthy • to be │ praised : – │ so shall • I be │ safe • from mine │ enemies.
mp	3	The sorrows of │ death │ compassed me : and the overflowings of un│godli•ness │ made • me a│fraid.
	4	The pains of │ hell • came a│bout me : the │ snares of │ death • over│took me.
p	5 ‡	In my trouble I will │ call up•on the │ Lord : – │ – and com│plain • unto my │ God.

mp	6	So shall he hear my voice out of his │ holy │ temple :
		   and my complaint shall come before him *
		   it shall │ enter • even │ into • his │ ears.

change chant (Full)

Psalm 18, continued

S. S. Wesley

Full *f*   7   The earth | trembled · and | quaked :
                             the very foundations also of the hills shook *
                             and were re|moved · be|cause · he was | wroth.

Full   8   There went a | smoke out · in his | presence :
                             and a consuming fire out of his mouth * |
                             so that | coals were | kindled at it.

Full   9   2nd part He bowed the heavens | also · and came | down :
                                           and it was | dark | under · his | feet.

         mf   10   He rode upon the | cherubins · and did | fly :
                             he came | flying up·on the | wings · of the | wind.

                    11   He made darkness his | secret | place :
                             his pavilion round about him *
                             with dark | water · and thick | clouds to | cover him.

         f   12 ‡ At the brightness of his presence his | clouds re|moved :
                             – | hailstones · and | coals of | fire.

                    13 ‡ The Lord also thundered out of heaven * and the | Highest · gave his | thunder :
                             – | hailstones · and | coals of | fire.

Full   14   He sent out his | arrows · and | scattered them :
                             he cast forth | lightnings | and de|stroyed them.

Full   15   The springs of waters were seen * and the foundations of the round world
                             were discovered at thy | chiding · O | Lord :
                             at the blasting of the | breath of | thy dis|pleasure.

change chant (Decani)

Psalm 18, continued

T. A. Walmisley

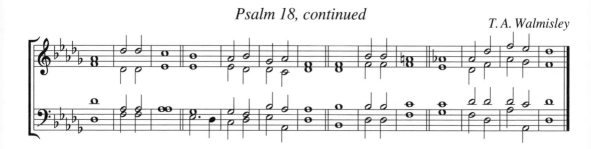

Dec. *mp* 16 He shall send down from on | high to | fetch me :
    and shall | take me • out of | many | waters.

17 He shall deliver me from my strongest enemy * and from | them which | hate me :
    for | they are • too | mighty | for me.

18 They prevented me in the | day of • my | trouble :
    but the | Lord was | my up | holder.

19 He brought me forth also into a | place of | liberty :
    he brought me forth * even be|cause he • had a | favour | unto me.

p 20 The Lord shall reward me after my | righteous | dealing :
    according to the | cleanness • of my | hands • shall he | recompense me.

21 Because I have kept the | ways • of the | Lord :
    and have not for|saken • my | God • as the | wicked doth.

mp 22 For I have an eye unto | all his | laws :
    and will not cast | out • his com|mandments | from me.

23 I was also uncor|rupt be|fore him :
    and es|chewed mine | own | wickedness.

24 **2nd part** Therefore shall the Lord reward me after my | righteous | dealing :
    and according unto the | cleanness • of my |
    hands • in his | eye-sight.

p 25 With the holy | thou shalt • be | holy :
    and with a | perfect • man | thou shalt • be | perfect.

26 With the clean | thou shalt • be | clean :
    and with the | froward | thou shalt • learn | frowardness.

mp 27 For thou shalt save the | people that are • in ad|versity :
    and shalt bring | down the | high looks • of the | proud.

mf 28 Thou also shalt | light my | candle :
    the Lord my God shall make my | darkness | to be | light.

Psalm 18, *continued*

T. A. Walmisley

29   For in thee I shall discomfit an | host of | men :
         and with the help of my | God · I shall leap | over · the | wall.

30   The way of God is an | unde·filed | way :
         the word of the Lord also is tried in the fire; *
         he is the defender of all | them that | put their | trust in him.

change chant (Full)

H. Smart

Full *f*   31   For who is | God · but the | Lord :
                      or who hath any | strength ex|cept our | God?

Full   32   It is God that girdeth me with | strength of | war :
                      and | maketh · my | way | perfect.

                 33   He maketh my | feet like | hart's feet :
                      and | setteth · me | up on | high.

                 34   He teacheth mine | hands to | fight :
                      and mine arms shall break | even · a | bow of | steel.

                 35   Thou hast given me the de|fence of thy · sal|vation :
                      thy right hand also shall hold me up *
                      and thy loving cor|rection · shall | make me | great.

                 36 ‡ Thou shalt make room enough | under me · for to | go :
                      – | – that my | footsteps · shall not | slide.

Psalm 18, continued

H. Smart

37 §   I will follow upon mine | enemies and • over|take them :

        neither will I | turn again • till I | have de|stroyed them.

38 §   I will smite them that they shall not be | able • to | stand :

        but | fall | under • my | feet.

39 §   Thou hast girded me with | strength • unto the | battle :

        thou shalt | throw down • mine | ene•mies | under me.

40 §‡ Thou hast made mine enemies also to | turn their • backs up|on me :

        – | – and I shall de|stroy • them that | hate me.

mf   41 §   They shall cry * but there shall be | none to | help them :

        yea even unto the Lord shall they | cry • but he | shall not | hear them.

42 §   I will beat them as small as the | dust be•fore the | wind :

        I will cast them | out as • the | clay • in the | streets.

43 §   Thou shalt deliver me from the | strivings • of the | people :

        and thou shalt | make me • the | head • of the | heathen.

44 ‡ | **4th quarter** | A people whom I | have not | known shall | serve me.

45   As soon as they hear of me | they shall • o|bey me :

        but the strange | children • shall dis|semble | with me.

46   The strange | children • shall | fail :

        and be a|fraid | out of • their | prisons.

change chant (Full)

§ *Omitted in the St Paul's Cathedral use*

Psalm 18, continued

J. Robinson

Full f   47   The Lord liveth * and blessed be my | strong | helper :
                     and praised be the | God of | my sal|vation;

Full   48   Even the God that seeth that I | be a|venged :
                     and sub|dueth • the | people | unto me.

              49   It is he that delivereth me from my cruel enemies *
                   and setteth me up a|bove mine | adversaries :
                     thou shalt | rid me • from the | wicked | man.

              50   For this cause will I give thanks unto thee O | Lord a•mong the | Gentiles :
                     and sing | praises | unto • thy | Name.

Full   51 | 2nd part | Great prosperity giveth he | unto • his | King :
                     and sheweth loving kindness unto David his Anointed *
                     and unto his | seed for | ever | more.

Full   Glory be to the Father | and to • the | Son :
                     and | to the | Holy | Ghost.

Full   As it was in the beginning is | now and • ever | shall be :
                     world without | end. A | . . | men.

PSALM 19

T. A. Walmisley

Cæli enarrant

Full *f* 1 The heavens declare the | glory • of | God :
and the | firma•ment | sheweth • his | handy-work.

Full 2 One day | telleth • an|other :
and one night | certi|fieth • an|other.

3 There is neither | speech nor | language :
but their | voices • are | heard a|mong them.

4 Their sound is gone | out • into all | lands :
and their | words • into the | ends • of the | world.

5 In them hath he set a | tabernacle • for the | sun :
which cometh forth as a bridegroom out of his chamber *
and rejoiceth as a | giant to | run his | course.

6 It goeth forth from the uttermost part of the heaven *
and runneth about unto the | end of it • a|gain :
and there is nothing | hid • from the | heat there|of.

mf 7 The law of the Lord is an undefiled law con|verting • the | soul :
the testimony of the Lord is sure and giveth | wisdom | unto • the | simple.

8 The statutes of the Lord are right and re|joice the | heart :
the commandment of the Lord is pure and giveth | light | unto • the | eyes.

mp 9 The fear of the Lord is clean and en|dureth • for | ever :
the judgements of the Lord are | true and | righteous • alto|gether.

10 More to be desired are they than gold * yea than | much fine | gold :
sweeter also than | honey | and the | honey-comb.

11 **2nd part** Moreover by them is thy | servant | taught :
and in | keeping of them • there is | great re|ward.

Psalm 19, continued

T. A. Walmisley

p	12	Who can tell how │ oft • he of│fendeth :
		O │ cleanse thou me • from my │ secret │ faults.
	13	Keep thy servant also from presumptuous sins *
		lest they get the do│minion │ over me :
		so shall I be undefiled and │ innocent • from the │ great of│fence.
Full mf	14	2nd part Let the words of my mouth and the meditation of my heart *
		be alway ac│ceptable • in thy │ sight :
cresc.	15	O Lord my │ strength and │ my re│deemer.
Full f		Glory be to the Father │ and to • the │ Son :
		and │ to the │ Holy │ Ghost.
Full		As it was in the beginning is │ now and • ever │ shall be :
		world without │ end. A │ . . │ men.

PSALM 20

R. Roseingrave

Exaudiat te Dominus

Full mp	1	The Lord hear thee in the │ day of │ trouble :
		the Name of the │ God of │ Jacob • de│fend thee;
Full	2	Send thee │ help • from the │ sanctuary :
		and │ strengthen • thee │ out of │ Sion;

Psalm 20, continued

R. *Roseingrave*

3   Re|member · all thy | offerings :
    and ac|cept thy | burnt | sacrifice;

4 ‡   Grant thee thy | heart's de|sire :
    – | – and ful|fil · all thy | mind.

mf   5   We will rejoice in thy salvation *
    and triumph in the Name of the | Lord our | God :
    the Lord per|form all | thy pe|titions.

f   6   Now know I that the Lord helpeth his Anointed *
    and will hear him from his | holy | heaven :
    even with the wholesome | strength · of his | right | hand.

mf   7   Some put their trust in | chariots and · some in | horses :
    but we will remember the | Name · of the | Lord our | God.

mp   8   They are brought | down and | fallen :
mf   but we are | risen · and | stand | upright.

mp   9 †‡   **2nd part** Save Lord and hear us O | King of | heaven ‖ – | – when we |
    call up|on thee.

Full   *mf*   Glory be to the Father | and to · the | Son :
    and | to the | Holy | Ghost.

Full   As it was in the beginning is | now and · ever | shall be :
    world without | end. A | . . | men.

PSALM 21

J. Goss

Domine, in virtute tua

| **Full** *f* | 1 | The King shall rejoice in thy \| strength O \| Lord : |
| | | exceeding \| glad • shall he \| be of • thy sal\|vation. |

| **Full** | 2 | Thou hast given him his \| heart's de\|sire : |
| | | and hast not de\|nied him • the re\|quest • of his \| lips. |

| *mf* | 3 | For thou shalt prevent him with the \| blessings • of \| goodness : |
| | | and shalt set a \| crown of • pure \| gold up•on his \| head. |

| | 4 ‡ | He asked life of thee * and thou gavest him a \| long \| life : |
| | | – \| even • for \| ever • and \| ever. |

| *f* | 5 | His honour is \| great in • thy sal\|vation : |
| | | glory and great \| worship • shalt thou \| lay up\|on him. |

| | 6 | For thou shalt give him ever\|lasting • fe\|licity : |
| | | and make him \| glad • with the \| joy • of thy \| countenance. |

| *mf* | 7 | And why? * because the King putteth his \| trust • in the \| Lord : |
| | | and in the mercy of the most \| Highest • he shall \| not mis\|carry. |

| | 8 | All thine enemies shall \| feel thy \| hand : |
| | | thy \| right hand • shall \| find out • them that \| hate thee. |

	9	Thou shalt make them like a fiery oven in | time • of thy | wrath :
		the Lord shall destroy them in his dis|pleasure • and the |
		fire • shall con|sume them.

| | 10 | Their fruit shalt thou root \| out of • the \| earth : |
| | | and their \| seed from a•mong the \| children • of \| men. |

Psalm 21, continued

J. Goss

mp	11	For they intended | mischief · a|gainst thee : and imagined such a device as they | are not | able · to per|form.
cresc.	12	Therefore shalt thou | put them · to | flight : and the strings of thy bow shalt thou make | ready · a|gainst the | face of them.
Full *f*	13	2nd part Be thou exalted | Lord in · thine own | strength : so will we | sing and | praise thy | power.
Full		Glory be to the Father | and to · the | Son : and | to the | Holy | Ghost.
Full		As it was in the beginning is | now and · ever | shall be : world without | end. A | . . | men.

PSALM 22

S. Wesley

Deus, Deus meus

Full	*p*	1	My God my God look upon me * | why hast · thou for|saken me :
			and art so far from my | health and · from the | words of · my com|plaint?
Full		2	O my God I cry in the | day-time · but thou | hearest not :
			and in the | night-season · also I | take no | rest.
	mp	3 †	And thou con|tinu·est | ho||ly * | O thou | worship · of | Israel.
		4	Our | fathers · hoped in | thee :
			they trusted in | thee and | thou · didst de|liver them.
	mf	5	They called upon | thee and · were | holpen :
			they put their trust in | thee · and were | not con|founded.
	p	6	But as for me * I am a | worm and · no | man :
			a very | scorn of men · and the | outcast · of the | people.
Full	*mf*	7	All they that see me | laugh me · to | scorn :
			they shoot out their | lips and | shake their | heads saying,
Full	*f*	8	He trusted in God that | he would · de|liver him :
			let him de|liver · him | if he · will | have him.
	mp	9	But thou art he that took me out of my | mother's | womb :
			thou wast my hope * when I hanged | yet up·on my | mother's | breasts.
		10	I have been left unto thee ever | since · I was | born :
			thou art my | God · even | from my · mother's | womb.
		11 ‡	O go not from me * for | trouble is · hard at | hand :
			– | – and there is | none to | help me.
		12	Many | oxen are · come a|bout me :
			fat bulls of | Basan · close me | in on · every | side.

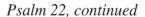

Psalm 22, continued

S. Wesley

mf   13   They gape up|on me • with their | mouths :
         as it were a | ramping • and a | roaring | lion.

p   14   I am poured out like water * and all my | bones are • out of | joint :
         my heart also in the midst of my body is | even • like | melting | wax.

    15   My strength is dried up like a potsherd * and my tongue | cleaveth • to my | gums :
         and thou shalt bring me | into • the | dust of | death.

    16   For many | dogs are • come a|bout me :
         and the council of the | wicked • layeth | siege a|gainst me.

pp   17   They pierced my hands and my feet; * I may | tell all • my | bones :
         they stand | staring • and | looking • up|on me.

    18   They part my | garments • a|mong them :
         and cast | lots up|on my | vesture.

mf   19   But be not thou | far from • me O | Lord :
         thou art my | succour * | haste thee • to | help me.

    20   Deliver my | soul • from the | sword :
         my | darling • from the | power • of the | dog.

    21   [*2nd part*] Save me from the | lion's | mouth :
         thou hast heard me also from a|mong the | horns • of the | unicorns.

change chant (Full)

Psalm 22, continued

H. Smart

Full *f*   22   I will declare thy │ name • unto my │ brethren :
                           in the midst of the congre│gation │ will I │ praise thee.

Full   23   O praise the │ Lord • ye that │ fear him :
                           magnify him all ye of the seed of Jacob *
                           and │ fear him • all ye │ seed of │ Israel.

Full   24   ┌─────┐ For he hath not despised nor abhorred the low e│state • of the │ poor :
                           │ 2nd │ he hath not hid his face from him *
                           │ part │
                           └─────┘ but when he │ called • unto │ him he │ heard him.

                       25   My praise is of thee in the │ great • congre│gation :
                           my vows will I per│form in • the │ sight of • them that │ fear him.

mf   26   The poor shall │ eat • and be │ satisfied :
cresc.   they that seek after the Lord shall praise him; *
                           your │ heart shall │ live for │ ever.

                       27   All the ends of the world shall remember themselves and be │
                           turned • unto the │ Lord :
                           and all the kindreds of the │ nations • shall │ worship • be│fore him.

                       28   For the │ kingdom • is the │ Lord's :
                           and he is the │ Governor • a│mong the │ people.

mf   29 † All │ such as • be │ fat up║on │ earth have │ eaten • and │ worshipped.

mp   30   All they that go down into the dust shall │ kneel be│fore him :
                           and │ no man • hath │ quickened • his own │ soul.

f   31   My │ seed shall │ serve him :
                           they shall be counted unto the │ Lord for • a │ gene│ration.

                       32   They shall come * and the heavens shall de│clare his │ righteousness :
                           unto a people that shall be │ born • whom the │ Lord hath │ made.

Full   Glory be to the Father │ and to • the │ Son :
                           and │ to the │ Holy │ Ghost.

Full   As it was in the beginning is │ now and • ever │ shall be :
                           world without │ end. A │ . . │ men.

PSALM 23

Dominus regit me

C. Hylton Stewart

1 The Lord is my shep - herd : therefore can I lack nothing.

2 He shall feed me in a green _ pas - ture : and lead me forth beside the wa-ters of com - fort.

3 He shall con-vert my soul : and bring me forth in the paths of righteousness for his Name's sake.

4 Yea though I walk through the valley of the shadow of death * I will fear no e - vil :

for thou art with me * thy rod and thy staff comfort me.

Psalm 23, continued

5 Thou shalt prepare a table before me * against them that trouble me :

thou hast anointed my head with oil * and my cup shall be full.

6 But thy loving kindness and mercy shall follow me * all the days of my life :

and I will dwell in the house of the Lord for e - ver.

Glory be to the Father and to the Son : and to the Holy Ghost.

As it was in the beginning is now and ever shall be : world with-out end. A - men.

Day 5: Morning

PSALM 24

J. Barnby

Domini est terra

Full f 1 The earth is the Lord's and │ all that • therein │ is :
  the compass of the │ world and │ they that │ dwell therein.

Full 2 For he hath │ founded it up•on the │ seas :
  and pre│pared it • up│on the │ floods.

  mf 3 Who shall ascend into the │ hill • of the │ Lord :
  or who shall rise │ up • in his │ holy │ place?

  4 Even he that hath clean │ hands • and a pure │ heart :
  and that hath not lift up his mind unto vanity *
  nor │ sworn • to de│ceive his │ neighbour.

  mp 5 He shall receive the │ blessing • from the │ Lord :
  and │ righteousness • from the │ God of • his sal│vation.

  6 This is the gene│ration of • them that │ seek him :
  even of │ them that • seek thy │ face O │ Jacob.

Full mf 7 Lift up your heads O ye gates * and be ye lift up ye │ ever•lasting │ doors :
  and the │ King of │ glory • shall come │ in.

Trebles mf 8 Who is the │ King of │ glory :
Full   it is the Lord strong and mighty * │ even the • Lord │ mighty • in │ battle.

Full unison f 9 Lift up your heads O ye gates * and be ye lift up ye │ ever•lasting │ doors :
  and the │ King of │ glory • shall come │ in.

Trebles f 10 Who is the │ King of │ glory :
Full unison   even the Lord of hosts * │ he • is the │ King of │ glory.

Full harmony   Glory be to the Father │ and to • the │ Son :
  and │ to the │ Holy │ Ghost.

Full   As it was in the beginning is │ now and • ever │ shall be :
  world without │ end. A │ • • │ men.

PSALM 25

J. Turle

Ad te, Domine, levavi

Full *mf* 1 Unto thee O Lord will I lift up my soul *
my God I have | put my | trust in thee :
O let me not be confounded *
neither let mine | ene•mies | triumph | over me.

Full 2 For all they that hope in thee | shall not • be a|shamed :
but such as transgress without a | cause • shall be | put to • con|fusion.

3 ‡ Shew me thy | ways O | Lord :
– | – and | teach me • thy | paths.

4 Lead me forth in thy | truth and | learn me :
for thou art the God of my salvation *
in thee hath been my | hope | all the • day | long.

mp 5 Call to remembrance O Lord thy | tender | mercies :
and thy loving-|kindnesses • which have been | ever • of | old.

6 O remember not the sins and of|fences • of my | youth :
but according to thy mercy *
think thou up|on me • O | Lord • for thy | goodness.

p 7 Gracious and | righteous • is the | Lord :
therefore will he | teach | sinners • in the | way.

8 Them that are meek shall he | guide in | judgement :
and such as are gentle * | them • shall he | learn his | way.

9 All the paths of the Lord are | mercy • and | truth :
unto such as keep his | cove•nant | and his | testimonies.

10 For thy | Name's sake • O | Lord :
be merciful unto my | sin for | it is | great.

Psalm 25, continued

J. Turle

11   What man is he that │ feareth • the │ Lord :
       him shall he │ teach • in the │ way that • he shall │ choose.

12   His │ soul shall • dwell at │ ease :
       and his │ seed • shall in│herit • the │ land.

p   13 ‡   **2nd part** The secret of the Lord is a│mong them • that │ fear him :
       – │ – and he will │ shew them • his │ covenant.

mp   14   Mine eyes are ever │ looking • unto the │ Lord :
       for he shall │ pluck my • feet │ out of • the │ net.

pp   15   Turn thee unto me and have │ mercy • up│on me :
       for I am │ deso•late │ and in │ misery.

p   16   The sorrows of my │ heart • are en│larged :
       O │ bring thou • me │ out of • my │ troubles.

pp   17 ‡   Look upon my ad│versity • and │ misery :
       – │ – and for│give me • all my │ sin.

mf   18   Consider mine enemies how │ many • they │ are :
       and they bear a │ tyran•nous │ hate a│gainst me.

19   O keep my │ soul • and de│liver me :
       let me not be con│founded • for I have │ put my │ trust in thee.

Full   20 ‡   Let perfectness and righteous │ dealing • wait up│on me :
       – │ – for my │ hope hath • been in │ thee.

Full   21 †‡   Deliver │ Israel • O │ God ‖ – │ – out of │ all his │ troubles.

Full   *mf*   Glory be to the Father │ and to • the │ Son :
       and │ to the │ Holy │ Ghost.

Full   As it was in the beginning is │ now and • ever │ shall be :
       world without │ end. A │ .. │ men.

PSALM 26

G. R. Sinclair

Judica me, Domine

Full   **mp**   1   Be thou my judge O Lord for | I have • walked | innocently :
                       my trust hath been also in the | Lord • therefore | shall I • not | fall.

Full   2 ‡   Examine me O | Lord and | prove me :
                       – | try out • my | reins • and my | heart.

                  3 ‡   For thy loving-kindness is | ever be•fore mine | eyes :
                       – | – and I will | walk in • thy | truth.

                  4   I have not | dwelt with • vain | persons :
                       neither will I have | fellow•ship | with the • de|ceitful.

    mf   5   I have hated the congre|gation • of the | wicked :
                       and will not | sit a|mong the • un|godly.

    mp   6   I will wash my hands in | innocency • O | Lord :
                       and | so • will I | go to • thine | altar;

    mf   7   That I may shew the | voice of | thanksgiving :
                       and | tell of • all thy | wondrous | works.

                  8   Lord I have loved the habi|tation • of thy | house :
                       and the | place • where thine | honour | dwelleth.

                  9 †   O shut not up my | soul • with the | sin‖ners * |
                       nor my | life • with the | blood-thirsty;

                10   In whose | hands is | wickedness :
                       and their | right hand • is | full of | gifts.

    mp   11   But as for me | I will • walk | innocently :
                       O de|liver me • and be | merci•ful | unto me.

    mf   12   My | foot • standeth | right :
                       I will praise the | Lord • in the | congre|gations.

Full   **f**   Glory be to the Father | and to • the | Son :
                       and | to the | Holy | Ghost.

Full   As it was in the beginning is | now and • ever | shall be :
                       world without | end. A | • • | men.

PSALM 27

v. 2

J. L. Hopkins

v. 2

Dominus illuminatio

Full *f*	1	The Lord is my light and my salvation * │ whom then • shall I │ fear :
		the Lord is the strength of my life *
		of │ whom then │ shall I • be a│fraid?
Full	2 ‡	When the wicked * even mine enemies and my foes came upon me to │
		eat up • my │ flesh :
		– │ – they │ stumbled • and │ fell.
	3	Though an host of men were laid against me *
		yet shall not my │ heart • be a│fraid :
		and though there rose up war against me * │
		yet will • I │ put my │ trust in him.
mf	4	One thing have I desired of the │ Lord which I • will re│quire :
		even that I may dwell in the house of the Lord all the days of my life *
		to behold the fair beauty of the │ Lord • and to │ visit • his │ temple.
mp	5	For in the time of trouble he shall │ hide me • in his │ tabernacle :
		yea in the secret place of his dwelling shall he hide me *
		and set me │ up up•on a │ rock of │ stone.
cresc.	6 †	And now shall he │ lift up • mine │ head a║bove mine │ ene•mies │ round a│bout me.
f	7	2nd part │ Therefore will I offer in his dwelling an ob║lation • with great │ gladness :
		I will sing and speak │ praises │ unto • the │ Lord.

change chant (Decani)

Psalm 27, continued

W. Wolstenholme

Dec.	*mp*	8	Hearken unto my voice O Lord when I | cry • unto | thee : have | mercy • up|on me • and | hear me.
		9	My heart hath talked of thee * | Seek ye • my | face : Thy | face Lord | will I | seek.
		10	O hide not | thou thy | face from me : nor cast thy | servant • a|way in • dis|pleasure.
	mf	11	Thou hast | been my | succour : leave me not neither forsake me O | God of | my sal|vation.
		12	**2nd part** When my father and my | mother • for|sake me : the | Lord | taketh • me | up.
	mp	13	Teach me thy | way O | Lord : and lead me in the right | way be|cause of • mine | enemies.
	mf	14	Deliver me not over into the | will of • mine | adversaries : for there are false witnesses risen up a|gainst me • and | such as • speak | wrong.
	mp *cresc.*	15	I should | utterly • have | fainted : but that I believe verily to see the goodness of the | Lord • in the | land • of the | living.
	f	16	O tarry thou the | Lord's | leisure : be strong and he shall comfort thine heart * and | put thou • thy | trust • in the | Lord.
Full			Glory be to the Father | and to • the | Son : and | to the | Holy | Ghost.
Full			As it was in the beginning is | now and • ever | shall be : world without | end. A | . . | men.

PSALM 28

E. J. Hopkins

Ad te, Domine

Full **p**   1   Unto thee will I │ cry O • Lord my │ strength :
  think no scorn of me ***** lest if thou make as though thou hearest not *****
  I become like │ them that • go │ down • into the │ pit.

Full   2   Hear the voice of my humble petitions when I │ cry • unto │ thee :
  when I hold up my hands towards the │ mercy-seat • of thy │ holy │ temple.

    mp   3   O pluck me not away ***** neither destroy me
with the un│godly and • wicked │ doers :
  which speak friendly to their neighbours *****
  but i│magine │ mischief • in their │ hearts.

                       4   Reward them ac│cording • to their │ deeds :
  and according to the │ wickedness • of their │ own in│ventions.

                       5   Recompense them after the │ work • of their │ hands :
  pay them │ that they │ have de│served.

                       6   For they regard not in their mind the works of the Lord *****
nor the ope│ration • of his │ hands :
  therefore shall he break them │ down • and not │ build them │ up.

change chant (Decani)

Psalm 28, continued

E. J. Hopkins

Dec. *f*   7   Praised | be the | Lord :
for he hath heard the | voice • of my | humble • pe|titions.

8   The Lord is my strength and my shield *
my heart hath trusted in | him and • I am | helped :
therefore my heart danceth for | joy and • in my |
song • will I | praise him.

9   The | Lord • is my | strength :
and he is the | wholesome • de|fence of • his A|nointed.

10 ‡   O save thy people * and give thy blessing unto | thine in|heritance :
– | feed them • and | set them • up for | ever.

Full   Glory be to the Father | and to • the | Son :
and | to the | Holy | Ghost.

Full   As it was in the beginning is | now and • ever | shall be :
world without | end. A | . . | men.

PSALM 29

H. G. Ley

Afferte Domino

Full *f*   1   Bring unto the Lord O ye mighty * bring young | rams • unto the | Lord :
ascribe unto the | Lord | worship • and | strength.

Full   2   Give the Lord the honour | due • unto his | Name :
worship the | Lord with | holy | worship.

Psalm 29, continued

H. G. Ley

mf 3 It is the Lord that com|mandeth · the | waters :
it is the glorious | God that | maketh · the | thunder.

4 It is the Lord that ruleth the sea *
the voice of the Lord is | mighty in · ope|ration :
the voice of the | Lord · is a | glorious | voice.

f 5 The voice of the Lord | breaketh · the | cedar-trees :
yea the Lord | breaketh · the | cedars · of | Libanus.

mf 6 He maketh them also to | skip · like a | calf :
Libanus also and | Siri·on | like a · young | unicorn.

f 7 The voice of the Lord divideth the flames of fire *
the voice of the Lord | shaketh · the | wilderness :
yea the Lord | shaketh · the | wilderness · of | Cades.

mf 8 The voice of the Lord maketh the hinds to bring forth young *
and dis|covereth · the thick | bushes :
in his temple doth | every · man | speak of · his | honour.

f 9 The Lord sitteth a|bove the | water-flood :
cresc. and the Lord re|maineth · a | King for | ever.

10 The Lord shall give | strength · unto his | people :
dim. the Lord shall give his | people · the | blessing · of | peace.

Full f Glory be to the Father | and to · the | Son :
and | to the | Holy | Ghost.

Full As it was in the beginning is | now and · ever | shall be :
world without | end. A | . . | men.

PSALM 30

C. H. Lloyd

Exaltabo te, Domine

Full *f* 1 I will magnify thee O Lord for thou hast | set me | up :
          and not made my | foes to | triumph | over me.

Full 2 ‡ O Lord my God I | cried • unto | thee :
          – | – and | thou hast | healed me.

mf 3 Thou Lord hast brought my | soul • out of | hell :
          thou hast kept my life from | them that • go | down • to the | pit.

4 Sing praises unto the | Lord • O ye | saints of his :
          and give thanks unto him for a re|membrance | of his | holiness.

5 For his wrath endureth but the twinkling of an eye * and in his | pleasure • is | life :
mp   heaviness may endure for a night *
mf   but | joy • cometh | in the | morning.

6 And in my prosperity I said I shall | never be • re|moved :
          thou Lord of thy | goodness • hast | made my • hill so | strong.

change chant (Decani)

John Scott

Dec. *mp* 7 Thou didst | turn thy | face from • me :
          and | I was | troubled.

8 Then cried I | unto • thee O | Lord :
          and gat me to my | Lord right | humbly.

Psalm 30, continued

John Scott

9   What profit is there | in my | blood :
        when I go | down · to the | pit?

10   Shall the dust give | thanks · unto | thee :
        or | shall it de·clare thy | truth?

mf   11   2nd part Hear O Lord and have | mercy · up|on me :
        Lord be | thou my | helper.

change chant (Decani)

C. H. Lloyd

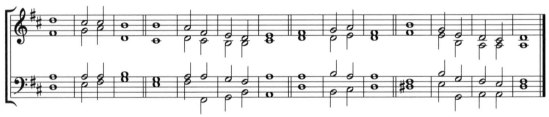

Dec. *f*   12   Thou hast turned my | heaviness · into | joy :
        thou hast put off my | sackcloth · and | girded · me with | gladness.

13   Therefore shall every good man sing of thy | praise with·out | ceasing :
        O my God I will give | thanks · unto | thee for | ever.

Full   Glory be to the Father | and to · the | Son :
        and | to the | Holy | Ghost.

Full   As it was in the beginning is | now and · ever | shall be :
        world without | end. A | . . | men.

PSALM 31

C. H. Lloyd

In te, Domine, speravi

Full	*mf*	1	In thee O Lord have I | put my | trust : let me never be put to confusion * de|liver • me | in thy | righteousness.
Full		2 ‡	Bow | down thine | ear to me : – | – make | haste • to de|liver me.
		3 ‡	And be thou my strong rock and | house • of de|fence : – | – that | thou • mayest | save me.
		4	For thou art my strong | rock • and my | castle : be thou also my | guide and | lead me • for thy | name's sake.
		5 ‡	Draw me out of the net that they have laid | privi•ly | for me : – | – for | thou art • my | strength.
mp *cresc.*		6	Into thy hands I com|mend my | spirit : for thou hast re|deemed me • O | Lord thou • God of | truth.
mf		7	I have hated them that hold of super|stitious | vanities : and my | trust hath | been • in the | Lord.
		8	I will be glad and re|joice • in thy | mercy : for thou hast considered my trouble * and hast | known my | soul • in ad|versities.
		9	2nd part Thou hast not shut me up into the | hand • of the | enemy : but hast set my | feet • in a | large | room.

change chant (Decani)

Psalm 31, *continued*

C. H. Lloyd

Dec. *mp*   10   Have mercy upon me O Lord for │ I am · in │ trouble :
           and mine eye is consumed for very heaviness * │
           yea my │ soul · and my │ body.

     11 ‡   For my life is waxen │ old with │ heaviness :
           – │ – and my │ years with │ mourning.

p   12 ‡   My strength faileth me be│cause of · mine in│iquity :
           – │ – and my │ bones · are con│sumed.

     13   I became a reproof among all mine enemies *
     but especially a│mong my │ neighbours :
           and they of mine acquaintance were afraid of me *
           and they that did see me with│out con│veyed them·selves │ from me.

pp   14   I am clean forgotten as a │ dead man · out of │ mind :
       I am be│come · like a │ broken │ vessel.

mp   15   For I have heard the │ blasphemy · of the │ multitude :
           and fear is on every side * while they conspire together against me *
           and take their │ counsel · to │ take a·way my │ life.

mf   16   But my hope hath been in │ thee O │ Lord :
       I have │ said * │ Thou art · my │ God.

     17 ‡   My time is in thy hand * deliver me from the │ hand · of mine │ enemies :
           – │ – and from │ them that │ persecute me.

     18   Shew thy servant the │ light · of thy │ countenance :
       and │ save me · for thy │ mercy's │ sake.

     19   Let me not be confounded O Lord * for I have │ called up│on thee :
           let the ungodly be put to confusion * and be put to │ silence │ in the │ grave.

     20   **2nd part**   Let the lying lips be │ put to │ silence :
           which cruelly disdainfully and de│spiteful·ly │
       speak a·gainst the │ righteous.

change chant (Full)

Psalm 31, continued

C. H. Lloyd

Full *mf* 21   O how plentiful is thy goodness which thou hast laid up for │ them that │ fear thee :
and that thou hast prepared for them that put their trust in thee * │
even be·fore the │ sons of │ men!

Full   22   Thou shalt hide them privily by thine own presence *
from the pro│voking · of │ all men :
thou shalt keep them secretly in thy │ tabernacle ·from the │
strife of │ tongues.

      f   23   Thanks │ be · to the │ Lord :
for he hath shewed me marvellous great │ kindness · in a │ strong │ city.

      mf   24   And when I made │ haste I │ said :
I am cast │ out of · the │ sight · of thine │ eyes.

             25 †   │2nd│ Nevertheless thou │ heardest · the │ voice ‖ of my │ prayer · when I │
                    │part│ cried │ unto thee.

Full *f* 26   O love the │ Lord · all ye his │ saints :
for the Lord preserveth them that are faithful *
and plenteously re│wardeth · the │ proud │ doer.

Full   27   Be strong and he shall e│stablish · your │ heart :
all ye that │ put your │ trust · in the │ Lord.

Full   Glory be to the Father │ and to · the │ Son :
and │ to the │ Holy │ Ghost.

Full   As it was in the beginning is │ now and · ever │ shall be :
world without │ end. A │ . . │ men.

Day 6: Evening

PSALM 32

W. Russell

Beati, quorum

Full *mp* 1 ‡ Blessed is he whose un|righteousness • is for|given :
– | – and whose | sin is | covered.

Full 2 Blessed is the man unto whom the Lord im|puteth • no | sin :
and in whose | spirit • there | is no | guile.

p 3 For while I | held my | tongue :
my bones consumed a|way • through my | daily • com|plaining.

4 For thy hand is heavy up|on me • day and | night :
and my | moisture is • like the | drought in | summer.

5 I will acknowledge my | sin • unto | thee :
and mine un|righteous•ness | have I • not | hid.

6 I said I will confess my | sins • unto the | Lord :
and so thou forgavest the | wicked•ness | of my | sin.

mp 7 For this shall everyone that is godly make his prayer unto thee *
in a time when thou | mayest • be | found :
cresc. but in the great | water-floods • they shall | not come | nigh him.

p 8 Thou art a place to hide me in * thou shalt pre|serve me • from | trouble :
thou shalt compass me a|bout with | songs • of de|liverance.

mf 9 I will inform thee and teach thee in the way where|in • thou shalt | go :
and I will | guide thee | with mine | eye.

10 Be ye not like to horse and mule which have | no • under|standing :
whose mouths must be held with bit and | bridle • lest they | fall up|on thee.

11 Great plagues re|main • for the un|godly :
cresc. but whoso putteth his trust in the Lord *
mercy em|braceth him • on | every | side.

Psalm 32, continued

W. Russell

f	12	Be glad O ye righteous and re|joice · in the | Lord : and be joyful all | ye · that are | true of | heart.
Full		Glory be to the Father | and to · the | Son : and | to the | Holy | Ghost.
Full		As it was in the beginning is | now and · ever | shall be : world without | end. A | . . | men.

PSALM 33

J. Turle

Exultate, justi

Full *f*	1	Rejoice in the | Lord · O ye | righteous : for it becometh | well the | just · to be | thankful.
Full	2	Praise the | Lord with | harp : sing praises unto him with the lute and | instrument · of | ten | strings.
	3	Sing unto the | Lord a · new | song : sing praises lustily unto | him · with a | good | courage.
	4	For the word of the | Lord is | true : and | all his | works are | faithful.
mf	5	He loveth | righteousness · and | judgement : the earth is full of the | goodness | of the | Lord.
	6	By the word of the Lord were the | heavens | made : and all the | hosts of them · by the | breath · of his | mouth.

Psalm 33, continued

J. Turle

7   He gathereth the waters of the sea together as it | were up•on an | heap :
          and layeth up the | deep as | in a | treasure-house.

mp   8   Let all the | earth • fear the | Lord :
          stand in awe of him all | ye that | dwell • in the | world.

mf   9   For he | spake and • it was | done :
          he com|manded • and it | stood | fast.

10   The Lord bringeth the counsel of the | heathen • to | nought :
          and maketh the devices of the people to be of none effect *
          and casteth | out the | counsels • of | princes.

f   11   The counsel of the Lord shall en|dure for | ever :
          and the thoughts of his heart from gene|ration • to | gene|ration.

12   Blessed are the people whose God is the | Lord Je|hovah :
          and blessed are the folk that he hath | chosen to • him to |
          be • his in|heritance.

mf   13   The Lord looked down from heaven and beheld all the | children • of | men :
          from the habitation of his dwelling he considereth all | them that |
          dwell • on the | earth.

14   He | fashioneth • all the | hearts of them :
          and under|standeth | all their | works.

15   There is no king that can be saved by the | multitude • of an | host :
          neither is any | mighty man • de|livered • by much | strength.

16   A horse is counted but a | vain thing • to | save a man :
          neither shall he deliver | any • man | by his • great | strength.

Psalm 33, continued

J. Turle

mp   17   Behold the eye of the Lord is upon | them that | fear him :
         and upon | them that · put their | trust · in his | mercy;

p   18   To deliver their | soul from | death :
         and to | feed them · in the | time of | dearth.

mf   19   Our soul hath patiently | tarried · for the | Lord :
         for | he is · our | help · and our | shield.

f   20   For our | heart · shall re|joice in him :
         because we have | hoped · in his | holy | Name.

Full   21   **2nd part** Let thy merciful kindness O | Lord · be up|on us :
         like as we do | put our | trust in | thee.

Full   Glory be to the Father | and to · the | Son :
         and | to the | Holy | Ghost.

Full   As it was in the beginning is | now and · ever | shall be :
         world without | end. A | · · | men.

PSALM 34

C. F. South

Benedicam Domino

Full *f*	1	I will alway give │ thanks • unto the │ Lord :	

his praise shall │ ever • be │ in my │ mouth.

Full   2   My soul shall make her │ boast • in the │ Lord :
the │ humble • shall │ hear thereof • and be │ glad.

Full   3   ┌─────┐ O praise the │ Lord with │ me :
         │ **2nd** │
         │ **part** │   and let us │ magnify • his │ Name to│gether.
         └─────┘

mf   4   I sought the │ Lord • and he │ heard me :
yea he de│livered me • out of │ all my │ fear.

5   They had an eye unto │ him • and were │ lightened :
and their │ faces • were │ not a│shamed.

mp   6   Lo the poor crieth and the │ Lord │ heareth him :
yea and │ saveth him • out of │ all his │ troubles.

7 †   The angel of the Lord tarrieth │ round a•bout │ them ‖ that │ fear him │
and de│livereth them.

p   8   O taste and see how │ gracious • the │ Lord is :
blessed is the │ man that │ trusteth • in │ him.

mf   9   O fear the Lord │ ye that • are his │ saints :
for │ they that │ fear him • lack │ nothing.

10   ┌─────┐ The lions do │ lack and • suffer │ hunger :
      │ **2nd** │
      │ **part** │   but they who seek the Lord shall want no │ manner • of │
      └─────┘   thing • that is │ good.

p   11   Come ye children and │ hearken │ unto me :
I will │ teach you • the │ fear • of the │ Lord.

mf   12 ‡   What man is he that │ lusteth • to │ live :
– │ and would │ fain • see good │ days?

Psalm 34, continued

C. F. South

mp   13   Keep thy | tongue from | evil :
       and thy | lips • that they | speak no | guile.

14   Eschew | evil • and do | good :
       seek | peace | and en|sue it.

15   The eyes of the Lord are | over • the | righteous :
       and his ears are | open | unto • their | prayers.

16   The countenance of the Lord is against | them that • do | evil :
       to root out the re|membrance • of them | from the | earth.

p   17   The righteous cry and the | Lord | heareth them :
       and de|livereth them • out of | all their | troubles.

18   The Lord is nigh unto them that are of a | contrite | heart :
       and will save | such as be • of an | humble | spirit.

mp   19   Great are the | troubles • of the | righteous :
cresc.   but the | Lord de|livereth him • out of | all.

mf   20 ‡   He | keepeth • all his | bones :
       – | so that • not | one of • them is | broken.

Full   f   21   But misfortune shall | slay the • un|godly :
       and they that | hate the | righteous • shall be | desolate.

Full   22   The Lord delivereth the | souls • of his | servants :
       and all they that put their | trust in him • shall | not be | destitute.

Full   Glory be to the Father | and to • the | Son :
       and | to the | Holy | Ghost.

Full   As it was in the beginning is | now and • ever | shall be :
       world without | end. A | . . | men.

PSALM 35

H. Stonex

Judica, Domine

Full   mf   1   Plead thou my cause O Lord with | them that | strive with me :
and | fight thou a•gainst | them that | fight against me.

Full   2 ‡   Lay hand upon the | shield and | buckler :
– | – and | stand up • to | help me.

3   Bring forth the spear * and stop the way against | them that | persecute me :
say unto my | soul * I am | thy sal|vation.

4 §   Let them be confounded and put to shame that | seek • after my | soul :
let them be turned back and brought to confusion that i|magine |
mischief | for me.

5 §   Let them be as the | dust be•fore the | wind :
and the | angel • of the | Lord | scattering them.

6 §   Let their way be | dark and | slippery :
and let the | angel • of the | Lord | persecute them,

7 §   For they have privily laid their net to de|stroy me with•out a | cause :
yea even without a cause have they | made a | pit • for my | soul.

8 §   Let a sudden destruction come upon him unawares *
and his net that he hath laid | privi•ly | catch himself :
that he may | fall • into his | own | mischief.

9   And my soul be | joyful • in the | Lord :
it shall re|joice in | his sal|vation.

10   **2nd part** All my bones shall say Lord who is like unto thee *
who deliverest the poor from | him that • is too | strong for him :
yea the poor and him that is in | misery • from |
him that | spoileth him?

§ *Omitted in the St Paul's Cathedral use*

Psalm 35, continued

H. Stonex

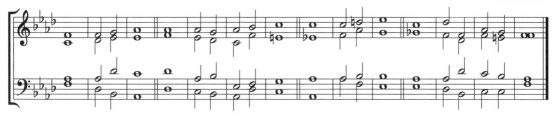

mf	11	False | witnesses did · rise | up :
		they laid to my | charge | things · that I | knew not.
	12	They rewarded me | evil · for | good :
		to the great dis|comfort | of my | soul.
p	13	Nevertheless when they were sick I put on sackcloth *
		and humbled my | soul with | fasting :
		and my prayer shall turn | into · mine | own | bosom.
	14	I behaved myself as though it had been my | friend · or my | brother :
		I went heavily as | one that | mourneth · for his | mother.
mp	15	But in mine adversity they rejoiced and gathered them|selves to|gether :
		yea the very abjects came together against me unawares *
		making | mouths at | me and | ceased not.
mf	16	With the flatterers were | busy | mockers :
		who | gnashed up·on me | with their | teeth.
	17	Lord how long wilt thou | look up·on | this :
		O deliver my soul from the calamities which they bring on me *
		and my | darling | from the | lions.
f	18	So will I give thee thanks in the | great · congre|gation :
		I will | praise thee · a|mong much | people.
mf	19	O let not them that are mine enemies triumph | over me · un|godly :
		neither let them wink with their eyes that | hate me · with|out a | cause.
	20	And why? * their communing is | not for | peace :
		but they imagine deceitful words against | them · that are |
		quiet · in the | land.

Psalm 35, continued

H. Stonex

21   They gaped upon me with their | mouths and | said :
       Fie on thee fie on thee we | saw it | with our | eyes.

22   This thou hast | seen O | Lord :
       hold not thy tongue then * | go not | far from • me O | Lord.

mf   23   Awake and stand up to | judge my | quarrel :
       avenge thou my | cause my | God • and my | Lord.

24   Judge me O Lord my God ac|cording • to thy | righteousness :
       and | let them • not | triumph | over me.

25   Let them not say in their hearts * There there | so • would we | have it :
       neither let them | say * | We have • de|voured him.

26   Let them be put to confusion and shame together that re|joice at • my | trouble :
       let them be clothed with rebuke and dis|honour • that |
       boast them•selves a|gainst me.

f   27   Let them be glad and rejoice that favour my | righteous | dealing :
       yea let them say alway *
       Blessed be the Lord who hath pleasure in the pro|speri•ty |
       of his | servant.

28   And as for my tongue it shall be | talking of • thy | righteousness :
       and of thy | praise | all the • day | long.

Full   *f*   Glory be to the Father | and to • the | Son :
       and | to the | Holy | Ghost.

Full   As it was in the beginning is | now and • ever | shall be :
       world without | end. A | . . | men.

PSALM 36

C. Hylton Stewart

Dixit injustus

Full	**mp**	1

My heart sheweth me the │ wickedness • of the un│godly :
    that there is no │ fear of │ God be•fore his │ eyes.

Full		2

For he flattereth him│self in his • own │ sight :
    until his a│bomina•ble │ sin be • found │ out.

3   The words of his mouth are unrighteous and │ full of • de│ceit :
    he hath left off to behave himself │ wisely │ and to • do │ good.

4   He imagineth mischief upon his bed * and hath set him│self in • no good │ way :
    neither doth he abhor │ any • thing │ that is │ evil.

change chant (Full)

E. J. Hopkins

Full	**f**	5

Thy mercy O Lord reacheth │ unto • the │ heavens :
    and thy │ faithful•ness │ unto • the │ clouds.

Full		6

Thy righteousness standeth │ like the • strong │ mountains :
    thy │ judgements • are │ like the • great │ deep.

	mf	7

Thou Lord shalt save both man and beast *
How excellent is thy │ mercy • O │ God :
    and the children of men shall put their │ trust • under the │
    shadow • of thy │ wings.

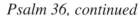

Psalm 36, continued

E. J. Hopkins

8   They shall be satisfied with the | plenteousness • of thy | house :
            and thou shalt give them drink of thy | pleasures • as | out of • the | river.

9   For with thee is the | well of | life :
            and in thy | light shall | we see | light.

10   O continue forth thy loving-kindness unto | them that | know thee :
            and thy righteousness unto | them • that are | true of | heart.

11   O let not the foot of | pride • come a|gainst me :
            and let not the | hand of • the un|godly • cast me | down.

12   There are they fallen | all that • work | wickedness :
            they are cast down and | shall not • be | able • to | stand.

Full f   Glory be to the Father | and to • the | Son :
            and | to the | Holy | Ghost.

Full   As it was in the beginning is | now and • ever | shall be :
            world without | end. A | . . | men.

PSALM 37

v. 6

H. N. Howells

Noli æmulari

Full *mf* 1 Fret not thyself be|cause of • the un|godly :
neither be thou | envious • a|gainst the • evil | doers.

Full 2 For they shall soon be cut | down • like the | grass :
and be | withered • even | as the • green | herb.

3 Put thou thy trust in the Lord and be | doing | good :
dwell in the land and | veri•ly | thou shalt • be | fed.

4 De|light thou • in the | Lord :
and he shall | give thee • thy | heart's de|sire.

5 Commit thy way unto the | Lord and • put thy | trust in him :
and | he shall | bring it • to | pass.

6 ‡ He shall make thy righteousness as | clear • as the | light :
– | – and thy just | dealing • as the | noon-day.

7 2nd part Hold thee still in the Lord and abide | patiently • up|on him :
but grieve not thyself at him whose way doth prosper *
against the man that | doeth • after | evil | counsels.

change chant (Decani)

H. N. Howells

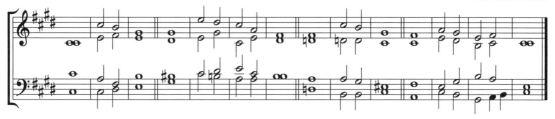

Dec. *mf* 8 Leave off from wrath and let | go dis|pleasure :
fret not thyself * else | shalt thou • be | moved to • do | evil.

9 Wicked doers shall be | rooted | out :
and they that patiently abide the Lord * | those • shall in|herit • the | land.

Psalm 37, *continued*

v. 15

H. N. Howells

mp	10	Yet a little while and the ungodly shall be | clean | gone :
		thou shalt look after his | place and | he shall • be a|way.
p	11	But the meek-spirited shall pos|sess the | earth :
		and shall be re|freshed • in the | multi•tude of | peace.
mf	12	The ungodly seeketh | counsel a•gainst the | just :
		and | gnasheth • up|on him • with his | teeth.
	13	The Lord shall | laugh him • to | scorn :
		for he hath | seen that • his | day is | coming.
	14	The ungodly have drawn out the sword and have | bent their | bow :
		to cast down the poor and needy *
		and to slay | such as are • of a | right • conver|sation.
	15 ‡	Their sword shall go | through their • own | heart :
		and their | – – | bow • shall be | broken.
mp	16	A small thing that the | righteous | hath :
		is better than great | riches | of the • un|godly.
mf	17	For the arms of the un|godly • shall be | broken :
		and the | Lord up|holdeth • the | righteous.
mp	18	The Lord knoweth the | days • of the | godly :
		and their in|heritance • shall en|dure for | ever.
	19	They shall not be confounded in the | peri•lous | time :
		and in the days of | dearth • they shall | have e|nough.
mf	20	**2nd part** As for the ungodly they shall perish *
		and the enemies of the Lord shall consume as the | fat of | lambs :
dim.		yea even as the | smoke shall • they con|sume a|way.
mp	21	The ungodly borroweth and | payeth • not a|gain :
		but the | righteous • is | merciful • and | liberal.
	22	Such as are blessed of God shall pos|sess the | land :
		and they that are | cursed of • him | shall be • rooted | out.

change chant (Decani)

Psalm 37, *continued*

H. N. Howells

Dec.   *mf*   23   The Lord ordereth a | good man's | going :
                    and maketh his | way ac|ceptable • to him|self.

               24   Though he fall he shall | not be • cast a|way :
                    for the Lord up|holdeth • him | with his | hand.

mp   25   I have been | young and • now am | old :
                    and yet saw I never the righteous forsaken * |
                    nor his • seed | begging • their | bread.

            26 ‡   The righteous is ever | merciful • and | lendeth :
                    – | – and his | seed is | blessed.

p   27 ‡   Flee from evil and do the | thing • that is | good :
                    – | – and | dwell for • ever|more.

            28   For the Lord loveth the | thing • that is | right :
                    he forsaketh not his that be godly * but | they are • pre|served for | ever.

mf   29   The un|righteous • shall be | punished :
                    as for the seed of the un|godly • it | shall be • rooted | out.

            30   The righteous shall in|herit • the | land :
                    and | dwell there|in for | ever.

mp   31   The mouth of the righteous is | exercised • in | wisdom :
                    and his | tongue • will be | talking • of | judgement.

           32 ‡   The law of his | God is • in his | heart :
                    – | – and his | goings • shall not | slide.

mf   33   The ungodly | seeth • the | righteous :
                    and | seeketh • oc|casion • to | slay him.

           34   The Lord will not | leave him • in his | hand :
                    nor con|demn him | when • he is | judged.

change chant (Decani)

Psalm 37, continued

H. N. Howells

Dec. *mf* 35 Hope thou in the Lord and keep his way *
and he shall promote thee that thou shalt pos|sess the | land :
when the un|godly • shall | perish • thou shalt | see it.

36 I myself have seen the un|godly in • great | power :
and | flourish•ing | like a • green | bay-tree.

37 [2nd part] I went by and | lo • he was | gone :
I sought him but his | place could | no where • be | found.

mp 38 Keep innocency and take heed unto the | thing • that is | right :
for that shall | bring a • man | peace at • the | last.

mf 39 As for the transgressors they shall | perish • to|gether :
and the end of the ungodly is * they shall be | rooted | out • at the | last.

Full *f* 40 But the salvation of the righteous | cometh • of the | Lord :
who is also their | strength • in the | time of | trouble.

Full 41 And the Lord shall | stand by • them and | save them :
he shall deliver them from the ungodly and shall save them *
be|cause they | put their | trust in him.

Full Glory be to the Father | and to • the | Son :
and | to the | Holy | Ghost.

Full As it was in the beginning is | now and • ever | shall be :
world without | end. A | . . | men.

PSALM 38

J. Barnby

Domine, ne in furore

Full	*p*	1	Put me not to rebuke O | Lord • in thine | anger : neither | chasten me • in thy | heavy • dis|pleasure.
Full		2	For thine | arrows • stick | fast in me : and thy | hand | presseth • me | sore.
		3	There is no health in my flesh be|cause of • thy dis|pleasure : neither is there any rest in my | bones by | reason • of my | sin.
		4	For my wickednesses are gone | over • my | head : and are like a sore burden too | heavy • for | me to | bear.
	mp	5 †‡	My wounds | stink and • are cor|rupt ‖ – | – – | through my | foolishness.
		6	I am brought into so great | trouble • and | misery : that I go | mourning | all the • day | long.
		7	For my loins are filled with a | sore di|sease : and there is | no whole | part • in my | body.
	p	8	I am | feeble and • sore | smitten : I have roared for the very dis|quiet•ness | of my | heart.
	mp	9	Lord thou knowest | all • my de|sire : and my | groaning | is not | hid from thee.
		10	My heart panteth my | strength hath | failed me : and the | sight • of mine | eyes is | gone from me.
	p	11	My lovers and my neighbours did stand looking up|on my | trouble : and my | kinsmen | stood a•far | off.
	mp	12	They also that sought after my | life laid | snares for me : and they that went about to do me evil talked of wickedness * and imagined de|ceit | all the • day | long.

Psalm 38, continued

J. Barnby

p   13   As for me I was like a | deaf man • and | heard not :
and as one that is | dumb who • doth not | open • his | mouth.

14   I became even as a | man that | heareth not :
and in whose | mouth are | no re|proofs.

mf   15   For in thee O Lord have I | put my | trust :
thou shalt | answer for • me O | Lord my | God.

16   I have required that they even mine enemies should not | triumph | over me :
for when my foot slipped they re|joiced | greatly • a|gainst me.

mp   17   And I truly am | set • in the | plague :
and my | heaviness • is | ever • in my | sight.

18 †‡   For I will con|fess my | wickedness ‖ – | – and be | sorry • for my | sin.

mf   19   But mine enemies | live • and are | mighty :
and they that hate me | wrongfully • are | many • in | number.

20   They also that reward evil for | good • are a|gainst me :
because I | follow • the | thing that | good is.

21 ‡   Forsake me not O | Lord my | God :
– | – – | be not • thou | far from me.

22 †‡   – | Haste thee • to | help me ‖ O Lord | God of | my sal|vation.

Full f   Glory be to the Father | and to • the | Son :
and | to the | Holy | Ghost.

Full   As it was in the beginning is | now and • ever | shall be :
world without | end. A | . . | men.

PSALM 39

I. A. Atkins

Dixi, custodiam

Full	*mp*	1	I said I will take | heed • to my | ways : that I of|fend not | in my | tongue.
Full		2	I will keep my mouth as it | were • with a | bridle : while the un|godly • is | in my | sight.
	p	3	I held my | tongue and • spake | nothing : I kept silence yea even from good words * | but it • was | pain and | grief to me.
	mp	4	My heart was hot within me * and while I was thus musing the | fire | kindled : and at the | last I | spake • with my | tongue;
	p	5	Lord let me know mine end and the | number • of my | days : that I may be | certified • how | long I • have to | live.
		6	Behold thou hast made my days as it | were a • span | long : and mine age is even as nothing in respect of thee * and verily every man | living • is | alto•gether | vanity.
		7	For man walketh in a vain shadow and disquieteth him|self in | vain : he heapeth up riches and | cannot • tell | who shall | gather them.
	mf	8	And now Lord | what is • my | hope : truly my | hope is | even • in | thee.
		9	Deliver me from | all • mine of|fences : and | make me not • a re|buke • unto the | foolish.
	p	10 ‡	I became dumb and | opened • not my | mouth : – | – for it was | thy | doing.
	mp	11	Take thy | plague a|way from me : I am even consumed by the | means • of thy | heavy | hand.
		12	When thou with rebukes dost chasten man for sin * thou makest his beauty to consume away * like as it were a moth | fretting • a | garment : every man | therefore | is but | vanity.

Psalm 39, continued

I. A. Atkins

p   13 ‡   Hear my prayer O Lord * and with thine ears con|sider • my | calling :
               – | hold not • thy | peace • at my | tears.

        14   For I am a | stranger • with | thee :
               and a | sojourner • as | all my | fathers were.

pp   15   2nd part   O spare me a little that I may re|cover • my | strength :
                 before I go | hence • and be | no more | seen.

Full p   Glory be to the Father | and to • the | Son :
               and | to the | Holy | Ghost.

Full   As it was in the beginning is | now and • ever | shall be :
               world without | end. A | • • | men.

PSALM 40

B. Harwood

Expectans expectavi

Full mf   1   I waited | patiently • for the | Lord :
               and he inclined unto | me and | heard my | calling.

Full   2   He brought me also out of the horrible pit * out of the | mire and | clay :
               and set my feet upon the | rock and | ordered • my | goings.

        3   And he hath put a new | song • in my | mouth :
               even a | thanks • giving | unto • our | God.

mp   4   Many shall | see it • and | fear :
cresc.   and shall | put their | trust • in the | Lord.

Psalm 40, *continued*

B. Harwood

f   5   Blessed is the man that hath set his | hope • in the | Lord :
            and turned not unto the proud * and to | such as • go a|bout with | lies.

         6   O Lord my God * great are the wondrous works which thou hast done *
           like as be also thy | thoughts which • are to | us-ward :
            and yet there is | no man • that | ordereth • them | unto • thee.

         7   **2nd part**   If I should de|clare them • and | speak of them :
               they should be | more than • I am | able • to ex|press.

mf   8 ‡   Sacrifice and meat-|offering • thou | wouldest not :
           but mine | – – | ears • hast thou | opened.

         9   Burnt-offerings and sacrifice for sin hast thou | not re|quired :
           then | said I * | Lo I | come.

       10   In the volume of the book it is written of me *
           that I should fulfil thy | will • O my | God :
            I am content to do it * yea thy | law • is with|in my | heart.

       11   I have declared thy righteousness in the | great • congre|gation :
            lo I will not refrain my lips O | Lord and | that thou | knowest.

       12   I have not hid thy | righteousness with•in my | heart :
            my talk hath been of thy | truth • and of | thy sal|vation.

    13 †   I have not kept back thy | loving | mercy ‖ and | truth • from the |
          great • congre|gation.

mp   14   Withdraw not thou thy | mercy • from me O | Lord :
            let thy loving-|kindness • and thy | truth • alway pre|serve me.

       15   For innumerable troubles are come about me *
           my sins have taken such hold upon me * that I am not | able to • look | up :
            yea they are more in number than the hairs of my |
            head • and my | heart hath | failed me.

Psalm 40, continued

B. Harwood

cresc.　16　O Lord let it be thy | pleasure · to de|liver me :
　　　　　　make | haste O | Lord to | help me.

17　Let them be ashamed and confounded together *
　　that seek after my | soul · to de|stroy it :
　　　　let them be driven backward and put to re|buke that | wish me | evil.

18　Let them be desolate and re|warded · with | shame :
　　　　that say unto me | Fie up·on thee * | fie up|on thee.

19　Let all those that seek thee be | joyful · and | glad in thee :
　　　　and let such as love thy salvation say | alway * The | Lord be | praised.

mp　　20 ‡　As for me I am | poor and | needy :
cresc.　　　　　but the | – – | Lord · careth | for me.

mf　　21　Thou art my | helper · and re|deemer :
　　　　　make no long | tarry·ing | O my | God.

Full　f　　Glory be to the Father | and to · the | Son :
　　　　　and | to the | Holy | Ghost.

Full　　　As it was in the beginning is | now and · ever | shall be :
　　　　　world without | end. A | . . | men.

PSALM 41

J. Stainer

Beatus qui intelligit

Full *mp* 1 Blessed is he that considereth the | poor and | needy :
the Lord shall de|liver him · in the | time of | trouble.

Full 2 The Lord preserve him and keep him alive *
that he may be | blessed up·on | earth :
and deliver not thou him | into · the | will · of his | enemies.

p 3 The Lord comfort him when he lieth | sick up·on his | bed :
make thou | all his | bed · in his | sickness.

4 I said Lord be | merci·ful | unto me :
heal my | soul for · I have | sinned a|gainst thee.

mf 5 Mine | enemies · speak | evil of me :
When shall he | die · and his | name | perish?

mp 6 And if he come to see me he | speaketh | vanity :
and his heart conceiveth falsehood within himself *
and | when he · cometh | forth he | telleth it.

7 All mine enemies whisper to|gether · a|gainst me :
even a|gainst me do · they i|magine · this | evil.

mf 8 Let the sentence of guiltiness pro|ceed a|gainst him :
and now that he lieth | let him · rise | up no | more.

p 9 2nd part Yea even mine own familiar | friend · whom I | trusted :
who did also eat of my | bread hath | laid great | wait for me.

mp 10 But be thou merciful | unto me · O | Lord :
raise thou me up a|gain and | I · shall re|ward them.

11 By this I | know thou | favourest me :
that mine | enemy · doth not | triumph · a|gainst me.

Psalm 41, continued

J. Stainer

mf	12	And when I am in my │ health · thou up│holdest me : and shalt set me be│fore thy │ face for │ ever.
Full	13	Blessed be the │ Lord · God of │ Israel : world without │ end. A │ · · │ men.
Full f		Glory be to the Father │ and to · the │ Son : and │ to the │ Holy │ Ghost.
Full		As it was in the beginning is │ now and · ever │ shall be : world without │ end. A │ · · │ men.

PSALM 42

S. Wesley

Quemadmodum

Full mf	1	Like as the hart de│sireth · the │ water-brooks : so longeth my │ soul · after │ thee O │ God.
Full	2	My soul is athirst for God * yea even for the │ living │ God : when shall I come to ap│pear be·fore the │ presence · of │ God?
mp	3	My tears have been my │ meat · day and │ night : while they daily say unto me * │ Where is │ now thy │ God?
	4	Now when I think thereupon * I pour out my │ heart · by my│self : for I went with the multitude * and brought them │ forth · into the │ house of │ God;
mf	5 ‡	⎡2nd⎤ In the voice of │ praise and │ thanksgiving : ⎣part⎦ among │ – – │ such as · keep │ holy-day.

change chant (Full)

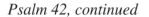

Psalm 42, continued

Anon. from S. Wesley

Full *p*   6   Why art thou so full of | heaviness • O my | soul :
                      and why art thou | so dis|quieted • with|in me?

Full *f*   7   Put thy | trust in | God :
                      for I will yet give him | thanks • for the | help of • his | countenance.

change chant (Decani)

S. Wesley

Dec. *mp*   8   My God my soul is | vexed with|in me :
                      therefore will I remember thee concerning the land of Jordan * |
                      and the • little | hill of | Hermon.

       9   One deep calleth another * because of the | noise • of the | water-pipes :
                      all thy | waves and | storms are • gone | over me.

   mf 10   The Lord hath granted his loving | kindness • in the | day-time :
                      and in the night-season did I sing of him *
                      and made my | prayer • unto the | God • of my | life.

       11   I will say unto the God of my strength * | Why hast • thou for|gotten me :
                      why go I thus | heavily • while the | enemy • op|presseth me?

       12   My bones are smitten asunder | as • with a | sword :
                      while mine enemies that | trouble • me | cast me • in the | teeth;

       13 † Namely | while they • say | daily ‖ unto me * | Where is | now thy | God?

change chant (Full)

Psalm 42, continued

Anon. from S. Wesley

Full   *p*   14   Why art thou so | vexed • O my | soul :

                      and why art thou | so dis|quieted • with | in me?

Full   *f*   15   O put thy | trust in | God :

                      for I will yet thank him *

                      which is the help of my | counte•nance | and my | God.

change chant (Decani)

PSALM 43

S. Wesley

Judica me, Deus

Dec.   *mf*   1   Give sentence with me O God *

                    and defend my cause against the un|godly | people :

                        O deliver me from the de|ceitful • and | wicked | man.

               2   For thou art the God of my strength * why hast thou | put me | from thee :

                        and why go I so | heavily • while the | enemy • op|presseth me?

               3   O send out thy light and thy | truth that • they may | lead me :

                        and bring me unto thy holy | hill and | to thy | dwelling.

               4   And that I may go unto the altar of God *

                        even unto the God of my | joy and | gladness :

                        and upon the harp will I give thanks unto | thee O | God my | God.

change chant (Full)

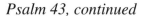

Psalm 43, continued

Anon. from S. Wesley

Full *p*   5   Why art thou so │ heavy • O my │ soul :
                    and why art thou │ so dis│quieted • with│in me?

Full *f*   6   O put thy │ trust in │ God :
                    for I will yet give him thanks *
                    which is the help of my │ counte•nance │ and my │ God.

change chant (Full)

S. Wesley

Full *f*   Glory be to the Father │ and to • the │ Son :
                    and │ to the │ Holy │ Ghost.

Full   As it was in the beginning is │ now and • ever │ shall be :
                    world without │ end. A │ . . │ men.

PSALM 44

J. Barnby

Deus, auribus

Full	*mf*	1	We have heard with our ears O God our | fathers • have | told us :
			what thou hast | done • in their | time of | old;
Full		2	How thou hast driven out the heathen with thy hand and | planted • them | in :
			how thou hast destroyed the | nations • and | cast them | out.
		3	For they gat not the land in possession | through their • own | sword :
			neither was it | their own | arm that | helped them;
		4	But thy right hand and thine arm and the | light • of thy | countenance :
			be|cause thou • hadst a | favour | unto them.
	f	5 ‡	Thou art my | King O | God :
			– | – send | help • unto | Jacob.
		6	Through thee will we over|throw our | enemies :
			and in thy Name will we tread them | under • that | rise up • a|gainst us.
	mf	7	For I will not | trust • in my | bow :
			it is | not my | sword • that shall | help me;
		8	But it is thou that | savest us • from our | enemies :
			and | puttest them • to con|fusion • that | hate us.
Full	*f*	9	[2nd part] We make our boast of | God • all day | long :
			and will | praise thy | Name for | ever.

change chant (Decani)

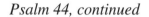

Psalm 44, continued

Anon. *("Cambridge Chant")*

Dec. *p*   10   But now thou art far off and | puttest us • to con|fusion :
                       and | goest • not | forth • with our | armies.

         11   Thou makest us to turn our | backs up•on our | enemies :
                       so that | they which | hate us • spoil our | goods.

         12   Thou lettest us be | eaten up • like | sheep :
                       and hast | scattered us • a|mong the | heathen.

         13   Thou sellest thy | people • for | nought :
                       and | takest • no | money | for them.

mf   14   Thou makest us to be re|buked • of our | neighbours :
                       to be laughed to scorn *
                       and had in derision of | them • that are | round a|bout us.

         15   Thou makest us to be a | by-word a•mong the | heathen :
                       and that the | people | shake their | heads at us.

         16   My confusion is | daily • be|fore me :
                       and the | shame • of my | face hath | covered me;

         17   For the voice of the | slanderer • and blas|phemer :
                       for the | ene•my | and a|venger.

mp   18   And though all this be come upon us * yet do we | not for|get thee :
                       nor behave ourselves | froward•ly | in thy | covenant.

         19   Our | heart is • not turned | back :
                       neither our | steps gone | out of • thy | way;

         20 | 2nd | No not when thou hast smitten us into the | place of | dragons :
              | part |
                       and | covered us • with the | shadow • of | death.

Psalm 44, continued

Anon. ("Cambridge Chant")

p   21   If we have forgotten the Name of our God *
and holden up our hands to | any • strange | god :
shall not God search it out? *
for he | knoweth the • very | secrets • of the | heart.

22   For thy sake also are we | killed • all the day | long
and are counted as | sheep ap|pointed • to be | slain.

change chant (Full)

J. Barnby

v. 26

Full f   23   Up | Lord why | sleepest thou :
awake and be not | absent • from | us for | ever.

Full   24   Wherefore | hidest • thou thy | face :
and for|gettest • our | misery • and | trouble?

mf   25   For our soul is brought low even | unto • the | dust :
our belly | cleaveth | unto • the | ground.

f   26   A|rise and | help us :
and de|liver • us | for thy | mercy's sake.

Full   Glory be to the Father | and to • the | Son :
and | to the | Holy | Ghost.

Full   As it was in the beginning is | now and • ever | shall be :
world without | end. A | . . | men.

PSALM 45

R. Cooke

Eructavit cor meum

Full   *mf*   1   My heart is inditing of a | good | matter :
           I speak of the | things which • I have | made • unto the | King.

Full   2 †‡   My | tongue • is the | pen ‖ – | – of a | ready | writer.

              3   Thou art fairer than the | children • of | men :
           full of grace are thy lips * because | God hath | blessed thee • for | ever.

              4   Gird thee with thy sword upon thy | thigh O • thou most | Mighty :
           ac|cording • to thy | worship • and re|nown.

              5   Good luck have | thou • with thine | honour :
           ride on because of the word of truth * of meekness and righteousness *
           and thy right hand shall | teach thee | terri•ble | things.

              6   Thy arrows are very sharp * and the people shall be sub|dued • unto | thee :
           even in the | midst a|mong the • King's | enemies.

     f   7   Thy seat O God en|dureth • for | ever :
           the sceptre of thy | kingdom • is a | right | sceptre.

              8   Thou hast loved righteousness and | hated • in|iquity :
           wherefore God even thy God *
           hath anointed thee with the oil of | gladness • a|bove thy | fellows.

   mf   9   All thy garments smell of myrrh | aloes • and | cassia :
           out of the ivory palaces where|by • they have | made thee | glad.

             10   Kings' daughters were among thy | honoura•ble | women :
           upon thy right hand did stand the queen in a vesture of gold *
           wrought a|bout with | divers | colours.

Psalm 45, continued

R. Cooke

mp 11 Hearken O daughter and consider * in|cline thine | ear :
     forget also thine own | people • and thy | father's | house.

12 So shall the King have | pleasure • in thy | beauty :
     for he is thy Lord | God and | worship • thou | him.

13 And the daughter of Tyre shall be | there • with a | gift :
     like as the rich also among the people shall |
     make their • suppli|cation • be|fore thee.

14 The King's daughter is all | glorious • with|in :
     her | clothing • is of | wrought | gold.

15 She shall be brought unto the King in | raiment • of | needle-work :
     the virgins that be her fellows shall bear her company * |
     and shall • be | brought | unto thee.

16 With joy and gladness | shall they • be | brought :
     and shall enter | into • the | King's | palace.

17 Instead of thy fathers | thou shalt • have | children :
     whom thou | mayest • make | princes • in all | lands.

18 I will remember thy Name from one gene|ration • to an|other :
     therefore shall the people give | thanks unto • thee * | world with•out | end.

Full f   Glory be to the Father | and to • the | Son :
     and | to the | Holy | Ghost.

Full   As it was in the beginning is | now and • ever | shall be :
     world without | end. A | . . | men.

PSALM 46

descant vv. 7, 11   *from M. Luther*

Deus noster refugium

Full *f*   1   God is our | hope and | strength :
          a very | present | help in | trouble.

Full   2   Therefore will we not fear though the | earth be | moved :
          and though the hills be carried | into • the | midst • of the | sea;

   3   Though the waters thereof | rage and | swell :
          and though the mountains | shake • at the | tempest • of the | same.

   4   The rivers of the flood thereof shall make glad the | city • of | God :
          the holy place of the | taberna•cle | of the • most | Highest.

mf   5   God is in the midst of her * therefore shall she | not • be re|moved :
          God shall | help her • and | that right | early.

   6   The heathen make much ado and the | kingdoms • are | moved :
dim.   but God hath shewed his | voice • and the | earth shall • melt a|way.

Full Unison *f*   7   ⌜2nd part⌝ The Lord of | hosts is | with us :
          the God of | Jacob | is our | refuge.

mf   8   O come hither and behold the | works • of the | Lord :
          what de|struction • he hath | brought up•on the | earth.

   9   He maketh wars to | cease in • all the | world :
          he breaketh the bow and knappeth the spear in sunder *
          and | burneth • the | chariots • in the | fire.

mp   10   Be still then and | know that • I am | God :
cresc.   I will be exalted among the heathen *
          and I will be ex|alted | in the | earth.

Full Unison *f*   11   The Lord of | hosts is | with us :
          the God of | Jacob | is our | refuge.

Full   Glory be to the Father | and to • the | Son :
          and | to the | Holy | Ghost.

Full   As it was in the beginning is | now and • ever | shall be :
          world without | end. A | .. | men.

PSALM 47

J. Davy

Omnes gentes, plaudite manibus

Full f 1 O clap your hands to|gether · all ye | people :
O sing unto | God · with the | voice of | melody.

Full 2 For the Lord is | high and · to be | feared :
he is the great | King up·on | all the | earth.

  mf 3 He shall sub|due the · people | under us :
and the | nations | under · our | feet.

   4 He shall choose out an | heri·tage | for us :
even the | worship · of | Jacob · whom he | loved.

  f 5 God is gone up with a | merry | noise :
and the | Lord with · the | sound · of the | trump.

   6 O sing praises sing | praises · unto our | God :
O sing praises sing | praises | unto · our | King.

  mf 7 For God is the | King of · all the | earth :
sing ye | praises · with | under|standing.

   8 God | reigneth · over the | heathen :
God | sitteth up·on his | holy | seat.

   9 ┌─────┐ The princes of the people are joined unto the people of the |
     │ **2nd** │
     │ **part** │ God of | Abraham :
     └─────┘
       for God which is very high exalted *
       doth defend the | earth · as it | were · with a | shield.

Full f Glory be to the Father | and to · the | Son :
and | to the | Holy | Ghost.

Full As it was in the beginning is | now and · ever | shall be :
world without | end. A | . . | men.

PSALM 48

J. Goss

Magnus Dominus

Full　*f*　1　Great is the Lord and | highly • to be | praised :
　　　　　　　　in the city of our God * | even up•on his | holy | hill.

Full　　　2　The hill of Sion is a fair place and the | joy of the • whole | earth :
　　　　　　　　upon the north-side lieth the city of the great King *
　　　　　　　　God is well known in her | palaces • as a | sure | refuge.

mf　　　3 †　For lo the | kings • of the | earth ‖ are | gathered • and gone | by to|gether.

　　　　　4　They | marvelled to • see such | things :
　　　　　　　　they were a|stonished • and | suddenly • cast | down.

mp　　　5 ‡　Fear came there up|on them • and | sorrow :
　　　　　　　　– | as upon • a | woman • in her | travail.

mf　　　6 †　Thou shalt | break the | ships ‖ of the | sea • through the | east | wind.

　　　　　7　2nd part　Like as we have heard * so have we seen in the city of the Lord of hosts *
　　　　　　　　in the | city of • our | God :
　　　　　　　　God up|holdeth • the | same for | ever.

mp　　　8 †　We wait for thy | loving | kindness ‖ O | God • in the | midst of • thy | temple.

mf　　　9　O God according to thy Name * so is thy praise unto the | world's | end :
　　　　　　　　thy | right hand • is | full of | righteousness.

　　　　　10 †　Let the mount Sion rejoice *
　　　　　　　　and the | daughters • of | Judah ‖ be | glad be|cause of • thy | judgements.

　　　　　11　Walk about Sion and go | round a|bout her :
　　　　　　　　and | tell the | towers • there|of.

f　　　12　Mark well her bulwarks * | set up • her | houses :
　　　　　　　　that ye may | tell | them that • come | after.

　　　　　13　For this God is our God for | ever • and | ever :
　　　　　　　　he shall be our | guide | unto | death.

Full　　　Glory be to the Father | and to • the | Son :
　　　　　　　　and | to the | Holy | Ghost.

Full　　　As it was in the beginning is | now and • ever | shall be :
　　　　　　　　world without | end. A | . . | men.

PSALM 49

T. A. Walmisley

Audite hæc, omnes

Full *p*	1	O hear ye │ this • all ye │ people :
		ponder it with your ears │ all ye • that │ dwell • in the │ world;
Full	2 †	High and │ low * │ rich ‖ and │ poor * │ one • with an│other.
	3	My │ mouth shall • speak of │ wisdom :
		and my │ heart shall │ muse of • under│standing.
	4	I will incline mine │ ear • to the │ parable :
		and │ shew my • dark │ speech up•on the │ harp.
mp	5	Wherefore should I fear in the │ days of │ wickedness :
		and when the wickedness of my heels │ compasseth • me │ round a│bout?
mf	6	There be some that put their │ trust • in their │ goods :
		and boast themselves in the │ multi•tude │ of their │ riches.
mp	7	But no man may de│liver • his │ brother;
		nor make a│greement • unto │ God │ for him;
	8	For it cost more to re│deem their │ souls :
		so that he must │ let that • a│lone for │ ever;
	9 ‡	Yea │ though he • live │ long :
		and │ see not – │ – the │ grave.
p	10	For he seeth that wise men also die and │ perish • to│gether :
		as well as the ignorant and foolish * and │ leave their │ riches • for │ other.
mp	11	And yet they think that their houses shall con│tinue • for │ ever :
		and that their dwelling-places shall endure from one generation
		to another * and │ call the • lands │ after their • own │ names.
Full Unison p	12	Nevertheless * man will not a│bide in │ honour :
		seeing he may be compared unto the beasts that │ perish * │
		this • is the │ way of them.

Psalm 49, continued

T. A. Walmisley

vv. 15,17,19

Dec.	*mp*	13	This │ is their │ foolishness :
			and their po│steri·ty │ praise their │ saying.
	mf	14	They lie in the hell like sheep * death gnaweth upon them *
			and the righteous shall have domination │ over them · in the │ morning :
	dim.		their beauty shall consume in the │ sepul·chre │ out of · their │ dwelling.
	mf	15 ‡	But God hath delivered my soul from the │ place of │ hell :
			for │ he shall – │ – re│ceive me.
		16	Be not thou afraid though │ one be · made │ rich :
			or if the │ glory · of his │ house · be in│creased;
	mp	17 ‡	For he shall carry nothing a│way with him · when he │ dieth :
			neither │ shall his – │ – pomp │ follow him.
		18	For while he lived he counted him│self an │ happy man :
			and so long as thou doest well unto thy│self * │
			men will · speak │ good of thee.
	p	19 ‡	He shall follow the gene│ration · of his │ fathers :
			and shall │ never – │ – see │ light.
Full Unison		20	Man being in honour hath │ no · under│standing :
			but is com│pared · unto the │ beasts that │ perish.
Full			Glory be to the Father │ and to · the │ Son :
			and │ to the │ Holy │ Ghost.
Full			As it was in the beginning is │ now and · ever │ shall be :
			world without │ end. A │ . . │ men.

PSALM 50

G. Thalben-Ball

Deus deorum

Full *f* 1 The Lord even the most mighty │ God hath │ spoken :
   and called the world *
   from the rising up of the │ sun • unto the │ going │ down thereof.

Full 2 † Out of │ Sion • hath │ God ‖ ap│peared in │ perfect │ beauty.

mf 3 Our God shall come and │ shall not • keep │ silence :
   there shall go before him a consuming fire *
   and a mighty │ tempest • shall be │ stirred up • round a│bout him.

  4 He shall call the │ heaven • from a│bove :
   and the │ earth that • he may │ judge his │ people.

  5 Gather my │ saints to•gether │ unto me :
   those that have made a │ covenant • with │ me with │ sacrifice.

  6 And the heavens shall de│clare his │ righteousness :
   for │ God is │ Judge him│self.

mp 7 ‡ Hear O my │ people and • I will │ speak :
   I myself will testify against thee O Israel *
   for I am │ – – │ God • even │ thy God.

  8 I will not reprove thee because of thy sacrifices * │ or for thy • burnt │ offerings :
   be│cause they • were not │ alway • be│fore me.

  9 I will take no │ bullock • out of thine │ house :
   nor │ he-goat │ out of • thy │ folds.

  10 For all the beasts of the │ forest • are │ mine :
   and so are the │ cattle up•on a │ thousand │ hills.

  11 I know all the │ fowls up•on the │ mountains :
   and the wild beasts of the │ field are │ in my │ sight.

  12 If I be │ hungry I • will not │ tell thee :
   for the whole world is │ mine and │ all that is • there│in.

Psalm 50, continued

G. Thalben-Ball

mf   13 ‡   Thinkest thou that I will | eat bulls' | flesh :
               – | – and | drink the • blood of | goats?

        14   Offer unto | God | thanksgiving :
               and pay thy | vows • unto the | most | Highest.

        15 | 2nd part | And call upon me in the | time of | trouble :
                   so will I | hear thee • and | thou shalt | praise me.

                                       change chant (Decani)

G. Thalben-Ball

Dec. *mp*   16   But unto the un|godly • said | God :
                   Why dost thou preach my laws *
                   and takest my | cove•nant | in thy | mouth;

        17   Whereas thou | hatest to • be re|formed :
               and hast | cast my | words be|hind thee?

        18   When thou sawest a thief thou con|sentedst | unto him :
               and hast been par|taker | with the • a|dulterers.

        19   Thou hast let thy | mouth speak | wickedness :
               and with thy | tongue • thou hast | set forth • de|ceit.

        20   Thou satest and spakest a|gainst thy | brother :
               yea and hast | slandered • thine | own • mother's | son.

Psalm 50, continued

G. Thalben-Ball

21   These things hast thou done and I held my tongue *

and thou thoughtest wickedly that I am even such a | one • as thy|self :

but I will reprove thee *

and set be|fore thee • the | things that • thou hast | done.

mf   22   O consider this | ye that for•get | God :

lest I pluck you a|way and • there be | none • to de|liver you.

cresc.   23   Whoso offereth me thanks and | praise he | honoureth me :

and to him that ordereth his conversation right will I |

shew the • sal|vation • of | God.

change chant (Full)

G. Thalben-Ball

Full   f   Glory be to the Father | and to • the | Son :

and | to the | Holy | Ghost.

Full   As it was in the beginning is | now and • ever | shall be :

world without | end. A | • • | men.

PSALM 51

E. C. Bairstow

Miserere mei, Deus

Full *p*   1   Have mercy upon me O God | after thy • great | goodness :
    according to the multitude of thy | mercies • do a|way • mine of|fences.

Full   2   Wash me | throughly • from my | wicked•ness :
    and | cleanse me | from my | sin.

3   For I ac|knowledge • my | faults :
    and my | sin is | ever • be|fore me.

4   Against thee only have I sinned * and done this | evil • in thy | sight :
    that thou mightest be justified in thy saying *
    and | clear when | thou art | judged.

5   Behold I was | shapen • in | wickedness :
    and in | sin • hath my | mother • con|ceived me.

6   But lo thou requirest truth in the | inward | parts :
    and shalt make me to | under•stand | wisdom | secretly.

mp   7   Thou shalt purge me with hyssop and | I shall • be | clean :
    thou shalt wash me and | I shall • be | whiter • than | snow.

mf   8   Thou shalt make me hear of | joy and | gladness :
    that the | bones which • thou hast | broken • may re|joice.

p   9   Turn thy | face • from my | sins :
    and | put out | all • my mis|deeds.

10   Make me a clean | heart O | God :
    and re|new a • right | spirit • with|in me.

mp   11   Cast me not a|way • from thy | presence :
    and | take not • thy | holy • Spirit | from me.

mf   12   O give me the comfort of thy | help a|gain :
    and | stablish me • with thy | free | Spirit.

13   **2nd part** Then shall I teach thy | ways • unto the | wicked :
    and | sinners shall • be con|verted | unto thee.

Psalm 51, continued

E. C. Bairstow

mf   14   Deliver me from blood-guiltiness O God *
thou that art the | God of · my | health :
and my | tongue shall | sing of · thy | righteousness.

        15   Thou shalt open my | lips O | Lord :
and my | mouth shall | shew thy | praise.

p   16   For thou desirest no sacrifice | else · would I | give it thee :
but thou de|lightest | not in · burnt | offerings.

pp   17   The sacrifice of God is a | troubled | spirit :
a broken and contrite heart O | God · shalt thou | not de|spise.

mf   18 ‡   O be favourable and | gracious · unto | Sion :
– | build thou · the | walls · of Je|rusalem.

        19   Then shalt thou be pleased with the sacrifice of righteousness *
with the burnt | offerings · and ob|lations :
then shall they offer young | bullocks · up|on thine | altar.

***Full* p**   Glory be to the Father | and to · the | Son :
and | to the | Holy | Ghost.

Full   As it was in the beginning is | now and · ever | shall be :
world without | end. A | . . | men.

PSALM 52

G. A. Scaife

Quid gloriaris?

***Full* f**   1 ‡   Why boastest thou thy|self thou | tyrant :
– | – that | thou canst · do | mischief;

Full   2 †‡   Whereas the | goodness · of | God ‖ – | – en|dureth · yet | daily.

Psalm 52, continued

G. A. Scaife

<table>
<tr><td>*mf*</td><td>3</td><td>Thy tongue i|magi·neth | wickedness :
    and with | lies thou · cuttest | like a · sharp | rasor.</td></tr>
<tr><td></td><td>4</td><td>Thou hast loved un|righteousness · more than | goodness :
    and to | talk of | lies · more than | righteousness.</td></tr>
<tr><td></td><td>5 ‡</td><td>Thou hast loved to speak all | words that · may do | hurt :
    – | – – | O thou · false | tongue.</td></tr>
<tr><td></td><td>6</td><td>Therefore shall God de|stroy thee · for | ever :
    he shall take thee and pluck thee out of thy dwelling *
    and root thee | out of · the | land of · the | living.</td></tr>
<tr><td></td><td>7 ‡</td><td>The righteous also shall | see this · and | fear :
    – | – and shall | laugh him · to | scorn;</td></tr>
<tr><td></td><td>8</td><td>Lo this is the man that took not | God · for his | strength :
    but trusted unto the multitude of his riches *
    and | strengthened · him|self in · his | wickedness.</td></tr>
</table>

change chant (Decani)

G. A. Scaife

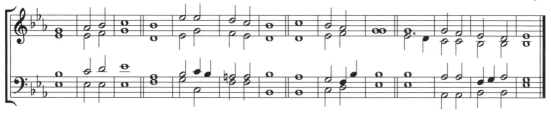

<table>
<tr><td>***Dec.*** *mf*</td><td>9</td><td>As for me I am like a green olive-tree in the | house of | God :
    my trust is in the tender mercy of | God for | ever · and | ever.</td></tr>
<tr><td></td><td>10</td><td>I will always give thanks unto thee for | that · thou hast | done :
    and I will hope in thy | Name * for thy | saints · like it | well.</td></tr>
<tr><td>***Full*** *f*</td><td></td><td>Glory be to the Father | and to · the | Son :
    and | to the | Holy | Ghost.</td></tr>
<tr><td>***Full***</td><td></td><td>As it was in the beginning is | now and · ever | shall be :
    world without | end. A | · · | men.</td></tr>
</table>

PSALM 53

T. Attwood

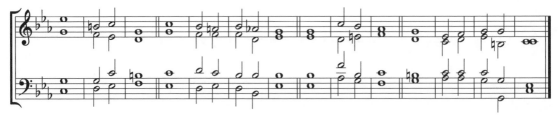

Dixit insipiens

Full *f* 1 † The foolish | body · hath | said ‖ in his | heart *
There | is no | God.

Full 2 Corrupt are they * and become a|bominable · in their | wickedness :
there is | none that | doeth | good.

mf 3 God looked down from heaven upon the | children · of | men :
to see if there were any that would under|stand and | seek · after | God.

f 4 But they are all gone out of the way *
they are alto|gether be·come a|bominable :
there is also | none that · doeth | good * no not | one.

mf 5 Are not they without under|standing that · work | wickedness :
eating up my people as if they would eat bread? *
they | have not | called up·on | God.

6 They were a|fraid · where no | fear was :
for God hath broken the bones of him that besieged thee *
thou hast put them to con|fusion be·cause | God · hath de|spised them.

f 7 O that the salvation were given unto | Israel · out of | Sion :
O that the Lord would deliver his | people | out of · cap|tivity!

8 Then should | Jacob · re|joice :
and | Isra·el | should be · right | glad.

Full Glory be to the Father | and to · the | Son :
and | to the | Holy | Ghost.

Full As it was in the beginning is | now and · ever | shall be :
world without | end. A | . . | men.

PSALM 54

M. Wise

Deus, in nomine

Full *p*   1 ‡   Save me O | God · for thy | Name's sake :
       – | – and a|venge me · in thy | strength.

Full   2   Hear my | prayer O | God :
       and | hearken · unto the | words · of my | mouth.

   mp   3   For strangers are | risen up · a|gainst me :
       and tyrants which have not God before their |
       eyes seek | after · my | soul.

   mf   4   Behold | God · is my | helper :
       the Lord is with | them · that up|hold my | soul.

       5   He shall reward | evil · unto mine | enemies :
       de|stroy thou | them · in thy | truth.

       6 ‡   An offering of a free heart will I give thee * and | praise thy · Name O | Lord :
       – | – be|cause it is · so | comfortable.

       7   For he hath delivered me | out of · all my | trouble :
       and mine eye hath seen his de|sire up|on mine | enemies.

Full *mp*   Glory be to the Father | and to · the | Son :
       and | to the | Holy | Ghost.

Full   As it was in the beginning is | now and · ever | shall be :
       world without | end. A | . . | men.

PSALM 55

J. Foster

Exaudi, Deus

Full **mp** 1 Hear my | prayer O | God :
    and hide not thy|self from | my pe|tition.

Full 2 Take heed | unto · me and | hear me :
    how I | mourn · in my | prayer · and am | vexed.

mf 3 The enemy crieth so * and the ungodly cometh | on so | fast :
    for they are minded to do me some mischief *
    so ma|liciously · are they | set a|gainst me.

mp 4 My heart is dis|quiet·ed with|in me :
    and the | fear of death · is | fallen · up|on me.

5 Fearfulness and | trembling are · come up|on me :
    and an horrible | dread hath | over|whelmed me.

p 6 And I said O that I had | wings · like a | dove :
    for then would I | flee a|way and · be at | rest.

7 Lo then would I get me a|way far | off :
    and re|main | in the | wilderness.

mp 8 I would make | haste · to es|cape :
    because of the | stormy | wind and | tempest.

mf 9 Destroy their tongues O | Lord · and di|vide them :
    for I have spied un|righteousness · and | strife · in the | city.

10 Day and night they go a|bout with·in the | walls thereof :
    mischief also and | sorrow · are | in the | midst of it.

11 ‡ **2nd part** − | Wickedness · is there|in :
    deceit and | guile · go not | out of · their | streets.

Psalm 55, continued

J. Foster

mp   12   For it is not an open enemy that hath | done me • this dis|honour :
            for | then I | could have | borne it.

       13   Neither was it mine adversary that did | magnify him•self a|gainst me :
            for then peradventure | I would • have | hid my•self | from him.

p   14   But it was even | thou • my com|panion :
            my | guide • and mine | own fa•miliar | friend.

       15   We took sweet | counsel • to|gether :
            and walked in the | house of | God as | friends.

mf   16 §   **2nd part**   Let death come hastily upon them *
              and let them go down | quick • into | hell :
              for wickedness is in their | dwellings | and a|mong them.

change chant (Decani)

G. C. Martin

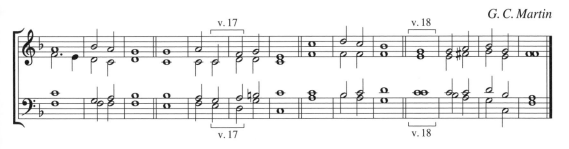

Dec. *mf*   17 ‡   As for me I will | call up•on | God :
                     and the | Lord – | – shall | save me.

             18 ‡   In the evening and morning and at noon-day will I | pray and • that | instantly :
                    – | and he • shall | hear my | voice.

mp   19 †   It is he that hath delivered my soul in peace from the |
                    battle that • was a|gainst ‖ me * | for there • were | many | with me.

mf   20   Yea even God that endureth for ever shall | hear me and • bring them | down :
                    for they will not | turn nor | fear | God.

§ Omitted in the St Paul's Cathedral use

Psalm 55, continued

G. C. Martin

p   21 †   He laid his hands upon │ such as • be at │ peace with ‖ him * │
                         and he │ brake his │ covenant.

mp   22   The words of his mouth were softer than butter *
mf   having │ war • in his │ heart :
mp   his words were smoother than oil *
mf   and │ yet • be they │ very │ swords.

             23   **2nd part** O cast thy burden upon the │ Lord and • he shall │ nourish thee :
                         and shall not suffer the │ righteous • to │ fall for │ ever.

Full *f* 24   And │ as for │ them :
                         thou O God shalt bring them │ into • the │ pit • of de│struction.

Full   25   The blood-thirsty and deceitful men shall not live out │ half their │ days :
                         nevertheless my │ trust shall • be in │ thee O │ Lord.

Full   Glory be to the Father │ and to • the │ Son :
                         and │ to the │ Holy │ Ghost.

Full   As it was in the beginning is │ now and • ever │ shall be :
                         world without │ end. A │ • • │ men.

PSALM 56

W. Bayley

Miserere mei, Deus

Full   **mp**   1   Be merciful unto me O God * for man goeth a|bout · to de|vour me :
              he is | daily | fighting · and | troubling me.

Full   2   Mine enemies are daily in hand to | swallow · me | up :
              for they be many that fight a|gainst me · O | thou most | Highest.

       mf   3   Nevertheless though I am | sometime · a|fraid :
              yet | put I · my | trust in | thee.

               4   I will praise God be|cause of · his | word :
              I have put my trust in God *
              and will not | fear what | flesh can | do unto me.

       mp   5   They daily mis|take my | words :
              all that they i|magine · is to | do me | evil.

               6   They hold all together and | keep them·selves | close :
              and mark my | steps · when they lay | wait · for my | soul.

       mf   7   Shall they es|cape · for their | wickedness :
              thou O God in thy dis|pleasure · shalt | cast them | down.

       p   8   Thou tellest my flittings * put my | tears · into thy | bottle :
              are not | these things | noted · in thy | book?

change chant (Full)

Psalm 56, continued

G. Thalben-Ball

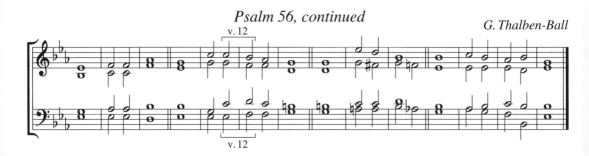

Full *f*   9   Whensoever I call upon thee * then shall mine enemies be | put to | flight :
this I | know * for | God is • on my | side.

Full   10   In | God's word • will I re|joice :
in the | Lord's word | will I | comfort me.

Full   11   2nd part   Yea in God have I | put my | trust :
I will not be a|fraid what | man can | do unto me.

mf   12 ‡   Unto thee O | God will I • pay my | vows :
unto | thee will – | – I give | thanks.

   13   For thou hast delivered my soul from death and my | feet from | falling :
that I may walk before | God • in the | light • of the | living.

Full *f*   Glory be to the Father | and to • the | Son :
and | to the | Holy | Ghost.

Full   As it was in the beginning is | now and • ever | shall be :
world without | end. A | . . | men.

PSALM 57

E. J. Hopkins

Miserere mei, Deus

Full	*mp*	1	Be merciful unto me O God be merciful unto me * for my soul │ trusteth • in │ thee : and under the shadow of thy wings shall be my refuge * until this │ tyranny • be │ over-│past.
Full		2	I will call unto the │ most high │ God : even unto the God that shall perform the │ cause • which I │ have in │ hand.
		3	He shall │ send from │ heaven : and save me from the reproof of │ him • that would │ eat me │ up.
		4	God shall send forth his │ mercy • and │ truth : my │ soul • is a│mong │ lions.
	mf	5 ‡	And I lie even among the children of men that are │ set on │ fire : whose teeth are spears and arrows * and their │ – – │ tongue a • sharp │ sword.
Full	*f*	6	Set up thyself O │ God a•bove the │ heavens : and thy │ glory a•bove │ all the │ earth.
Can.	*mf*	7	[2nd part] They have laid a net for my feet and pressed │ down my │ soul : they have digged a pit before me * and are │ fallen • into the │ midst of it • them│selves.

change chant (Full)

Psalm 57, continued

E. J. Hopkins

Full *f*   8 ‡   My heart is fixed O God my | heart is | fixed :
            I will | – – | sing and • give | praise.

Full   9   Awake up my glory * awake | lute and | harp :
            I my|self • will a|wake right | early.

      mf   10   I will give thanks unto thee O | Lord a•mong the | people :
            and I will | sing • unto | thee a•mong the | nations.

          11 ‡   For the greatness of thy mercy reacheth | unto • the | heavens :
            – | – and thy | truth • unto the | clouds.

Full *f*   12   **2nd part** Set up thyself O | God a•bove the | heavens :
                and thy | glory a•bove | all the | earth.

Full   Glory be to the Father | and to • the | Son :
            and | to the | Holy | Ghost.

Full   As it was in the beginning is | now and • ever | shall be :
            world without | end. A | • • | men.

PSALM 58

vv. 2,5

S. S. Wesley

vv. 2,5

Si vere utique

Full *mf*   1 §   Are your minds set upon righteousness | O ye • congre|gation :
and do you judge the thing that is | right • O ye | sons of | men?

Full   2 §‡ Yea ye imagine mischief in your | heart up•on the | earth :
– | – and your | hands • deal with | wickedness.

3 §   The ungodly are froward * even | from their • mother's | womb :
as soon as they are | born they • go a|stray and • speak | lies.

4 §   They are as venomous as the | poison • of a | serpent :
even like the deaf | adder • that | stoppeth • her | ears.

5 §‡ Which refuseth to hear the | voice • of the | charmer :
– | – charm he | never • so | wisely.

f   6 §   Break their teeth O God in their mouths *
smite the jaw-bones of the | lions O | Lord :
let them fall away like water that runneth apace *
and when they shoot their arrows | let them • be | rooted | out.

mf   7 §   Let them consume away like a snail *
and be like the untimely | fruit • of a | woman :
and | let them • not | see the | sun.

8 §   Or ever your pots be made | hot with | thorns :
so let indignation vex him * | even • as a | thing • that is | raw.

f   9 §   The righteous shall rejoice when he | seeth • the | vengeance :
he shall wash his | footsteps • in the | blood of • the un|godly.

10 § So that a man shall say * Verily there is a re|ward • for the | righteous :
doubtless there is a | God that | judgeth • the | earth.

Full   Glory be to the Father | and to • the | Son :
and | to the | Holy | Ghost.

Full   As it was in the beginning is | now and • ever | shall be :
world without | end. A | . . | men.

§ *Omitted in the St Paul's Cathedral use*

PSALM 59

C. V. Stanford

Eripe me de inimicis

Full	*mf*	1	Deliver me from mine | enemies · O | God : defend me from | them that | rise up · a|gainst me.
Full		2	O deliver me from the | wicked | doers : and | save me · from the | blood·thirsty | men.
		3	For lo they lie | waiting · for my | soul : the mighty men are gathered against me * without any of|fence or | fault of me · O | Lord.
		4	They run and prepare them|selves with·out my | fault : arise thou | therefore · to | help me · and be|hold.
	f	5	Stand up O Lord God of Hosts thou God of Israel * to | visit · all the | heathen : and be not merciful unto them that of|fend · of ma|licious | wickedness.
		6	They go to and | fro · in the | evening : they grin like a | dog and · run a|bout · through the | city.
	mf	7 ‡	Behold they speak with their mouth * and | swords are · in their | lips : for | – – | who doth | hear?
		8	But thou O Lord shalt | have them · in de|rision : and thou shalt | laugh · all the | heathen · to | scorn.
Full	*f*	9	2nd part My strength will I a|scribe · unto | thee : for | thou art · the | God · of my | refuge.

Psalm 59, continued

C. V. Stanford

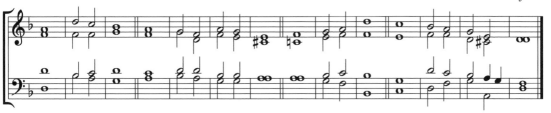

Dec. **mf**   10   God sheweth me his | goodness | plenteously :
                          and God shall let me see my de|sire up|on mine | enemies.

              11   Slay them not lest my | people • for|get it :
                          but scatter them abroad among the people *
                          and put them | down O | Lord • our de|fence.

              12   For the sin of their mouth and for the words of their lips *
                          they shall be | taken • in their | pride :
                          and why * their | preaching • is of | cursing • and | lies.

     f   13   Consume them in thy wrath * con|sume them that • they may | perish :
                          and know that it is God that ruleth in Jacob *
                          and | unto • the | ends • of the | world.

              14   And in the | evening • they will re|turn :
                          grin like a | dog • and will | go a•bout the | city.

              15   They will run here and | there for | meat :
                          and | grudge • if they | be not | satisfied.

Full   16   As for me I will sing of thy power *
                    and will praise thy mercy be|times • in the | morning :
                          for thou hast been my defence and | refuge • in the | day of • my | trouble.

Full   17   Unto thee O my | strength • will I | sing :
                          for thou O God art my | refuge • and my | merci•ful | God.

Full   Glory be to the Father | and to • the | Son :
                          and | to the | Holy | Ghost.

Full   As it was in the beginning is | now and • ever | shall be :
                          world without | end. A | • • | men.

PSALM 60

J. Goss

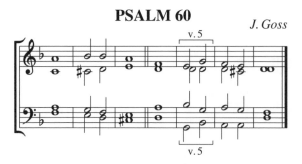

Deus, repulisti nos

Full	*p*	1	O God thou hast cast us out and │ scattered us • a│broad :
			thou hast also been displeased * O │ turn thee • unto │ us a│gain.
Full		2	Thou hast moved the │ land • and di│vided it :
			heal the │ sores there•of │ for it │ shaketh.
	mp	3	Thou hast shewed thy │ people • heavy │ things :
			thou hast │ given us • a │ drink of • deadly │ wine.
		4	Thou hast given a token for │ such as │ fear thee :
			that they may │ triumph • be│cause of • the │ truth.
	mf	5 ‡	Therefore were thy be│loved • de│livered :
			help me with thy │ – – │ right hand • and │ hear me.

change chant (Cantoris)

R. P. Stewart

Can.	*f*	6	God hath │ spoken • in his │ holiness :
			I will rejoice and divide Sichem * and │ mete out • the │ valley • of │ Succoth.
		7	Gilead is mine and Ma│nasses • is │ mine :
			Ephraim also is the strength of my head * │ Judah │ is my │ law-giver;
		8	Moab is my wash-pot * over Edom will I │ cast out • my │ shoe :
			Phi│listi•a │ be thou │ glad of me.
		9	Who will lead me into the │ strong │ city :
			who will │ bring me │ into │ Edom?

change chant (Cantoris)

Psalm 60, continued

J. Harrison

Can.	*p*	10	Hast not thou cast us │ out O │ God :
			wilt not thou O │ God go │ out • with our │ hosts?
	mp	11	O be thou our │ help in │ trouble :
			for │ vain • is the │ help of │ man.
	mf	12	Through God will we │ do great │ acts :
			for it is │ he • that shall │ tread down • our │ enemies.

change chant (Full)

J. Harrison

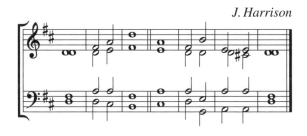

Full	*f*	Glory be to the Father │ and to • the │ Son :
		and │ to the │ Holy │ Ghost.
Full		As it was in the beginning is │ now and • ever │ shall be :
		world without │ end. A │ • • │ men.

PSALM 61

C. Hylton Stewart

Exaudi, Deus

Full   **mp**   1   Hear my | crying • O | God :
                          give | ear | unto • my | prayer.

Full   2 †‡   From the ends of the | earth • will I | call upon thee ‖ when my |
                          − − | heart • is in | heaviness.

                  3   O set me up upon the rock that is | higher • than | I :
                          for thou hast been my hope *
                          and a strong | tower for me • a|gainst the | enemy.

                  4   I will dwell in thy | tabernacle • for | ever :
                          and my trust shall be under the | cover•ing | of thy | wings.

          mf   5   For thou O Lord hast | heard • my de|sires :
                          and hast given an | heritage • unto | those that • fear thy | Name.

                  6   Thou shalt grant the | King a • long | life :
                          that his years may en|dure • throughout | all • gene|rations.

          mp   7   He shall dwell before | God for | ever :
                          O prepare thy loving mercy and |
                          faithfulness • that | they may • pre|serve him.

          mf   8   So will I always sing | praise • unto thy | Name :
          dim.   that I may | daily • per|form my | vows.

Full   **p**   Glory be to the Father | and to • the | Son :
                          and | to the | Holy | Ghost.

Full   As it was in the beginning is | now and • ever | shall be :
                          world without | end. A | . . | men.

PSALM 62

W. Boyce

Nonne Deo?

Full	*mf*	1	My soul truly waiteth │ still up‧on │ God :
			for of │ him ‧ cometh │ my sal│vation.
Full		2	He verily is my │ strength and ‧ my sal│vation :
			he is my defence * │ so that ‧ I │ shall not ‧ greatly │ fall.
	mp	3	How long will ye imagine mischief a│gainst ‧ every │ man :
			ye shall be slain all the sort of you *
			yea as a tottering wall shall ye │ be and ‧ like a │ broken │ hedge.
		4	Their device is only how to put him out whom │ God ‧ will ex│alt :
			their delight is in lies *
			they give good words with their │ mouth but │ curse with ‧ their │ heart.
	mf	5 ‡	Nevertheless my soul wait thou │ still up‧on │ God :
			– │ – for my │ hope ‧ is in │ him.
		6	He truly is my │ strength and ‧ my sal│vation :
			he is my defence │ so that ‧ I │ shall not │ fall.
	f	7	In God is my │ health ‧ and my │ glory :
			the rock of my │ might ‧ and in │ God is ‧ my │ trust.
		8	O put your trust in him │ alway ‧ ye │ people :
			pour out your hearts be│fore him ‧ for │ God is ‧ our │ hope.
	mp	9	As for the children of men │ they are ‧ but │ vanity :
			the children of men are deceitful upon the weights *
			they are altogether │ lighter ‧ than │ vanity ‧ it│self.
		10	O trust not in wrong and robbery * give not your│selves ‧ unto │ vanity :
			if riches increase │ set not ‧ your │ heart up│on them.

Psalm 62, continued

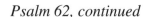

W. Boyce

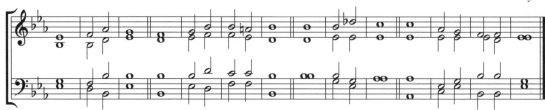

mf 11 God spake once * and twice I have │ also • heard the │ same :
that │ power be│longeth • unto │ God;

12 And that │ thou • Lord art │ merciful :
for thou rewardest │ every man • ac│cording • to his │ work.

Full f Glory be to the Father │ and to • the │ Son :
and │ to the │ Holy │ Ghost.

Full As it was in the beginning is │ now and • ever │ shall be :
world without │ end. A │ . . │ men.

PSALM 63

I. A. Atkins

Deus, Deus meus

Full f 1 ‡ O God │ thou art • my │ God :
– │ early │ will I │ seek thee.

Full 2 My soul thirsteth for thee * my flesh also │ longeth │ after thee :
in a barren and │ dry land │ where no │ water is.

mf 3 Thus have I │ looked for thee • in │ holiness :
that I might be│hold thy │ power and │ glory.

4 ‡ For thy loving-kindness is better than the │ life it│self :
my │ – – │ lips shall │ praise thee.

Psalm 63, *continued*

I. A. Atkins

5   As long as I live will I | magnify thee • on this | manner :
     and | lift up • my | hands • in thy | Name.

6   My soul shall be satisfied * even as it were with | marrow • and | fatness :
     when my mouth | praiseth thee • with | joyful | lips.

mp   7   Have I not re|membered thee • in my | bed :
     and thought up|on thee | when I • was | waking?

cresc.   8   Because | thou hast • been my | helper :
     therefore under the | shadow of • thy | wings will • I re|joice.

mf   9   My soul | hangeth • up|on thee :
     thy | right hand | hath up|holden me.

10 ‡   These also that seek the | hurt • of my | soul :
     they shall go | – – | under • the | earth.

11   Let them fall upon the | edge • of the | sword :
     that | they may • be a | portion • for | foxes.

f   12   But the King shall rejoice in God *
     all they also that swear by | him shall • be com|mended :
     for the mouth of | them that • speak | lies • shall be | stopped.

Full   Glory be to the Father | and to • the | Son :
     and | to the | Holy | Ghost.

Full   As it was in the beginning is | now and • ever | shall be :
     world without | end. A | . . | men.

PSALM 64

G. J. Bennett

Exaudi, Deus

Full	*mp*	1	Hear my voice O | God • in my | prayer :
			preserve my | life from | fear • of the | enemy.
Full		2	Hide me from the gathering to|gether • of the | froward :
			and from the insur|rection • of | wicked | doers;
	mf	3	Who have whet their | tongue • like a | sword :
			and shoot out their | arrows • even | bitter | words;
		4	That they may privily shoot at | him • that is | perfect :
			suddenly | do they | hit him • and | fear not.
	mp	5	They en|courage them•selves in | mischief :
			and commune among themselves how they may lay snares *
			and | say that | no man • shall | see them.
		6	They imagine | wickedness • and | practise • it :
			that they keep secret among themselves * | every man • in the |
			deep • of his | heart.
	f	7 ‡	But God shall suddenly shoot at them | with a • swift | arrow :
			– | – that | they shall • be | wounded.
		8	Yea their own | tongues shall • make them | fall :
			insomuch that whoso | seeth them • shall | laugh them • to | scorn.
		9	And all men that see it shall say * | This hath • God | done :
			for they shall per|ceive that | it is • his | work.
		10	The righteous shall rejoice in the | Lord and • put his | trust in • him :
			and all they that are | true of | heart • shall be | glad.
Full			Glory be to the Father | and to • the | Son :
			and | to the | Holy | Ghost.
Full			As it was in the beginning is | now and • ever | shall be :
			world without | end. A | . . | men.

PSALM 65

E. J. Hopkins

Te decet hymnus

Full *f* 1 Thou O God art | praised in | Sion :
  and unto thee shall the | vow • be per|formed • in Je|rusalem.

Full 2 Thou that | hearest • the | prayer :
  unto | thee shall | all flesh | come.

mp 3 My mis|deeds pre•vail a|gainst me :
  O be thou | merci•ful | unto • our | sins.

4 Blessed is the man whom thou choosest and re|ceivest | unto thee :
  he shall dwell in thy court *
  and shall be satisfied with the pleasures of thy house * |
  even • of thy | holy | temple.

mf 5 Thou shalt shew us wonderful things in thy righteousness O |
  God of • our sal|vation :
  thou that art the hope of all the ends of the earth *
  and of them that re|main • in the | broad | sea.

f 6 Who in his strength setteth | fast the | mountains :
  and is | girded • a|bout with | power.

mp 7 Who stilleth the | raging • of the | sea :
  and the noise of his | waves • and the | madness • of the | people.

8 They also that dwell in the uttermost parts of the earth
  shall be a|fraid at • thy | tokens :
  thou that makest the outgoings of the | morning • and |
  evening • to | praise thee.

9 Thou visitest the | earth and | blessest it :
  thou | makest • it | very | plenteous.

10 The river of | God is • full of | water :
  thou preparest their corn * for | so • thou pro|videst • for the | earth.

Psalm 65, continued

E. J. Hopkins

p   11   Thou waterest her furrows * thou sendest rain into the little │ valleys • there│of :
              thou makest it soft with the drops of rain and │ blessest • the │
              increase │ of it.

mf   12 † Thou │ crownest • the │ year ‖ with thy │ goodness *
              and thy │ clouds drop │ fatness.

         13   They shall drop upon the │ dwellings • of the │ wilderness :
              and the little │ hills • shall re│joice on • every │ side.

f   14   The folds shall be │ full of │ sheep :
              the valleys also shall stand so thick with │ corn that • they shall │
              laugh and │ sing.

Full   Glory be to the Father │ and to • the │ Son :
              and │ to the │ Holy │ Ghost.

Full   As it was in the beginning is │ now and • ever │ shall be :
              world without │ end. A │ . . │ men.

PSALM 66

I. A. Atkins

Jubilate Deo

Full *f*   1   O be joyful in | God · all ye | lands :
    sing praises unto the honour of his Name * |
    make his | praise · to be | glorious.

Full   2   Say unto God * O how wonderful art | thou in · thy | works :
    through the greatness of thy power shall thine |
    enemies be · found | liars | unto thee.

3 †   For all the | world shall | worship ‖ thee * |
    sing of thee · and | praise thy | Name.

4   O come hither and be|hold the · works of | God :
    how wonderful he is in his | doing to·ward the | children · of | men.

mf   5   He turned the | sea into · dry | land :
    so that they went through the water on foot * |
    there did | we re|joice thereof.

6   He ruleth with his power for ever * his | eyes be·hold the | people :
    and such as will not be|lieve shall · not be | able · to ex|alt themselves.

f   7   O | praise our · God ye | people :
    and make the | voice of · his | praise · to be | heard;

8   Who | holdeth our · soul in | life :
    and | suffereth · not our | feet to | slip.

mf   9   For thou O | God hast | proved us :
    thou also hast | tried us | like as | silver is tried.

10   Thou broughtest us | into · the | snare :
    and laidest | trouble · up|on our | loins.

Psalm 66, continued   *I. A. Atkins*

f   11   Thou sufferedst men to ride │ over • our │ heads :
we went through fire and water *****
and thou broughtest us │ out • into a │ wealthy │ place.

    12   I will go into thine │ house with • burnt │ offerings :
and will pay thee my vows *****
which I promised with my lips and spake with my │
mouth • when I │ was in │ trouble.

mf   13   I will offer unto thee fat burnt-sacrifices with the │ incense • of │ rams :
I will │ offer │ bullocks • and │ goats.

mp   14   O come hither and hearken all │ ye that • fear │ God :
and I will tell you │ what he • hath │ done • for my │ soul.

mf   15   I │ called unto him • with my │ mouth :
and │ gave him │ praises • with my │ tongue.

   16 ‡   If I incline unto │ wickedness • with mine │ heart :
− │ − the │ Lord • will not │ hear me.

Full f   17   But │ God hath │ heard me :
and con│sidered • the │ voice • of my │ prayer.

Full   18 ‡   Praised be God who hath not │ cast out • my │ prayer :
− │ − nor │ turned his • mercy │ from me.

Full   Glory be to the Father │ and to • the │ Son :
and │ to the │ Holy │ Ghost.

Full   As it was in the beginning is │ now and • ever │ shall be :
world without │ end. A │ . . │ men.

PSALM 67

B. Luard Selby

Deus misereatur

Full *p*	1	God be merciful unto | us and | bless us :
		and shew us the light of his | countenance · and be |
		merci·ful | unto us.
Full	2	That thy way may be | known up·on | earth :
		thy saving | health a|mong all | nations.
Full Unison mf	3 ‡	Let the people | praise thee · O | God :
		– | – yea let | all the · people | praise thee.
Dec.	4	O let the nations re|joice and · be | glad :
		for thou shalt judge the folk righteously *
		and | govern · the | nations up·on | earth.
Full Unison f	5 ‡	Let the people | praise thee · O | God :
		– | – let | all the · people | praise thee.
Can. *mp*	6	Then shall the | earth bring · forth her | increase :
		and God * even our | own God · shall | give us · his | blessing.
Dec. *p*	7 ‡	– | God shall | bless us :
		and all the | ends · of the | world shall | fear him.
Full *mp*		Glory be to the Father | and to · the | Son :
		and | to the | Holy | Ghost.
Full		As it was in the beginning is | now and · ever | shall be :
		world without | end. A | · · | men.

PSALM 68

W. Crotch

Exsurgat Deus

Full f   1   Let God arise and let his | enemies • be | scattered :
let them | also • that | hate him • flee be|fore him.

Full   2   Like as the smoke vanisheth * so shalt thou | drive • them a|way :
and like as wax melteth at the fire *
so let the ungodly | perish • at the | presence • of | God.

3   But let the righteous be glad and re|joice be•fore | God :
let them | also • be | merry • and | joyful.

4   O sing unto God and sing praises | unto • his | Name :
magnify him that rideth upon the heavens as it were upon an horse *
praise him in his Name | JAH • and re|joice be|fore him.

mf   5   He is a father of the fatherless * and defendeth the | cause • of the | widows :
even | God • in his | holy • habi|tation.

6   He is the God that maketh men to be of one mind in an house *
and bringeth the prisoners | out of • cap|tivi•ty :
but letteth the | runa•gates con|tinue • in | scarceness.

change chant (Decani)

Psalm 68, continued

H. Smart

Dec. *f*   7 ‡   O God when thou wentest | forth be•fore the | people :
       – | – when thou | wentest • through the | wilderness;

       8   The earth shook * and the heavens dropped at the | presence • of | God :
       even as Sinai also was moved at the presence of |
       God who • is the | God of | Israel.

mf   9   Thou O God sentest a gracious rain upon | thine in|heritance :
       and re|freshedst • it | when it • was | weary.

       10   Thy congregation shall | dwell there|in :
       for thou O God hast of thy | goodness • pre|pared • for the | poor.

Full *f*   11   The | Lord • gave the | word :
       great was the | compa•ny | of the | preachers.

Full   12   Kings with their armies did | flee and • were dis|comfited :
       and they of the | household • di|vided • the | spoil.

mf   13   Though ye have lien among the pots * yet shall ye be as the | wings • of a | dove :
       that is covered with silver | wings • and her | feathers • like | gold.

       14   When the Almighty scattered | kings • for their | sake :
       then were they as | white as | snow in | Salmon.

       15   As the hill of | Basan • so is | God's hill :
       even an | high hill • as the | hill of | Basan.

       16   Why hop ye so ye high hills? *
       this is God's hill in the which it | pleaseth • him to | dwell :
       yea the | Lord • will a|bide in it • for | ever.

       17   The chariots of God are twenty thousand * even | thousands • of | angels :
       and the Lord is among them as in the | holy | place of | Sinai.

       18   Thou art gone up on high *
       thou hast led captivity captive and received | gifts for | men :
       yea even for thine enemies *
       that the Lord | God might | dwell a|mong them.

Psalm 68, continued

H. Smart

f   19   Praised be the | Lord | daily :

       even the God who helpeth us and | poureth · his | benefits · up|on us.

      20   He is our God * even the God of whom | cometh · sal|vation :

       God is the | Lord by · whom | we es·cape | death.

      21 §   God shall wound the | head · of his | enemies :

       and the hairy scalp of such a one as | goeth · on | still · in his | wickedness.

      22 §   The Lord hath said * I will bring my people again as I | did from | Basan :

       mine own will I bring again * as I did | sometime · from the |

       deep · of the | sea.

      23 §   **2nd part**   That thy foot may be dipped in the | blood · of thine | enemies :

       and that the tongue of thy | dogs · may be |

       red · through the | same.

mf   24   It is well seen O | God · how thou | goest :

       how thou my | God and · King | goest · in the | sanctuary.

      25   The singers go before * the | minstrels · follow | after :

       in the midst are the | damsels | playing · with the | timbrels.

f   26 ‡   Give thanks O Israel unto God the Lord in the | congre|gations :

       – | – from the | ground · of the | heart.

      27   There is little Benjamin their ruler * and the princes of | Judah · their | counsel :

       the princes of Za|bulon · and the | princes · of | Nephthali.

mf   28   Thy God hath | sent forth | strength for thee :

       stablish the thing O | God that | thou hast | wrought in us.

      29   For thy | temple's sake · at Je|rusalem :

       so shall | kings bring | presents | unto thee.

§ *Omitted in the St Paul's Cathedral use*

Psalm 68, continued

H. Smart

30   When the company of the spear-men and multitude of the mighty *
      are scattered abroad among the beasts of the people *
      so that they humbly bring | pieces • of | silver :
            and when he hath scattered the | people • that de|light in | war;

31   Then shall the | princes • come out of | Egypt :
            the Morians' land shall soon | stretch out • her | hands • unto | God.

change chant (Full)

W. Crotch

Full   f   32   Sing unto God O ye | kingdoms • of the | earth :
                    O sing | praises | unto • the | Lord;

Full   33   Who sitteth in the heavens over | all from • the be|ginning :
                        lo he doth send out his voice * | yea and | that a | mighty voice.

              34   Ascribe ye the power to | God • over | Israel :
                        his | worship • and | strength is • in the | clouds.

              35   O God wonderful art thou in thy | holy | places :
                        even the God of Israel *
                        he will give strength and power unto his | people * | blessed • be | God.

Full   Glory be to the Father | and to • the | Son :
                        and | to the | Holy | Ghost.

Full   As it was in the beginning is | now and • ever | shall be :
                        world without | end. A | • • | men.

PSALM 69

J. Barnby

Salvum me fac

Full *p*   1   Save │ me O │ God :
for the waters are come │ in · even │ unto · my │ soul.

Full   2   I stick fast in the deep │ mire · where no │ ground is :
I am come into deep │ waters · so that the │ floods run │ over me.

3   I am weary of crying my │ throat is │ dry :
my sight faileth me for │ waiting · so │ long up·on my │ God.

4   They that hate me without a cause are more than the │ hairs · of my │ head :
they that are mine enemies and would de│stroy me │ guiltless · are │ mighty.

mp   5   I paid them the things that I │ never │ took :
God thou knowest my │ simpleness · and my │ faults · are not │
hid from thee.

mf   6   Let not them that trust in thee O Lord God of hosts be a│shamed · for my │ cause :
let not those that seek thee be con│founded through · me O │
Lord · God of │ Israel.

p   7 ‡   And why? * for thy sake have I │ suffered · re│proof :
– │ shame hath │ covered · my │ face.

8   I am become a │ stranger · unto my │ brethren :
even an │ alien · unto my │ mother's │ children.

9   For the zeal of thine │ house hath · even │ eaten me :
and the rebukes of them that re│buked thee · are │ fallen · up│on me.

10   I wept and │ chastened my·self with │ fasting :
and that was │ turned to │ my re│proof.

11 ‡   I put on │ sackcloth │ also :
– │ and they │ jested · up│on me.

12   They that sit in the │ gate · speak a│gainst me :
and the │ drunkards · make │ songs up│on me.

Psalm 69, continued

J. Barnby

mp　　13 ‡　But Lord I make my | prayer • unto | thee :
　　　　　　　　　– | in an • ac|cepta•ble | time.

　　　　14　Hear me O God in the | multitude • of thy | mercy :
　　　　　　　　　even in the | truth of | thy sal|vation.

mf　　15　Take me out of the | mire • that I | sink not :
　　　　　　　　　O let me be delivered from them that hate me and |
　　　　　　　　　out of • the | deep | waters.

　　　　16　Let not the water-flood drown me * neither let the deep | swallow • me | up :
　　　　　　　　　and let not the | pit • shut her | mouth up|on me.

p　　17　Hear me O Lord for thy loving | kindness • is | comfortable :
　　　　　　　　　turn thee unto me ac|cording • to the | multitude • of thy | mercies.

　　　　18 ‡　And hide not thy face from thy servant for | I am • in | trouble :
　　　　　　　　　– | – O | haste thee • and | hear me.

　　　　19　Draw nigh unto my | soul and | save it :
　　　　　　　　　O de|liver me • be|cause of • mine | enemies.

　　　　20　Thou hast known my reproof my | shame and • my dis|honour :
　　　　　　　　　mine | adversaries • are | all • in thy | sight.

pp　　21　Thy rebuke hath broken my heart * I am | full of | heaviness :
　　　　　　　　　I looked for some to have pity on me *
　　　　　　　　　but there was no man * | neither • found I | any • to | comfort me.

　　　　22　They gave me | gall to | eat :
　　　　　　　　　and when I was | thirsty they • gave me | vinegar • to | drink.

Psalm 69, continued

J. Barnby

mf

23 §   Let their table be made a snare to | take themselves • with|al :
          and let the things that should have been for their wealth be |
          unto them • an oc|casion • of | falling.

24 §   Let their eyes be | blinded • that they | see not :
          and ever | bow thou | down their | backs.

25 §   Pour out thine indig|nation • up|on them :
          and let thy | wrathful • dis|pleasure • take | hold of them.

26 §   Let their habi|tation • be | void :
          and | no man • to | dwell • in their | tents.

27 §   For they persecute | him whom • thou hast | smitten :
          and they talk how they may | vex them • whom | thou hast | wounded.

28 §‡   Let them fall from one | wickedness • to an|other :
          – | – and not | come into • thy | righteousness.

29 §   **2nd part** Let them be wiped out of the | book • of the | living :
          and not be | written • a|mong the | righteous.

change chant (Full)

§ *Omitted in the St Paul's Cathedral use*

Psalm 69, continued

T. Attwood

Full	mf	30	As for me when I am | poor · and in | heaviness : thy help O | God shall | lift me | up.
Full	f	31 ‡	I will praise the name of | God · with a | song : – | – and | magnify it · with | thanksgiving.
	mf	32	This also shall | please the | Lord : better than a | bullock · that hath | horns and | hoofs.
		33	The humble shall con|sider this · and be | glad : seek ye after | God · and your | soul shall | live.
		34 ‡	For the Lord | heareth · the | poor : – | – and de|spiseth · not his | prisoners.
		35	Let | heaven and · earth | praise him : the | sea and · all that | moveth · there|in.
	f	36	For God will save Sion and build the | cities · of | Judah : that men may | dwell there · and | have it · in pos|session.
		37	The posterity also of his | servants · shall in|herit it : and they that | love his | Name shall | dwell therein.
Full			Glory be to the Father | and to · the | Son : and | to the | Holy | Ghost.
Full			As it was in the beginning is | now and · ever | shall be : world without | end. A | . . | men.

PSALM 70

W. Hine

Deus, in adjutorium

Full	*p*	1	Haste thee O | God · to de|liver me : make | haste to | help me · O | Lord.
Full		2	Let them be ashamed and confounded that | seek · after my | soul : let them be turned backward and put to con|fusion · that | wish me | evil.
		3	Let them for their reward be | soon · brought to | shame : that cry | over · me * | There | there.

change chant (Cantoris)

H. Aldrich

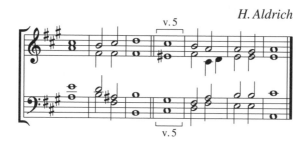

Can.	*mf*	4	But let all those that seek thee be | joyful · and | glad in thee : and let all such as delight in thy salvation say | alway * The | Lord be | praised.
	mp	5 ‡	As for me I am | poor · and in | misery : – | haste thee · unto | me O | God.
	cresc.	6	Thou art my | helper and · my re|deemer : O | Lord make | no long | tarrying.
Full	*mf*		Glory be to the Father | and to · the | Son : and | to the | Holy | Ghost.
Full			As it was in the beginning is | now and · ever | shall be : world without | end. A | . . | men.

PSALM 71

E. F. Day

In te, Domine, speravi

Full	*mf*	1	In thee O Lord have I put my trust * let me never be | put to · con|fusion : but rid me and deliver me in thy righteousness * incline thine | ear · unto | me and | save me.
Full		2	Be thou my stronghold whereunto I may | alway · re|sort : thou hast promised to help me * for thou art my | house of · de|fence · and my | castle.
		3	Deliver me O my God out of the | hand of the · un|godly : out of the hand of the un|righteous · and | cruel | man.
		4	For thou O Lord God art the | thing · that I | long for : thou art my | hope | even · from my | youth.
		5	Through thee have I been holden up ever | since · I was | born : thou art he that took me out of my mother's womb * my | praise · shall be | always · of | thee.
		6	I am become as it were a | monster · unto | many : but my | sure trust | is in | thee.
	f	7	O let my mouth be | filled · with thy | praise : that I may sing of thy glory and | honour | all the · day | long.
	mp	8	Cast me not away in the | time of | age : forsake me | not · when my | strength | faileth me.
	mf	9	For mine enemies speak against me * and they that lay wait for my soul take their | counsel to·gether | saying : God hath forsaken him * persecute him and | take him · for there is | none · to de|liver him.
		10	Go not | far from me · O | God : my | God | haste thee · to | help me.

Psalm 71, continued

E. F. Day

11   Let them be confounded and perish that are a|gainst my | soul :
     let them be covered with shame and dis|honour • that | seek to • do me | evil.

mp 12   As for me I will patiently a|bide | alway :
     and will | praise thee | more and | more.

   13 ‡   My mouth shall daily speak of thy | righteousness • and sal|vation :
     – | – for I | know no | end thereof.

cresc. 14   I will go forth in the | strength of the • Lord | God :
     and will make | mention • of thy | righteous•ness | only.

change chant (Full)

Maurice Bevan

Full   mf 15   Thou O God hast taught me from my | youth up • until | now :
     therefore will I | tell of • thy | wondrous | works.

Full 16   Forsake me not O God in mine old age | when I am • gray-|headed :
     until I have shewed thy strength unto this generation *
     and thy power to all | them • that are | yet for • to | come.

   17   Thy righteousness O | God is • very | high :
     and great things are they that thou hast done *
     O | God • who is | like • unto | thee?

mp cresc. 18   O what great troubles and adversities hast thou shewed me *
     and yet didst thou | turn • and re|fresh me :
     yea and broughtest me from the | deep • of the | earth a|gain.

Psalm 71, continued

Maurice Bevan

mf   19   Thou hast │ brought me to • great │ honour :
           and │ comforted • me on │ every │ side.

f   20   Therefore will I praise thee and thy faithfulness O God *
           playing upon an │ instrument • of │ musick :
              unto thee will I sing upon the │ harp • O thou │ Holy One • of │ Israel.

    21   My lips will be fain when I │ sing • unto │ thee :
           and so will my │ soul whom │ thou hast • de│livered.

    22   My tongue also shall talk of thy righteousness │ all the • day │ long :
           for they are confounded and brought unto │ shame that │
           seek to • do me │ evil.

Full   Glory be to the Father │ and to • the │ Son :
           and │ to the │ Holy │ Ghost.

Full   As it was in the beginning is │ now and • ever │ shall be :
           world without │ end. A │ . . │ men.

PSALM 72

W. Boyce

Deus, judicium

Full *f*　1　Give the King thy | judgements · O | God :
　　　　　　　and thy | righteousness · unto the | King's | son.

Full　2 †　Then shall he judge thy | people · ac|cording ‖ unto | right · and de|fend the | poor.

mp　3　The mountains | also · shall bring | peace :
　　　　　　and the little hills | righteous·ness | unto · the | people.

　4　He shall keep the | simple folk · by their | right :
　　　　　　defend the children of the | poor and | punish · the | wrong-doer.

　5　They shall fear thee as long as the | sun and · moon en|dureth :
　　　　　　from | one · gene|ration · to an|other.

　6　He shall come down like the rain into a | fleece of | wool :
　　　　　　even as the | drops that | water · the | earth.

cresc.　7　2nd part　In his time shall the | righteous | flourish :
dim.　　　　　　yea and abundance of peace so | long · as the | moon en|dureth.

f　8　His dominion shall be also from the | one sea · to the | other :
　　　　　　and from the | flood · unto the | world's | end.

　9　They that dwell in the wilderness shall | kneel be|fore him :
　　　　　　his | enem·ies shall | lick the | dust.

mf　10　The kings of Tharsis and of the | isles · shall give | presents :
　　　　　　the kings of A|rabia · and | Saba · shall bring | gifts.

　11　All kings shall fall | down be|fore him :
　　　　　　all | nations · shall | do him | service.

p　12　For he shall deliver the | poor · when he | crieth :
　　　　　　the needy | also · and | him that · hath no | helper.

　13　He shall be favourable to the | simple · and | needy :
　　　　　　and shall pre|serve the | souls · of the | poor.

Psalm 72, continued

W. Boyce

mp 14 He shall deliver their souls from | falsehood · and | wrong :
and | dear · shall their | blood be · in his | sight.

cresc. 15 He shall live * and unto him shall be given of the | gold · of A|rabia :
prayer shall be made ever unto him * and | daily · shall | he be | praised.

mf 16 There shall be an heap of corn in the earth | high up·on the | hills :
his fruit shall shake like Libanus *
and shall be green in the | city · like | grass up·on the | earth.

17 His Name shall endure for ever *
his Name shall remain under the sun a|mong the · po|sterities :
which shall be blessed through him *
and | all the | heathen · shall | praise him.

Full* *f 18 Blessed be the Lord God * even the | God of | Israel :
which | only · doeth | wondrous | things.

Full 19 And blessed be the Name of his | Majesty · for | ever :
and all the earth shall be filled with his Majesty | Amen * | A|men.

Full Glory be to the Father | and to · the | Son :
and | to the | Holy | Ghost.

Full As it was in the beginning is | now and · ever | shall be :
world without | end. A | · · | men.

PSALM 73

W. Crotch

Quam bonus Israel!

Full *mf* 1 Truly God is │ loving • unto │ Israel :
   even unto │ such • as are │ of a • clean │ heart.

Full 2 Nevertheless my │ feet were • almost │ gone :
   my │ treadings • had │ well-nigh │ slipt.

3 And why? * I was │ grieved • at the │ wicked :
   I do also see the un│godly • in │ such pro│sperity.

4 ‡ For they are in no │ peril • of │ death :
   – │ – but are │ lusty • and │ strong.

5 ‡ They come in no mis│fortune • like │ other folk :
   – │ neither • are they │ plagued like │ other men.

6 ‡ And this is the cause that they are so │ holden • with │ pride :
   – │ – and over│whelmed with │ cruelty.

7 ‡ Their │ eyes • swell with │ fatness :
   – │ and they • do │ even • what they │ lust.

8 They corrupt other and │ speak of • wicked │ blasphemy :
   their │ talking • is a│gainst the • most │ High.

9 For they stretch forth their │ mouth • unto the │ heaven :
   and their │ tongue • goeth │ through the │ world.

10 Therefore fall the │ people │ unto them :
   and thereout │ suck they • no │ small ad│vantage.

Psalm 73, continued

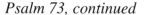

W. Crotch

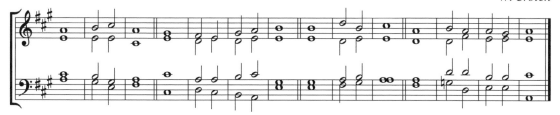

mp	11	Tush say they * | how should · God per|ceive it :
		is there | knowledge | in the · most | High?
mf	12	Lo these are the ungodly * these prosper in the world *
		and these have | riches · in pos|session :
		and I said * Then have I cleansed my heart in |
		vain and · washed mine | hands in | innocency.
	13	All the day | long have · I been | punished :
		and | chastened | every | morning.
	14	Yea and I had almost said | even · as | they :
		but lo then I should have con|demned the · gene|ration · of thy | children.
mp	15 †	Then | thought I · to | under‖stand | this · but it | was too | hard for me,
cresc.	16	Until I went into the | sanctuary · of | God :
		then under|stood I · the | end of · these | men;
mf	17	Namely how thou dost set them in | slippe·ry | places :
		and | castest · them | down · and de|stroyest them.
	18	O how | suddenly do · they con|sume :
		perish and | come · to a | fearful | end.
	19	[2nd part] Yea even like as a | dream when · one a|waketh :
dim.		so shalt thou make their image to | vanish | out of · the | city.
p	20	Thus my | heart was | grieved :
		and it went | even | through my | reins.
	21	So | foolish was · I and | ignorant :
		even as it | were a | beast be|fore thee.

change chant (Full)

Psalm 73, continued

F. A. G. Ouseley

Full *f* 22 Nevertheless I am │ alway • by │ thee :
for thou hast │ holden • me │ by my • right │ hand.

Full 23 Thou shalt │ guide me • with thy │ counsel :
and │ after • that re│ceive me • with │ glory.

mf 24 Whom have I in │ heaven but │ thee :
and there is none upon earth that I de│sire • in com│pari•son of │ thee.

mp 25 My flesh and my │ heart │ faileth :
mf but God is the strength of my │ heart • and my │ portion • for │ ever.

26 For lo they that for│sake thee • shall │ perish :
thou hast destroyed all them that com│mit • forni│cation • a│gainst thee.

f 27 But it is good for me to hold me fast by God *
to put my trust in the │ Lord │ God :
and to speak of all thy works in the │ gates of • the │ daughter • of │ Sion.

Full Glory be to the Father │ and to • the │ Son :
and │ to the │ Holy │ Ghost.

Full As it was in the beginning is │ now and • ever │ shall be :
world without │ end. A │ • • │ men.

PSALM 74

H. Smart

Ut quid, Deus?

Full *p* 1 O God wherefore art thou | absent from us • so | long :
   why is thy wrath so | hot a•gainst the | sheep • of thy | pasture?

Full 2 O think upon thy | congre|gation :
   whom thou hast | purchased • and re|deemed of | old.

3 Think upon the | tribe of • thine in|heritance :
   and mount | Sion • where|in • thou hast | dwelt.

cresc. 4 ‡ Lift up thy feet * that thou mayest utterly de|stroy • every | enemy :
   – | – which hath done | evil • in thy | sanctuary.

mf 5 Thine adversaries roar in the | midst of thy • congre|gations :
   and | set up • their | banners • for | tokens.

6 He that hewed timber afore out of the | thick | trees :
   was known to | bring it • to an | excel•lent | work.

p 7 ‡ But now they break down | all the • carved | work thereof :
   – | – with | axes • and | hammers.

8 They have set fire upon thy | holy | places :
   and have defiled the dwelling-place of thy | Name • even |
   unto • the | ground.

mp 9 Yea they said in their hearts * Let us make | havock of them • alto|gether :
   thus have they burnt up all the | houses • of | God • in the | land.

10 We see not our tokens * there is not | one • prophet | more :
   no not one is there among us that under|standeth | any | more.

Psalm 74, continued

H. Smart

p   11   O God how long shall the adversary | do this • dis|honour :
                   how long shall the | enemy • blas|pheme thy • Name for | ever?

pp   12   Why with|drawest • thou thy | hand :
                   why pluckest thou not thy right hand out of thy |
                   bosom • to con|sume the | enemy?

change chant (Full)

T. T. Noble

Full   *f*   13   For God is my | King of | old :
                   the help that is done upon | earth he | doeth it • him|self.

Full   14   Thou didst divide the | sea • through thy | power :
                   thou brakest the | heads • of the | dragons • in the | waters.

           15   Thou smotest the heads of Le|viathan • in | pieces :
                   and gavest him to be | meat • for the | people • in the | wilderness.

           16   Thou broughtest out fountains and waters | out of the • hard | rocks :
                   thou | driedst • up | mighty | waters.

mf   17   The | day is thine • and the | night is thine :
                   thou hast pre|pared the | light • and the | sun.

         18 ‡   Thou hast set all the | borders • of the | earth :
                   – | thou hast • made | summer • and | winter.

change chant (Decani)

Psalm 74, continued

H. Smart

Dec. *mp* 19 Remember this O Lord how the | enemy • hath re|buked :
                and how the foolish | people • hath blas|phemed thy | Name.

            20 O deliver not the soul of thy turtle-dove unto the | multitude • of the | enemies :
                and forget not the congre|gation • of the | poor for | ever.

  p 21 ‡ – | Look upon • the | covenant :
                for all the earth is full of | darkness • and | cruel • habi|tations.

  cresc. 22 O let not the simple go a|way a|shamed :
                but let the poor and | needy • give | praise • unto thy | Name.

change chant (Full)

T. T. Noble

Full *f* 23 Arise O God main|tain thine • own | cause :
                remember how the | foolish man • blas|phemeth • thee | daily.

Full 24 Forget not the | voice • of thine | enemies :
                the presumption of them that hate thee in|creaseth • ever |
                more and | more.

Full Glory be to the Father | and to • the | Son :
                and | to the | Holy | Ghost.

Full As it was in the beginning is | now and • ever | shall be :
                world without | end. A | . . | men.

PSALM 75

C. H. Lloyd

Confitebimur tibi

Full *f*	1	Unto thee O | God do • we give | thanks :	
		yea unto | thee do | we give | thanks.	
Full	2	Thy Name | also is • so | nigh :	
		and that do thy | wondrous | works de|clare.	
mf	3	When I re|ceive the • congre|gation :	
		I shall | judge ac|cording • unto | right.	
	4	The earth is weak * and all the in|habiters • there|of :	
		I | bear up • the | pillars | of it.	
	5	I said unto the fools | Deal not • so | madly :	
		and to the un|godly * Set not | up your | horn.	
	6	Set not up your | horn on | high :	
		and | speak not | with a • stiff | neck.	
7 ‡		For promotion cometh neither from the | east nor • from the | west :	
		nor | – – | yet • from the | south.	
f	8	And why? * | God • is the | Judge :	
		he putteth down | one and | setteth • up an|other.	
mf	9	For in the hand of the Lord there is a cup and the | wine is | red :	
		it is full mixed * and he | poureth | out • of the | same.	
	10	As for the | dregs there|of :	
		all the ungodly of the earth shall | drink them • and | suck them | out.	
Full *f*	11 ‡	But I will talk of the | God of | Jacob :	
		and | – – | praise him • for | ever.	
Full	12	All the horns of the ungodly | also • will I | break :	
		and the | horns • of the | righteous • shall be ex|alted.	
Full		Glory be to the Father | and to • the | Son :	
		and | to the | Holy | Ghost.	
Full		As it was in the beginning is | now and • ever | shall be :	
		world without | end. A | . . | men.	

PSALM 76

S. H. Nicholson

Notus in Judæa

Full	*f*	1	In	Jewry is • God	known : his	Name is • great in	Israel.
Full		2	At	Salem • is his	tabernacle : and his	dwelling • in	Sion.
	mf	3	There brake he the	arrows • of the	bow : the shield the	sword • and the	battle.
		4 †	Thou art of more	honour • and	might ‖ than the	hills • of the	robbers.
		5	The proud are robbed * they have	slept their	sleep : and all the men whose hands were	mighty • have found	nothing.
		6	At thy re	buke O • God of	Jacob : both the chariot and	horse are	fallen.
	f	7	Thou even	thou art • to be	feared : and who may stand in thy	sight when • thou art	angry?
		8	Thou didst cause thy judgement to be	heard from	heaven :
	dim.		the earth	trembled • and was	still;
	f	9	When God a	rose to	judgement : and to help all the	meek up•on	earth.
		10	The fierceness of man shall	turn • to thy	praise : and the fierceness of them	shalt thou • re	frain.
	mf	11	Promise unto the Lord your God and keep it * all ye that are	round a	bout him : bring presents unto him that	ought to • be	feared.
		12	He shall refrain the	spirit • of	princes : and is wonderful among the	kings • of the	earth.
Full	*f*		Glory be to the Father	and to • the	Son : and to the	Holy	Ghost.
Full			As it was in the beginning is	now and • ever	shall be : world without	end. A	men.

PSALM 77

J. Stainer

Voce mea ad Dominum

Full p   1   I will cry unto │ God • with my │ voice :
                   even unto God will I cry with my │ voice and • he shall │ hearken │ unto • me.

Full   2   In the time of my │ trouble I • sought the │ Lord :
                   my sore ran and ceased not in the │ night-season *
                   my │ soul re•fused │ comfort.

              3   When I am in heaviness I will │ think up•on │ God :
                   when my │ heart is │ vexed • I will com│plain.

              4   Thou holdest mine │ eyes │ waking :
                   I am so │ feeble • that I │ cannot │ speak.

              5 † I have con│sidered • the │ days ‖ of │ old • and the │ years • that are │ past.

              6   I call to re│membrance • my │ song :
                   and in the night I commune with mine own │
                   heart and │ search out • my │ spirits.

mp   7   Will the Lord ab│sent himself • for │ ever :
                   and │ will he • be no │ more in│treated?

              8   Is his mercy clean │ gone for │ ever :
                   and is his promise come utterly to an │ end for │ ever│more?

              9   Hath God for│gotten • to be │ gracious :
                   and will he shut up his loving-│kindness │ in dis│pleasure?

p   10   And I said It is mine │ own in│firmity :
                   but I will remember the years of the │ right hand │ of the • most │ Highest.

mp   11   I will remember the │ works • of the │ Lord :
                   and call to │ mind thy │ wonders • of │ old time.

             12   I will think │ also of • all thy │ works :
                   and my │ talking • shall be │ of thy │ doings.

Psalm 77, continued

J. Stainer

13 Thy way O | God is | holy :

cresc.   who is so | great a | God as | our God?

mf   14 Thou art the | God that • doeth | wonders :
                    and hast declared thy | power • a|mong the | people.

15 Thou hast mightily de|livered • thy | people :
                    even the | sons of | Jacob • and | Joseph.

16 ‡   The waters saw thee O God * the waters | saw thee and • were a|fraid :
                    – | – the depths | also • were | troubled.

Full *f*   17 The clouds poured out water the | air | thundered :
                    and thine | arrows | went a|broad.

Full   18 The voice of thy thunder was | heard • round a|bout :
                    the lightnings shone upon the ground *
                    the earth was | moved and | shook with|al.

mf   19 Thy way is in the sea and thy paths in the | great | waters :
                    and thy | footsteps | are not | known.

mp   20 Thou leddest thy | people • like | sheep :
                    by the | hand of | Moses • and | Aaron.

Full *p*   Glory be to the Father | and to • the | Son :
                    and | to the | Holy | Ghost.

Full   As it was in the beginning is | now and • ever | shall be :
                    world without | end. A | . . | men.

PSALM 78

A. H. Mann

Attendite, popule

Full *f*	1	Hear my | law • O my | people :	
		incline your | ears • unto the | words • of my | mouth.	
Full	2	I will open my | mouth • in a | parable :	
		I will de|clare hard | senten•ces of | old;	
Full	3	Which we have | heard and | known :	
		and | such • as our | fathers • have | told us;	
Full	4	That we should not hide them from the children of the gene|rations • to | come :	
		but to shew the honour of the Lord *	
		his mighty and wonderful | works that | he hath | done.	

change chant (Decani)

Psalm 78, continued

J. Pring

Dec. *mf*   5   He made a covenant with Jacob and gave | Israel • a | law :
           which he commanded our | forefathers • to | teach their | children;

        6   That their po|sterity • might | know it :
           and the | children • which were | yet un|born;

        7   To the intent that | when they • came | up :
           they might | shew their | children • the | same;

        8   That they might put their | trust in | God :
           and not to forget the works of | God • but to |
           keep his • com|mandments;

        9   And not to be as their forefathers * a faithless and | stubborn • gene|ration :
           a generation that set not their heart aright *
           and whose spirit cleaveth not | stedfast•ly | unto | God;

      10   Like as the | children • of | Ephraim :
           who being harnessed and carrying bows *
           turned themselves | back • in the | day of | battle.

      11   They kept not the | covenant • of | God :
           and | would not | walk in • his | law;

      12   But for|gat what • he had | done :
           and the | wonder•ful | works that • he had | shewed for them.

change chant (Full)

Psalm 78, continued

C. V. Stanford

Full *f*	13 ‡	Marvellous things did he in the sight of our forefathers * in the | land of | Egypt : – | even • in the | field of | Zoan.
Full	14	He divided the sea and | let them • go | through : he made the | waters • to | stand • on an | heap.
Full	15	In the day-time also he | led them • with a | cloud : and all the night | through • with a | light of | fire.
Full	16	He clave the hard | rocks • in the | wilderness : and gave them drink thereof * as it had been | out of • the | great | depth.
Full	17	[**2nd part**] He brought waters out of the | stony | rock : so that it | gushed out | like the | rivers.

change chant (Decani)

J. Barnby

Dec. *p*	18	Yet for all this they | sinned • more a|gainst him : and pro|voked the • most | Highest • in the | wilderness.
	19 ‡	They tempted | God • in their | hearts : – | and re•quired | meat • for their | lust.
	20	They spake against | God • also | saying : Shall | God pre•pare a | table • in the | wilderness?
	21	He smote the stony rock indeed * that the waters gushed out and the | streams • flowed with|al : but can he give bread also * | or pro•vide | flesh • for his | people?

change chant (Full)

Psalm 78, continued

I. A. Atkins

Full *f*   22   When the Lord heard | this • he was | wroth :
                                 so the fire was kindled in Jacob *
                                 and there came up | heavy • dis|pleasure a•gainst | Israel;

Full   23   Because they be|lieved not • in | God :
                                 and | put not • their | trust • in his | help.

         mf   24   So he com|manded the • clouds a|bove :
                                 and | opened • the | doors of | heaven.

                25   He rained down manna also up|on them • for to | eat :
                                 and | gave them | food from | heaven.

                26   So man did eat | angels' | food :
                                 for he | sent them | meat e|nough.

                27   He caused the east-wind to | blow • under | heaven :
                                 and through his power he | brought in • the | south-west | wind.

                28   He rained flesh upon them as | thick as | dust :
                                 and feathered | fowls • like as the | sand • of the | sea.

                29   He let it | fall a•mong their | tents :
                                 even round a|bout their | habi|tation.

Full *f*   30   **2nd part**   So they did eat and were well filled *
                                 for he | gave them their • own de|sire :
                                 they were | not • disap|pointed • of their | lust.

change chant (Decani)

Psalm 78, continued

J. Goss

Dec. **p**   31   But while the meat was yet in their mouths *
     cresc.   the heavy wrath of God came upon them and slew the | wealthi·est | of them :
                         yea and smote down the | chosen men · that | were in | Israel.

      p   32   But for all this they | sinned yet | more :
                         and be|lieved not · his | wondrous | works.

                   33 †   Therefore their | days did · he con|sume ‖ in | vanity · and their |
                         years in | trouble.

                   34   When he | slew them · they | sought him :
                         and turned them | early · and in|quired · after | God.

      mf   35   And they remembered that | God · was their | strength :
                         and that the high | God was | their re|deemer.

      p   36   Nevertheless they did but | flatter him · with their | mouth :
                         and dis|sembled · with him | in their | tongue.

                   37   For their | heart · was not | whole with him :
                         neither con|tinued · they | stedfast · in his | covenant.

      mp   38 †   But he was so | merciful · that he for|gave ‖
                         their mis|deeds · and de|stroyed them | not.

      p   39   Yea many a time | turned he his · wrath a|way :
                         and would not | suffer his · whole dis|pleasure · to a|rise.

      pp   40   For he considered that they | were but | flesh :
                         and that they were even a wind that passeth a|way and |
                         cometh · not a|gain.

change chant (Full)

Psalm 78, continued

A. H. Mann

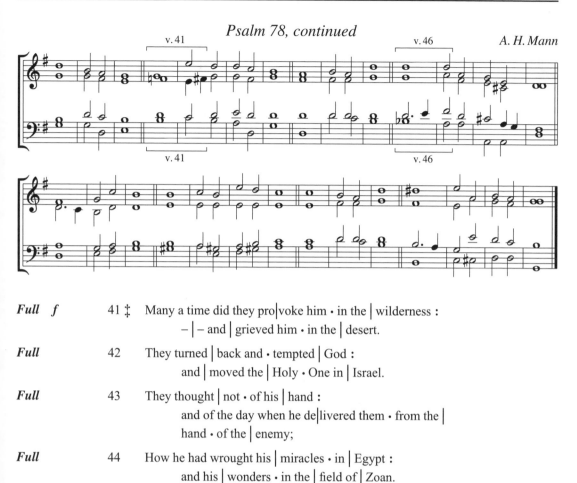

Full *f*   41 ‡   Many a time did they pro|voke him • in the | wilderness :
                 – | – and | grieved him • in the | desert.

Full   42   They turned | back and • tempted | God :
                 and | moved the | Holy • One in | Israel.

Full   43   They thought | not • of his | hand :
                 and of the day when he de|livered them • from the |
                 hand • of the | enemy;

Full   44   How he had wrought his | miracles • in | Egypt :
                 and his | wonders • in the | field of | Zoan.

Full   45   He turned their | waters • into | blood :
                 so that they | might not | drink of • the | rivers.

Full   46 ‡   He sent lice among them and de|voured them | up :
                 – | – and | frogs • to de|stroy them.

Full   47   He gave their | fruit • unto the | caterpillar :
                 and their | labour | unto • the | grasshopper.

Full   48   He destroyed their | vines with | hail-stones :
                 and their | mulber•ry-|trees • with the | frost.

Psalm 78, continued

A. H. Mann

Full Unison	49 ‡	He smote their │ cattle • also with │ hail-stones : – │ – and their │ flocks with • hot │ thunderbolts.
Full Unison	50	He cast upon them the furiousness of his wrath * anger dis│pleasure • and │ trouble : and sent │ evil │ angels • a│mong them.
Full Unison	51	He made a way to his indignation and spared not their │ soul from │ death : but │ gave their • life │ over • to the │ pestilence;
Full Unison	52	And smote all the │ first-born • in │ Egypt : the most principal and │ mightiest • in the │ dwellings • of │ Ham.

change chant (Decani)

G. Cooper

Dec. **mp**	53	But as for his own people * he │ led them • forth like │ sheep : and carried them in the │ wilder•ness │ like a │ flock.
	54	He brought them out safely that they │ should not │ fear : and overwhelmed their │ ene•mies │ with the │ sea.

Psalm 78, continued

G. Cooper

55   And brought them within the | borders • of his | sanctuary :
        even to his mountain which he | purchased | with his • right | hand.

56   He cast out the | heathen • also be|fore them :
        caused their land to be divided among them for an heritage *
        and made the tribes of | Israel • to | dwell • in their | tents.

change chant (Decani)

J. Goss

Dec.   *mf*   57 ‡ So they tempted and dis|pleased the • most high | God :
                – | – and | kept not • his | testimonies;

58   But turned their backs and fell a|way • like their | forefathers :
        starting a|side • like a | broken | bow.

59   2nd part For they | grieved him • with their | hill-altars :
              and pro|voked him • to dis|pleasure • with their | images.

f   60   When God heard | this • he was | wroth :
        and took | sore dis|pleasure • at | Israel.

61   So that he forsook the | tabernacle • in | Silo :
        even the | tent that • he had | pitched a•mong | men.

Psalm 78, continued

mf   62 He delivered their | power • into cap|tivity :
        and their | beauty • into the | ene•my's | hand.

63 ‡ He gave his people over | also • unto the | sword :
        – | – and was | wroth with • his in|heritance.

64 The fire con|sumed their • young | men :
        and their | maidens • were not | given • to | marriage.

65 Their priests were | slain • with the | sword :
        and there were no | widows • to | make • lamen|tation.

change chant (Full)

H. J. Gauntlett

Full *f*   66 So the Lord awaked as | one • out of | sleep :
        and like a | giant • re|freshed with | wine.

Full   67 He smote his enemies in the | hinder | parts :
        and | put them • to a per|petu•al | shame.

68 He refused the | tabernacle • of | Joseph :
        and | chose not • the | tribe of | Ephraim;

69 But chose the | tribe of | Judah :
        even the | hill of | Sion • which he | loved.

Psalm 78, continued

H. J. Gauntlett

mf   70   And there he built his | temple • on | high :
                 and laid the foundation of it like the | ground which • he hath |
                 made con|tinually.

         71   He chose | David • also his | servant :
                 and | took him • a|way • from the | sheep-folds.

         72   As he was following the ewes great with | young ones • he | took him :
                 that he might feed Jacob his | people • and | Israel • his in|heritance.

Full *f*   73   So he fed them with a | faithful and • true | heart :
                 and ruled them | prudently • with | all his | power.

Full   Glory be to the Father | and to • the | Son :
                 and | to the | Holy | Ghost.

Full   As it was in the beginning is | now and • ever | shall be :
                 world without | end. A | • • | men.

PSALM 79

C. Hylton Stewart

Deus, venerunt

Full **mp**   1   O God the heathen are come | into • thine in|heritance :
        thy holy temple have they defiled *
        and made Je|rusalem • an | heap of | stones.

Full   2   The dead bodies of thy servants have they given to be meat unto the |
        fowls • of the | air :
        and the flesh of thy | saints • unto the | beasts • of the | land.

          3 ‡   Their blood have they shed like water on every | side • of Je|rusalem :
        – | – and there was | no man • to | bury them.

          4   We are become an open | shame • to our | enemies :
        a very scorn and derision unto | them • that are | round a|bout us.

mf   5   Lord how | long wilt • thou be | angry :
        shall thy | jealousy • burn like | fire for | ever?

          6   Pour out thine indignation upon the | heathen that • have not | known thee :
        and upon the | kingdoms that • have not | called up•on thy | Name.

mp   7 ‡   For they have de|voured | Jacob :
        – | – and laid | waste his | dwelling-place.

p   8   O remember not our old sins * but have mercy up|on us • and that | soon :
        for we are | come to | great | misery.

mf   9   Help us O God of our salvation * for the | glory • of thy | Name :
        O deliver us and be | merciful • unto our | sins • for thy | Name's sake.

cresc.   10 †   Wherefore | do the | heathen ‖ say * | Where is | now their | God?

Psalm 79, continued

C. Hylton Stewart

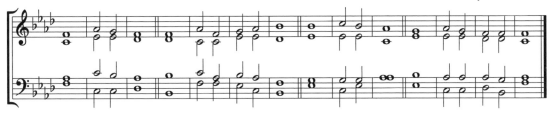

mf	11	O let the vengeance of thy servants' | blood · that is | shed : be openly | shewed up·on the | heathen · in our | sight.
mp	12	O let the sorrowful sighing of the | prisoners · come be|fore thee : according to the greatness of thy power * preserve thou | those that · are ap|pointed · to | die.
mf	13	And for the blasphemy wherewith our | neighbours · have blas|phemed thee : reward thou them O Lord | seven-·fold | into · their | bosom.
Full	14	So we that are thy people and sheep of thy pasture * shall give thee | thanks for | ever : and will alway be shewing forth thy praise from gene|ration · to | gene|ration.
Full f		Glory be to the Father | and to · the | Son : and | to the | Holy | Ghost.
Full		As it was in the beginning is | now and · ever | shall be : world without | end. A | . . | men.

PSALM 80

I. A. Atkins

Qui regis Israel

Full mf	1	Hear O thou shepherd of Israel * thou that leadest | Joseph · like a | sheep : shew thyself also * thou that | sittest · up|on the | cherubims.
Full	2 ‡	Before Ephraim | Benjamin · and Ma|nasses : – | stir up · thy | strength and · come and | help us.
Full f	3	**2nd part** Turn us a|gain O | God : shew the light of thy | countenance · and | we shall · be | whole.

Psalm 80, continued

I. A. Atkins

mp	4	O Lord | God of | hosts :
		how long wilt thou be | angry • with thy | people • that | prayeth?
	5	Thou feedest them with the | bread of | tears :
		and givest them | plenteousness • of | tears to | drink.
mf	6	Thou hast made us a very | strife • unto our | neighbours :
		and our | ene•mies | laugh us • to | scorn.
Full f	7	Turn us again thou | God of | hosts :
		shew the light of thy | countenance • and | we shall • be | whole.
mf	8	Thou hast brought a | vine • out of | Egypt :
		thou hast | cast out • the | heathen • and | planted it.
	9	Thou | madest | room for it :
		and when it had taken | root it | filled the | land.
	10	The hills were | covered • with the | shadow of it :
		and the | boughs thereof • were | like the • goodly | cedar-trees.
	11 ‡	She stretched out her | branches • unto the | sea :
		– | – and her | boughs • unto the | river.
mp	12	Why hast thou then | broken down • her | hedge :
		that all | they that go • by | pluck off • her | grapes?
mf	13	The wild boar out of the | wood doth • root it | up :
		and the wild | beasts • of the | field de|vour it.
Full f	14	2nd part Turn thee again thou God of hosts * look | down from | heaven :
		be|hold and | visit • this | vine;

Psalm 80, continued

I. A. Atkins

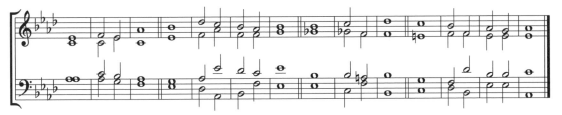

mf 15 And the place of the vineyard that thy │ right hand • hath │ planted :
and the branch that thou │ madest • so │ strong • for thy│self.

16 It is burnt with │ fire • and cut │ down :
and they shall │ perish • at the re│buke • of thy │ countenance.

17 Let thy hand be upon the │ man • of thy │ right hand :
and upon the son of man *
whom thou │ madest • so │ strong for • thine own │ self.

18 And so │ will not we • go │ back from thee :
O let us │ live and • we shall │ call up•on thy │ Name.

Full f 19 2nd part │ Turn us again O Lord │ God of │ hosts :
shew the light of thy │ countenance • and │ we shall • be │ whole.

Full Glory be to the Father │ and to • the │ Son :
and │ to the │ Holy │ Ghost.

Full As it was in the beginning is │ now and • ever │ shall be :
world without │ end. A │ • • │ men.

PSALM 81

R. P. Goodenough

Exultate Deo

Full f 1 Sing we merrily unto │ God our │ strength :
make a cheerful │ noise un•to the │ God of │ Jacob.

Full 2 Take the psalm bring │ hither • the │ tabret :
the │ merry │ harp • with the │ lute.

Psalm 81, *continued*

R. P. Goodenough

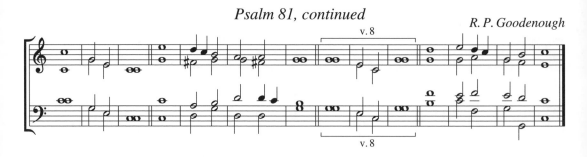

3 Blow up the | trumpet · in the new-|moon :
even in the time appointed * | and up·on our | solemn | feast-day.

4 For this was made a | statute · for | Israel :
and a | law · of the | God of | Jacob.

mf 5 This he ordained in | Joseph · for a | testimony :
when he came out of the land of | Egypt · and had |
heard a · strange | language.

6 I eased his | shoulder · from the | burden :
and his hands were de|livered · from | making · the | pots.

7 Thou calledst upon me in | troubles and · I de|livered thee :
and heard thee what | time as · the | storm · fell up|on thee.

8 ‡ 4th quarter I proved thee | also · at the | waters · of | strife.

f 9 Hear O my people and I will as|sure thee · O | Israel :
if | thou wilt | hearken | unto me,

10 There shall no | strange · god be | in thee :
neither shalt thou | worship | any · other | god.

11 2nd part I am the Lord thy God who brought thee | out of the · land of | Egypt :
open thy mouth | wide and | I shall | fill it.

change chant (Decani)

Psalm 81, continued

David Willcocks

Dec.   *mp*   12   But my people would not | hear my | voice :
                                    and | Israel • would | not o|bey me.

                       13   So I gave them up unto their | own hearts' | lusts :
                                    and let them | follow • their | own i•magi|nations.

                       14   O that my people would have | hearkened | unto me :
                                    for if | Israel • had | walked • in my | ways,

mf   15   I should soon have put | down their | enemies :
                                    and turned my | hand a|gainst their | adversaries.

                       16   The haters of the Lord should have been | found | liars :
                                    but their | time • should have en|dured for | ever.

                       17   He should have fed them also with the | finest | wheat-flour :
                                    and with honey out of the stony | rock should | I have | satisfied thee.

change chant (Full)

R. P. Goodenough

Full   *f*   Glory be to the Father | and to • the | Son :
                                    and | to the | Holy | Ghost.

Full   As it was in the beginning is | now and • ever | shall be :
                                    world without | end. A | . . | men.

Day 16: Evening

PSALM 82

W. Parratt

Deus stetit

<table>
<tr><td>***Full***   *f*</td><td>1 ‡</td><td>God standeth in the congre|gation · of | princes :
     – | he is · a | Judge a·mong | gods.</td></tr>
<tr><td>***Full***</td><td>2</td><td>How long will ye | give wrong | judgement :
     and accept the | persons | of the · un|godly?</td></tr>
<tr><td>*mf*</td><td>3</td><td>Defend the | poor and | father·less :
     see that such as are in | need · and ne|cessity · have | right.</td></tr>
<tr><td></td><td>4 ‡</td><td>Deliver the | outcast · and | poor :
     – | save them · from the | hand of the · un|godly.</td></tr>
<tr><td>*mp*</td><td>5</td><td>They will not be learned nor understand * but | walk on · still in | darkness :
     all the foun|dations · of the | earth are · out of | course.</td></tr>
<tr><td>*mf*</td><td>6</td><td>I have | said · Ye are | gods :
     and ye are all the | children · of the | most | Highest.</td></tr>
<tr><td>*mp*</td><td>7</td><td>But ye shall | die like | men :
     and | fall like | one of · the | princes.</td></tr>
<tr><td>*f*</td><td>8</td><td>Arise O God and | judge thou · the | earth :
     for thou shalt take all | heathen · to | thine in|heritance.</td></tr>
<tr><td>***Full***</td><td></td><td>Glory be to the Father | and to · the | Son :
     and | to the | Holy | Ghost.</td></tr>
<tr><td>***Full***</td><td></td><td>As it was in the beginning is | now and · ever | shall be :
     world without | end. A | .. | men.</td></tr>
</table>

PSALM 83

David Willcocks

Deus, quis similis?

Full *mf*   1   Hold not thy tongue O God | keep not · still | silence :
            refrain not thy|self O | God.

Full   2   For lo thine | enemies · make a | murmur·ing :
            and they that hate thee have | lift up · their | head.

    p   3   They have imagined | craftily a·gainst thy | people :
            and taken counsel a|gainst thy | secret ones.

        4   They have said come and let us root them out *
            that they be no | more a | people :
            and that the name of Israel may be no | more · in re|membrance.

   mf   5   For they have cast their heads to|gether with · one con|sent :
            and are con|federate · a|gainst thee;

        6   The tabernacles of the | Edomites · and the | Ismae·lites :
            the | Moabites · and | Hagarenes;

        7   Gebal and | Ammon · and | Ama·lek :
            the Philistines with | them that · dwell at | Tyre.

        8   Assur | also · is | joined with · them :
            and have holpen the | children · of | Lot.

        9   But do thou to them as | unto · the | Madian·ites :
            unto Sisera and unto Jabin at the | brook of | Kison;

      10   Who | perished · at | Endor :
            and became as the | dung · of the | earth.

Psalm 83, continued

David Willcocks

11 Make them and their princes like | Oreb · and | Zeb :
   yea make all their princes like as | Zeba · and Sal|mana;

12 † Who say let us | take · to our|selves the ‖ houses of | God · in pos|session.

f 13 O my God make them | like · unto a | wheel :
   and as the | stubble be·fore the | wind;

14 Like as the fire that | burneth · up the | wood :
   and as the flame that con|sumeth · the | mountains.

15 Persecute them even | so · with thy | tempest :
   and make them a|fraid · with thy | storm.

16 Make their | faces a·shamed O | Lord :
   that they may | seek thy | name.

17 Let them be confounded and vexed ever | more and | more :
   let them be put to | shame and | perish.

18 And they shall know that thou whose | name · is Je|hovah :
   art only the most Highest | over · all the | earth.

Full Glory be to the Father | and to · the | Son :
   and to the | Holy | Ghost.

Full As it was in the beginning is | now and · ever | shall be :
   world without | end. A|men.

PSALM 84

C. H. H. Parry

Quam dilecta!

Full *mf*   1 †   O how | amia·ble | are ‖ thy | dwellings · thou | Lord of | hosts!

Full   2   My soul hath a desire and longing to enter into the | courts · of the | Lord :
            my heart and my flesh re|joice · in the | living | God.

mp   3   Yea the sparrow hath found her an house *
        and the swallow a nest | where she may · lay her | young :
          even thy altars O Lord of | hosts my | King · and my | God.

4 ‡   Blessed are they that | dwell · in thy | house :
        they will be | – – | alway | praising thee.

mf   5 ‡   Blessed is the man whose | strength · is in | thee :
        – | in whose | heart · are thy | ways.

mp   6   Who going through the vale of misery | use it · for a | well :
        and the | pools are | filled with | water.

mf   7 | **2nd part** | They will go from | strength to | strength :
        and unto the God of gods appeareth | every · one of | them in | Sion.

p   8 ‡   O Lord God of | hosts · hear my | prayer :
        – | hearken · O | God of | Jacob.

mp   9   Behold O | God · our de|fender :
        and look upon the | face of | thine A|nointed.

mf   10 † For | one day · in thy | courts ‖ is | better | than a | thousand.

Psalm 84, continued

C. H. H. Parry

11   I had rather be a door-keeper in the │ house • of my │ God :
           than to │ dwell in • the │ tents • of un│godliness.

12   For the Lord God is a │ light • and de│fence :
           the Lord will give grace and worship * and no good thing shall he
           with│hold from │ them that • live a │ godly • life.

13   O Lord │ God of │ hosts :
           blessed is the │ man that │ putteth • his │ trust in thee.

Full   Glory be to the Father │ and to • the │ Son :
           and │ to the │ Holy │ Ghost.

Full   As it was in the beginning is │ now and • ever │ shall be :
           world without │ end. A │ • • │ men.

PSALM 85

W. Parratt

Benedixisti, Domine

Full   *mp*   1   Lord thou art become │ gracious • unto thy │ land :
                  thou hast turned a│way the • cap│tivity • of │ Jacob.

Full   2 ‡   Thou hast forgiven the of│fence • of thy │ people :
                  – │ – and │ covered • all their │ sins.

Full   3   **2nd part**   Thou hast taken away │ all • thy dis│pleasure :
                  and │ turned thyself • from thy │ wrathful • indig│nation.

Psalm 85, continued

W. Parratt

p	4	Turn us then O | God our | Saviour :
		and | let thine | anger | cease from us.
mp	5	Wilt thou be dis|pleased at us • for | ever :
		and wilt thou stretch out thy wrath from |
		one • gene|ration • to an|other?
mf	6	Wilt thou not | turn again • and | quicken us :
		that thy | people | may re|joice in thee?
	7 ‡	Shew us thy | mercy • O | Lord :
		– | – and | grant us • thy sal|vation.
p	8	I will hearken what the Lord | God will • say con|cerning me :
		for he shall speak peace unto his people and to his |
		saints • that they | turn not • a|gain.
mf	9	For his salvation is | nigh • them that | fear him :
		that | glory • may | dwell in • our | land.
p	10	Mercy and | truth are • met to|gether :
		righteousness and | peace have | kissed each | other.
	11	Truth shall | flourish • out of the | earth :
		and | righteousness • hath looked | down from | heaven.
mf	12	Yea the Lord shall shew | loving | kindness :
		and our | land shall | give her | increase.
	13	Righteousness shall | go be|fore him :
dim.		and he shall di|rect his | going • in the | way.
Full *p*		Glory be to the Father | and to • the | Son :
		and | to the | Holy | Ghost.
Full		As it was in the beginning is | now and • ever | shall be :
		world without | end. A | . . | men.

PSALM 86

J. Turle

Inclina, Domine

Full *mp*   1 ‡   Bow down thine ear O │ Lord and │ hear me :
for I am │ – – │ poor • and in │ misery.

Full   2   Preserve thou my │ soul for • I am │ holy :
my God save thy │ servant • that │ putteth • his │ trust in thee.

   3 ‡   Be merciful │ unto me • O │ Lord :
for I will call │ – – │ daily • up│on thee.

   4   Comfort the │ soul • of thy │ servant :
for unto thee O │ Lord • do I │ lift up • my │ soul.

   5   For thou Lord art │ good and │ gracious :
and of great mercy unto │ all • them that │ call up│on thee.

   6   Give ear │ Lord • unto my │ prayer :
and ponder the │ voice • of my │ humble • de│sires.

   7 †   **2nd part**   In the │ time • of my │ trouble ‖ I will │ call up•on │ thee • for thou │ hearest me.

mf   8   Among the gods there is none like unto │ thee O │ Lord :
there is not │ one • that can │ do as │ thou doest.

   9 ‡   All nations whom thou hast made shall come and │ worship thee • O │ Lord :
– │ – and shall │ glori•fy thy │ Name.

   10 ‡   For thou art great and doest │ wondrous │ things :
thou art │ – – │ God a│lone.

   11   Teach me thy way O Lord and I will │ walk in • thy │ truth :
O knit my heart unto │ thee that • I may │ fear thy │ Name.

Psalm 86, continued

J. Turle

Full *f* 12 I will thank thee O Lord my | God with • all my | heart :
  and will | praise thy | Name for • ever|more.

Full 13 For great is thy | mercy • to|ward me :
  and thou hast delivered my | soul • from the | nether•most | hell.

mf 14 O God the proud are | risen • a|gainst me :
  and the congregations of naughty men have sought after my soul *
  and have not | set thee • be|fore their | eyes.

  15 But thou O Lord God art full of com|passion • and | mercy :
  long-suffering | plenteous • in | goodness • and | truth.

mp 16 O turn thee then unto me and have | mercy • up|on me :
  give thy strength unto thy | servant and • help the |
  son of • thine | handmaid.

mf 17 Shew some token upon me for good *
  that they who hate me may | see it and • be a|shamed :
  because | thou Lord • hast | holpen • me and | comforted me.

Full Glory be to the Father | and to • the | Son :
  and | to the | Holy | Ghost.

Full As it was in the beginning is | now and • ever | shall be :
  world without | end. A | . . | men.

PSALM 87

J. Battishill

(abbreviated)

Fundamenta ejus

Full *f*   1   Her foundations are up|on the · holy | hills :
the Lord loveth the gates of Sion more than all the |
dwellings · of | Jacob.

Full   2 †   Very excellent things are | spoken · of | thee ‖ thou | city · of | God.

mf   3   I will think upon | Rahab · and | Babylon :
with | them that | know me.

4   Behold ye the | Phili·stines | also :
and they of Tyre with the Morians * lo | there · was he | born.

5   And of Sion it shall be re|ported that · he was | born in her :
and the most | High shall | stablish her.

6   The Lord shall rehearse it when he | writeth · up the | people :
that | he was · born | there.

Full *f*   7   The singers also and | trumpeters shall · he re|hearse :
All my fresh | springs shall · be in | thee.

Full   Glory be to the Father | and to · the | Son :
and to the | Holy | Ghost.

Full   As it was in the beginning is | now and · ever | shall be :
world without | end. A | men.

PSALM 88

L. Flintoft

Domine Deus

Full *p* 1 O Lord God of my salvation * I have cried | day and · night be|fore thee :
O let my prayer enter into thy presence *
in|cline thine | ear · unto my | calling.

Full   2 For my | soul is · full of | trouble :
and my | life · draweth | nigh · unto | hell.

3 I am counted as one of them that go | down · into the | pit :
and I have been | even · as a | man that · hath no | strength.

4 Free among the dead * like unto them that are wounded and |
lie · in the | grave :

dim.   who are out of remembrance * | and are · cut a|way · from thy | hand.

5 Thou hast laid me in the | lowest | pit :
in a place of | darkness | and in · the | deep.

cresc. 6 Thine indignation lieth | hard up|on me :
and thou hast | vexed me · with | all thy | storms.

pp   7 Thou hast put away mine ac|quaintance | far from me :
and | made me · to | be ab|horred of them.

8 †‡ I am so | fast in | prison ‖ – | – that I | cannot · get | forth.

p   9 My sight | faileth for · very | trouble :
Lord I have called daily upon thee *
I have | stretched forth · my | hands · unto | thee.

cresc. 10 Dost thou shew | wonders a·mong the | dead :
or shall the | dead · rise up a|gain and | praise thee?

Psalm 88, continued

L. Flintoft

p   11 ‡   Shall thy loving-kindness be | shewed · in the | grave :
                 – | – or thy | faithfulness · in de|struction?

        12   Shall thy wondrous works be | known · in the | dark :
                 and thy righteousness in the | land where | all things · are for|gotten?

mp   13   Unto thee have I | cried O | Lord :
                 and | early · shall my | prayer · come be|fore thee.

        14 ‡   Lord why ab|horrest · thou my | soul :
                 – | – and | hidest · thou thy | face from me?

p   15   I am in misery * and like unto him that is at the | point to | die :
                 even from my youth up *
                 thy terrors have I | suffered · with a | troubled | mind.

mp   16 ‡   Thy wrathful dis|pleasure · goeth | over me :
                 – | – and the | fear of thee · hath un|done me.

p   17   They came round about me | daily · like | water :
                 and | compassed me · to|gether on · every | side.

pp   18   My lovers and friends hast thou | put a|way from me :
                 and hid mine ac|quaintance | out of · my | sight.

Full p   Glory be to the Father | and to · the | Son :
                 and | to the | Holy | Ghost.

Full   As it was in the beginning is | now and · ever | shall be :
                 world without | end. A | · · | men.

PSALM 89

Anon. from J. Battishill

Misericordias Domini

Full   *mf*   1   My song shall be alway of the loving │ kindness • of the │ Lord :
         with my mouth will I ever be shewing thy truth from │
         one • gene│ration • to an│other.

Full   2   For I have said Mercy shall be set │ up for │ ever :
         thy │ truth • shalt thou │ stablish • in the │ heavens.

        3   I have made a │ covenant • with my │ chosen :
         I have │ sworn • unto │ David • my │ servant;

        4   Thy seed will I │ stablish • for │ ever :
         and set up thy throne from │ one • gene│ration • to an│other.

change chant (Decani)

vv. 6, 7   *T. Norris*

vv. 6, 7

Dec.   *f*   5   O Lord the very heavens shall │ praise thy • wondrous │ works :
         and thy │ truth in the • congre│gation • of the │ saints.

    6 †‡   For who is │ he a•mong the │ clouds ‖ that shall be
      com│ – – │pared • unto the │ Lord?

    7 †‡   **2nd part** And what is │ he a•mong the │ gods ‖ that shall be │ – – │
      like • unto the │ Lord?

Psalm 89, *continued*

T. Norris

mf	8	God is very greatly to be feared in the | council • of the | saints :
		and to be had in reverence of all | them • that are | round a|bout him.
	9	O Lord God of hosts who is | like • unto | thee :
		thy truth most mighty | Lord • is on | every | side.
	10	Thou rulest the | raging • of the | sea :
mp		thou stillest the | waves there•of | when they • a|rise.
	11	Thou hast subdued | Egypt • and de|stroyed it :
cresc.		thou hast scattered thine enemies a|broad • with thy | mighty | arm.
mf	12	The heavens are thine * the | earth • also is | thine :
		thou hast laid the foundation of the round | world and | all that • therein | is.
	13	Thou hast made the | north • and the | south :
		Tabor and | Hermon • shall re|joice in • thy | name.
f	14	Thou hast a | mighty | arm :
		strong is thy | hand and | high is • thy | right hand.
	15	Righteousness and equity are the habi|tation • of thy | seat :
		mercy and | truth shall | go be•fore thy | face.
mf	16	Blessed is the people O | Lord that • can re|joice in thee :
		they shall | walk in • the | light of • thy | countenance.
	17	Their delight shall be | daily • in thy | name :
		and in thy | righteousness • shall they | make their | boast.
f	18	For thou art the | glory • of their | strength :
		and in thy loving-|kindness • thou shalt | lift up • our | horns.
	19	For the | Lord is • our de|fence :
		the Holy One of | Isra•el | is our | King.

change chant (Decani)

Psalm 89, continued

W. Russell

Dec. *mf* 20   Thou spakest sometime in visions unto thy | saints and | saidst :
                          I have laid help upon one that is mighty *
                          I have exalted | one · chosen | out of · the | people.

           21   I have found | David · my | servant :
                          with my | holy | oil have · I a|nointed him.

           22 ‡ My | hand shall · hold him | fast :
                          – | – and my | arm shall | strengthen him.

           23   The enemy shall not be | able to · do him | violence :
                          the son of | wicked·ness | shall not | hurt him.

           24 ‡ [2nd part] I will smite down his | foes be·fore his | face :
                          – | – and | plague them · that | hate him.

mp   25   My truth also and my | mercy · shall be | with him :
                          and in my | name · shall his | horn be · ex|alted.

           26 ‡ I will set his dominion | also · in the | sea :
                          – | – and his | right hand · in the | floods.

mf   27   He shall call me * | Thou art · my | Father :
                          my | God · and my | strong sal|vation.

           28   And I will | make him · my | first-born :
                          higher | than the | kings · of the | earth.

mp   29   My mercy will I | keep for him for · ever|more :
                          and my | cove·nant | shall stand | fast with him.

           30   His seed also will I make to en|dure for | ever :
                          and his | throne · as the | days of | heaven.

change chant (Decani)

Psalm 89, *continued*

J. Battishill

Dec.   *p*   31 ‡   But if his | children for·sake my | law :
                            and | – – | walk not · in my | judgements;

       32   If they break my statutes and | keep not · my com|mandments :
                            I will visit their offences with the | rod · and their | sin with | scourges.

change chant (Decani)

Anon. from J. Battishill

Dec.   *mf*   33   Nevertheless my loving-kindness will I not | utter·ly | take from him :
                            nor | suffer · my | truth to | fail.

       34   My covenant will I not break *
            nor alter the thing that is gone | out of · my | lips :
                            I have sworn once by my | holiness · that I | will not · fail | David.

       35   His seed shall en|dure for | ever :
                            and his seat is | like as · the | sun be|fore me.

       36   He shall stand fast for ever|more · as the | moon :
                            and as the | faithful | witness · in | heaven.

change chant (Decani)

Psalm 89, *continued*

J. Battishill

Dec.   ***p***   37 ‡   But thou hast abhorred and for|saken • thine A|nointed :
                           and | – – | art dis|pleased at • him.

          38   Thou hast broken the | covenant • of thy | servant :
                           and | cast his | crown • to the | ground.

          39 ‡   Thou hast over|thrown • all his | hedges :
                           and | – – | broken • down his | strongholds.

          40   All | they that go • by | spoil him :
                           and he is be|come • a re|proach • to his | neighbours.

          41 ‡   Thou hast set up the | right hand • of his | enemies :
                           and made all his | – – | adversaries • to re|joice.

          42   Thou hast taken away the | edge • of his | sword :
                           and givest him not | victo•ry | in the | battle.

          43   Thou hast put | out his | glory :
                           and | cast his | throne • down to the | ground.

          44   The days of his | youth • hast thou | shortened :
                           and | covered • him | with dis|honour.

mp   45 ‡   Lord how long wilt thou | hide thyself • for | ever :
                           and shall thy | – – | wrath • burn like | fire?

          46   O re|member how • short my | time is :
                           wherefore | hast thou • made | all • men for | nought?

p   47   What man is he that liveth and | shall not • see | death :
                           and shall he deliver his | soul • from the | hand of | hell?

          48   Lord where are thy | old • loving-|kindnesses :
                           which thou | swarest • unto | David • in thy | truth?

Psalm 89, continued

J. Battishill

mf   49   Remember Lord the re|buke • that thy | servants have :
          and how I do bear in my | bosom • the re|bukes of • many | people.

       50a   Wherewith thine | enemies • have blas|phemed thee :
          and slandered the | footsteps • of | thine A|nointed.

change chant (Full)

Anon. from J. Battishill

Full *f*   50b   **2nd part**   Praised be the | Lord for • ever|more :
          A|men * and | A|men.

Anon. from J. Battishill

Full   Glory be to the Father | and to • the | Son :
          and | to the | Holy | Ghost.

Full   As it was in the beginning is | now and • ever | shall be :
          world without | end. A | . . | men.

PSALM 90

A. H. Mann

Domine, refugium

Full   *mf*   1   Lord | thou hast · been our | refuge :
from | one · gene|ration · to an|other.

Full   2   Before the mountains were brought forth *
or ever the earth and the | world were | made :
thou art God from ever|lasting · and | world with·out | end.

mp   3   Thou turnest | man · to de|struction :
again thou sayest * Come a|gain ye | children · of | men.

4   For a thousand years in | thy sight · are but as | yesterday :
seeing that is | past · as a | watch · in the | night.

p   5   As soon as thou scatterest them they are | even · as a | sleep :
and fade away | sudden·ly | like the | grass.

cresc.   6   In the morning it is | green and · groweth | up :
dim.   but in the evening it is | cut down | dried up · and | withered.

mp   7   For we consume a|way in · thy dis|pleasure :
and are a|fraid at · thy | wrathful · indig|nation.

8   Thou hast set our mis|deeds be|fore thee :
and our secret | sins · in the | light of · thy | countenance.

9   For when thou art angry all our | days are | gone :
we bring our years to an end | as it were · a | tale · that is | told.

mf   10   The days of our age are threescore years and ten *
and though men be so strong that they | come to · fourscore | years :
yet is their strength then but labour and sorrow *
dim.   so soon | passeth it · a|way and · we are | gone.

Psalm 90, continued

vv. 16, 17   A. H. Mann

mf   11   But who regardeth the | power · of thy | wrath :
for even thereafter as a man | feareth | so is · thy dis|pleasure.

mp   12   So teach us to | number · our | days :
that we may ap|ply our | hearts · unto | wisdom.

      13   Turn thee again O | Lord · at the | last :
and be | gracious | unto · thy | servants.

cresc.   14   O satisfy us with thy | mercy and · that | soon :
so shall we rejoice and be | glad · all the | days of · our | life.

mf   15   Comfort us again now after the | time that · thou hast | plagued us :
and for the years where|in · we have | suffered · ad|versity.

      16 ‡   Shew thy | servants · thy | work :
and their | – – | children · thy | glory.

Full f   17 ‡   2nd part   And the glorious majesty of the Lord our | God · be up|on us :
prosper thou the work of our hands upon us *
O | – – | prosper thou · our | handy-work.

Full   Glory be to the Father | and to · the | Son :
and | to the | Holy | Ghost.

Full   As it was in the beginning is | now and · ever | shall be :
world without | end. A | . . | men.

PSALM 91

H. *Walford Davies*

Qui habitat

Full *mf* 1 Whoso dwelleth under the de|fence of the • most | High :
　　　　　　　　shall a|bide • under the | shadow • of the Al|mighty.

Full *cresc.* 2 I will say unto the Lord * Thou art my | hope • and my | stronghold :
　　　　　　　　my | God in | him • will I | trust.

mp 3 ‡ For he shall deliver thee from the | snare • of the | hunter :
　　　　　　　　– | – and from the | noisome | pestilence.

4 He shall defend thee under his wings *
　　and thou shalt be | safe • under his | feathers :
　　　　　　　　his faithfulness and | truth shall • be thy | shield and | buckler.

mf 5 Thou shalt not be afraid for any | terror • by | night :
　　　　　　　　nor for the | arrow • that | flieth • by | day;

6 For the pestilence that | walketh • in | darkness :
　　　　　　　　nor for the | sickness • that de|stroyeth • in the | noon-day.

7 ‡ A thousand shall fall beside thee * and ten thousand | at thy • right | hand :
　　　　　　　　– | – but it shall | not come | nigh thee.

8 Yea with thine | eyes shalt • thou be|hold :
　　　　　　　　and | see the • re|ward of • the un|godly.

9 For | thou Lord • art my | hope :
　　　　　　　　thou hast set thine | house of • de|fence • very | high.

10 There shall no | evil • happen | unto • thee :
　　　　　　　　neither shall any | plague come | nigh thy | dwelling.

p 11 For he shall give his | angels • charge | over • thee :
　　　　　　　　to | keep thee • in | all thy | ways.

12 They shall | bear thee • in their | hands :
　　　　　　　　that thou | hurt not • thy | foot a•gainst a | stone.

Psalm 91, continued

H. *Walford Davies*

cresc.	13	Thou shalt go upon the	lion • and	adder : the young lion and the	dragon • shalt thou	tread • under thy	feet.
mf	14	Because he hath set his love upon me *	therefore • will I de	liver • him : I will set him up be	cause he • hath	known my	Name.
	15	He shall call up	on me and • I will	hear him : yea I am with him in trouble * I will de	liver him • and	bring him • to	honour.
f	16 ‡	With long	life • will I	satisfy • him : –	– and	shew him • my sal	vation.
Full		Glory be to the Father	and to • the	Son : and	to the	Holy	Ghost.
Full		As it was in the beginning is	now and • ever	shall be : world without	end. A	. .	men.

PSALM 92

W. *Crotch*

Bonum est confiteri

Full f	1	It is a good thing to give	thanks • unto the	Lord : and to sing	praises • unto thy	Name • O most	Highest.
Full	2 ‡	To tell of thy loving-kindness	early • in the	morning : –	– and of thy	truth • in the	night-season.

Psalm 92, *continued*

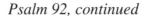

W. Crotch

3   Upon an instrument of ten strings and up|on the | lute :
    upon a loud | instru•ment | and up•on the | harp.

4   For thou Lord hast made me | glad • through thy | works :
    and I will rejoice in giving | praise for the • ope|rations • of thy | hands.

5 ‡ O Lord how | glorious • are thy | works :
    thy | thoughts are – | – very | deep.

6   An unwise man doth not | well con|sider this :
    and a | fool • doth not | under|stand it.

mf   7   When the ungodly are green as the grass *
    and when all the workers of | wickedness • do | flourish :
        then shall they be destroyed for ever *
        but thou Lord art the most | Highest • for | ever|more.

8 § For lo thine enemies O Lord * lo thine | enemies • shall | perish :
    and all the workers of | wickedness • shall | be de|stroyed.

9 §‡ But mine horn shall be exalted like the | horn • of an | unicorn :
    for I am a|nointed with – | – fresh | oil.

10 § Mine eye also shall see his | lust • of mine | enemies :
    and mine ear shall hear his desire of the |
    wicked • that a|rise up • a|gainst me.

cresc. 11   The righteous shall | flourish • like a | palm-tree :
    and shall spread a|broad • like a | cedar • in | Libanus.

12   **2nd part** Such as are planted in the | house • of the | Lord :
    shall flourish in the | courts • of the | house of • our | God.

§ Omitted in the St Paul's Cathedral use

Psalm 92, continued

W. Crotch

f   13 ‡   They also shall bring forth more | fruit • in their | age :
and shall be | fat and – | – well-|liking.

14   That they may shew how | true the • Lord my | strength is :
and that there is | no un|righteous•ness | in him.

Full   Glory be to the Father | and to • the | Son :
and | to the | Holy | Ghost.

Full   As it was in the beginning is | now and • ever | shall be :
world without | end. A | . . | men.

PSALM 93

G. A. Macfarren

Dominus regnavit

Full	*f*	1	The Lord is King * and hath put on │ glorious • ap│parel : the Lord hath put on his apparel and │ girded • him│self with │ strength.
Full		2 †	He hath │ made the • round │ world ‖ so │ sure • that it │ cannot • be │ moved.
	mf	3 ‡	Ever since the world began hath thy │ seat • been pre│pared : – │ thou art • from │ ever│lasting.
	f	4	The floods are risen O Lord * the │ floods have lift • up their │ voice : the │ floods lift │ up their │ waves.
	cresc.	5	The waves of the sea are │ mighty and • rage │ horribly : but yet the Lord who │ dwelleth • on │ high is │ mightier.
dim.	*mf*	6	Thy testimonies O │ Lord are • very │ sure : holiness be│cometh • thine │ house for │ ever.
Full	*f*		Glory be to the Father │ and to • the │ Son : and │ to the │ Holy │ Ghost.
Full			As it was in the beginning is │ now and • ever │ shall be : world without │ end. A │ . . │ men.

PSALM 94

R. Clark

Deus ultionum

Full	*mf*	1	O Lord God to whom | vengeance · be|longeth :
			thou God to whom | vengeance · be|longeth | shew thyself.
Full	*f*	2	Arise thou | Judge · of the | world :
			and reward the | proud · after | their de|serving.
	mf	3	Lord how | long shall · the un|godly :
			how | long shall · the un|godly | triumph?
		4 †‡	How long shall all wicked doers | speak · so dis|dainfully ‖
			– | – and | make such · proud | boasting?
		5 †	They | smite down · thy | people ‖ O | Lord and | trouble · thine | heritage.
		6 ‡	They murder the | widow · and the | stranger :
			– | – and put the | fatherless · to | death.
	p	7	And yet they say Tush the | Lord · shall not | see :
			neither shall the | God of | Jacob · re|gard it.
		8	Take heed ye un|wise a·mong the | people :
			O ye | fools · when will ye | under|stand?
	mp	9	He that planted the | ear shall · he not | hear :
			or he that made the | eye shall | he not | see?
		10	Or he that | nurtureth · the | heathen :
			it is he that teacheth man | knowledge | shall not · he | punish?
	mf	11 †	[2nd part] The Lord | knoweth · the | thoughts ‖ of | man · that they | are but | vain.

change chant (Decani)

Psalm 94, continued

R. Woodward

| Dec. | *mp* | 12 ‡ | Blessed is the man whom thou │ chastenest • O │ Lord : and │ – – │ teachest him • in thy │ law; |

Dec. **mp** 12 ‡ Blessed is the man whom thou │ chastenest • O │ Lord :
and │ – – │ teachest him • in thy │ law;

13 That thou mayest give him patience in │ time • of ad│versity :
until the │ pit be • digged │ up for • the un│godly.

mf 14 For the Lord will not │ fail his │ people :
neither │ will he • for│sake • his in│heritance;

15 Until righteousness turn a│gain • unto │ judgement :
all │ such as • are │ true in heart • shall │ follow it.

f 16 Who will rise up with me a│gainst the │ wicked :
or who will take my │ part a•gainst the │ evil │ doers?

17 If the │ Lord • had not │ helped me :
dim. it had not failed but my │ soul • had been │ put to │ silence.

mp 18 But when I said My │ foot hath │ slipt :
thy │ mercy • O │ Lord • held me │ up.

p 19 In the multitude of the sorrows that I │ had in • my │ heart :
cresc. thy │ comforts • have re│freshed my │ soul.

mf 20 Wilt thou have anything to do with the │ stool of │ wickedness :
which i│magin•eth │ mischief • as a │ law?

21 They gather them together against the │ soul • of the │ righteous :
and con│demn the │ inno•cent │ blood.

Full **f** 22 ⌐2nd¬ │part│ But the │ Lord • is my │ refuge :
and my │ God • is the │ strength of • my │ confidence.

Full 23 § He shall recompense them their wickedness *
and de│stroy them • in their own │ malice :
yea the │ Lord our │ God • shall de│stroy them.

Full Glory be to the Father │ and to • the │ Son :
and │ to the │ Holy │ Ghost.

Full As it was in the beginning is │ now and • ever │ shall be :
world without │ end. A │ . . │ men.

§ *Omitted in the St Paul's Cathedral use. When v.23 is sung, v.22 should be sung to the first part of the chant, and v.23 to the second part.*

Day 19: Morning

PSALM 95

"Per recte et retro"

W. Crotch

Venite, exultemus

Full *f*   1   O come let us | sing • unto the | Lord :
            let us heartily re|joice • in the | strength of • our sal|vation.

Full   2   Let us come before his | presence • with | thanksgiving :
            and | shew our•selves | glad in him • with | psalms.

       mf   3   For the | Lord is • a | great God :
            and a | great | King a•bove | all gods.

              4   In his hand are all the | corners • of the | earth :
            and the | strength of • the | hills • is his | also.

              5   The sea is | his and • he | made it :
            and his | hands pre|pared the • dry | land.

       mp   6   O come let us | worship • and fall | down :
            and | kneel before • the | Lord our | Maker.

              7   [2nd part] For | he is the • Lord our | God :
            and we are the people of his | pasture • and the | sheep • of his | hand.

       mf   8   Today if ye will hear his voice * | harden • not your | hearts :
            as in the provocation *
            and as in the | day of • temp|tation • in the | wilderness;

              9 †   When your | fathers | tempted ‖ me * |
            proved me • and | saw my | works.

              10   Forty years long was I grieved with this gene|ration • and | said :
            It is a people that do err in their hearts * |
            for they • have not | known my | ways;

              11   Unto whom I | sware • in my | wrath :
            that they should not | enter | into • my | rest.

Full *f*   Glory be to the Father | and to • the | Son :
            and | to the | Holy | Ghost.

Full   As it was in the beginning is | now and • ever | shall be :
            world without | end. A | . . | men.

PSALM 96

A. Gray

Cantate Domino

Full   *f*   1   O sing unto the | Lord a · new | song :
         sing unto the | Lord · all the | whole | earth.

Full   2   Sing unto the | Lord and · praise his | Name :
         be telling of his sal|vation · from | day to | day.

      mf   3   Declare his | honour · unto the | heathen :
         and his | wonders · unto | all | people.

         4   For the Lord is great and cannot | worthily · be | praised :
         he is | more · to be | feared than | all gods.

         5   As for all the gods of the | heathen · they are but | idols :
         but it is the | Lord that | made the | heavens.

         6   Glory and | worship · are be|fore him :
         power and | honour · are | in his | sanctuary.

Full   *f*   7   Ascribe unto the Lord O ye | kindreds · of the | people :
         ascribe unto the | Lord | worship · and | power.

Full   8   Ascribe unto the Lord the | honour · due unto his | Name :
         bring | presents · and | come · into his | courts.

      mp   9   O worship the Lord in the | beauty · of | holiness :
         let the | whole earth | stand in | awe of him.

      mf   10   Tell it out among the heathen that the | Lord is | King :
         and that it is he who hath made the round world so fast that
         it cannot be moved *
         and | how that · he shall | judge the · people | righteously.

Psalm 96, continued

A. Gray

> *f* 11 Let the heavens rejoice and let the | earth be | glad :
> let the sea make a | noise and | all that • therein | is.

> 12 Let the field be joyful and | all that • is | in it :
> then shall all the trees of the | wood re|joice be•fore the | Lord.

> 13 **2nd part** For he cometh * for he | cometh to • judge the | earth :
> and with righteousness to judge the |
> world • and the | people • with his | truth.

Full

> Glory be to the Father | and to • the | Son :
> and | to the | Holy | Ghost.

Full

> As it was in the beginning is | now and • ever | shall be :
> world without | end. A | • • | men.

PSALM 97

J. Stainer

Dominus regnavit

Full f 1 The Lord is King * the | earth • may be | glad thereof :
> yea the | multitude • of the | isles • may be | glad there•of.

Full 2 Clouds and | darkness are • round a|bout him :
> righteousness and | judgement are the • habi|tation • of his | seat.

Psalm 97, continued

J. Stainer

mf   3   There shall go a | fire be|fore him :
                and burn up his | enemies • on | every | side.

        4   His lightnings gave | shine • unto the | world :
                the earth | saw it | and was • a|fraid.

        5   The hills melted like wax at the | presence • of the | Lord :
                at the presence of the | Lord • of the | whole | earth.

        6   The heavens have de|clared his | righteousness :
                and all the | people • have | seen his | glory.

f   7   Confounded be all they that worship carved images *
            and that de|light in • vain | gods :
                worship | him | all ye | gods.

        8   Sion | heard of it • and re|joiced :
                and the daughters of Judah were glad be|cause of • thy |
                judgements • O | Lord.

        9   For thou Lord art higher than | all that are • in the | earth :
                thou art ex|alted | far a•bove | all gods.

mf   10   O ye that love the Lord * see that ye hate the | thing • which is | evil :
            the Lord preserveth the souls of his saints *
            he shall de|liver them • from the | hand of the • un|godly.

      11   There is sprung up a | light • for the | righteous :
            and joyful | gladness • for | such as are • true-|hearted.

      12   Rejoice in the | Lord ye | righteous :
            and give | thanks • for a re|membrance • of his | holiness.

Full *f*   Glory be to the Father | and to • the | Son :
            and | to the | Holy | Ghost.

Full   As it was in the beginning is | now and • ever | shall be :
            world without | end. A | . . | men.

Day 19: Evening

PSALM 98

J. Randall

Cantate Domino

Full *f*   1   O sing unto the | Lord a · new | song :
　　　　　　　　for | he hath · done | marvel·lous | things.

Full   2   With his own right hand and with his | holy | arm :
　　　　　　　　hath he | gotten · him|self the | victory.

mf   3   The Lord de|clared · his sal|vation :
　　　　　　　　his righteousness hath he openly | shewed in · the |
　　　　　　　　sight · of the | heathen.

mp   4   He hath remembered his mercy and truth to|ward the · house of | Israel :
　　　　　　　　and all the ends of the world have | seen the · sal|vation · of our | God.

f   5 ‡   Shew yourselves joyful unto the | Lord · all ye | lands :
　　　　　　　　– | sing re|joice and · give | thanks.

6   Praise the | Lord up·on the | harp :
　　　　　　　　sing to the | harp · with a | psalm of | thanksgiving.

7   With | trumpets · also and | shawms :
　　　　　　　　O shew yourselves | joyful be·fore the | Lord the | King.

8   Let the sea make a noise and | all that · therein | is :
　　　　　　　　the round | world and | they that | dwell therein.

9   Let the floods clap their hands *
　　　　　　　and let the hills be joyful to|gether be·fore the | Lord :
　　　　　　　　for he is | come to | judge the | earth.

mf   10 †‡   With righteousness shall he | judge the | world ‖ – | – and the |
　　　　　　　people · with | equity.

Full *f*   Glory be to the Father | and to · the | Son :
　　　　　　　　and | to the | Holy | Ghost.

Full   As it was in the beginning is | now and · ever | shall be :
　　　　　　　　world without | end. A | . . | men.

PSALM 99

E. F. Day

Dominus regnavit

Full	*f*	1	The Lord is King * be the people | never · so un|patient :
			he sitteth between the cherubims * be the | earth | never · so un|quiet.
Full		2 ‡	The Lord is | great in | Sion :
			and | – – | high above · all | people.
		3	They shall give | thanks · unto thy | name :
			which is | great | wonderful · and | holy.
		4	The King's power loveth judgement * | thou hast pre·pared | equi·ty :
			thou hast executed | judgement · and | righteousness · in | Jacob.
Full		5	**2nd part** O magnify the | Lord our | God :
			and fall down before his | footstool · for | he is | holy.
	mf	6	Moses and Aaron among his priests *
			and Samuel among such as | call up·on his | name :
			these | called up·on the | Lord · and he | heard them.
		7	He spake unto them out of the | cloudy | pillar :
			for they kept his | testimonies · and the | law · that he | gave them.
		8	Thou heardest them O | Lord our | God :
			thou forgavest them O God and | punishedst · their | own in|ventions.
Full	*f*	9	O magnify the Lord our God * and worship him upon his | holy | hill :
			for the | Lord our | God is | holy.
Full	*f*		Glory be to the Father | and to · the | Son :
			and | to the | Holy | Ghost.
Full			As it was in the beginning is | now and · ever | shall be :
			world without | end. A | · · | men.

PSALM 100

T. Attwood

Jubilate Deo

Full   *f*   1   O be joyful in the | Lord · all ye | lands :
                                serve the Lord with gladness *
                                and | come before · his | presence · with a | song.

Full   2   Be ye sure that the | Lord · he is | God :
                                it is he that hath made us and not we ourselves *
                                we are his | people · and the | sheep · of his | pasture.

                   3   O go your way into his gates with thanksgiving *
                                and into his | courts with | praise :
                                be thankful unto | him and · speak | good · of his | name.

          mf   4   For the Lord is gracious * his | mercy is · ever|lasting :
                                and his truth endureth from gene|ration · to | gene|ration.

Full   *f*   Glory be to the Father | and to · the | Son :
                                and | to the | Holy | Ghost.

Full   As it was in the beginning is | now and · ever | shall be :
                                world without | end. A | . . | men.

PSALM 101

S. H. Nicholson

Misericordiam et judicium

Full	*mp*	1	My song shall be of | mercy • and | judgement : unto thee O | Lord • will I | sing.
Full		2 †	O let me have | under|standing ‖ in the | way of | godliness.
	p	3	When wilt thou | come • unto | me : I will walk in my | house • with a | perfect heart.
		4	I will take no wicked thing in hand * I hate the | sins • of un|faithfulness : there shall | no such | cleave unto me.
	mp	5	A froward | heart • shall de|part from me : I will not | know a • wicked | person.
	mf	6 ‡	Whoso privily | slandereth • his | neighbour : – | him will • I de|stroy.
		7 ‡	**2nd part** Whoso hath also a proud | look and • high | stomach : – | I will • not | suffer him.
	p	8	Mine eyes look upon such as are | faithful • in the | land : that | they may | dwell with me.
		9 ‡	Whoso | leadeth • a | godly life : – | he shall • be my | servant.
	mp	10	There shall no deceitful person | dwell • in my | house : he that telleth lies shall not | tarry in • my | sight.
	mf	11	I shall soon destroy the un|godly that are • in the | land : that I may root out all wicked doers from the | city • of the | Lord.
Full	*p*		Glory be to the Father | and to • the | Son : and to the | Holy | Ghost.
Full			As it was in the beginning is | now and • ever | shall be : world without | end. A | men.

PSALM 102

P. A. Tranchell

Domine, exaudi

Full	*mp*	1	Hear my | prayer O | Lord :
			and | let my | crying • come | unto thee.
Full		2	Hide not thy face from me in the | time • of my | trouble :
			incline thine ear unto me when I call *
			O | hear me • and | that right | soon.
	p	3	For my days are con|sumed away • like | smoke :
			and my bones are | burnt up | as it were • a | fire-brand.
		4	My heart is smitten down and | withered • like | grass :
			so that I for|get to | eat my | bread.
	mp	5	For the | voice of • my | groaning :
			my | bones will • scarce | cleave • to my | flesh.
		6	I am become like a | pelican • in the | wilderness :
			and like an | owl • that is | in the | desert.
		7	I have watched and am even | as it were • a | sparrow :
			that | sitteth • a|lone up•on the | house-top.
	mf	8	Mine enemies revile me | all the • day | long :
			and they that are mad upon me are | sworn to|gether • a|gainst me.
	mp	9	For I have eaten | ashes • as it were | bread :
			and | mingled • my | drink with | weeping;
	mf	10	And that because of thine indig|nation • and | wrath :
			for thou hast taken me | up and | cast me | down.
	mp	11 ‡	[2nd part] My days are | gone • like a | shadow :
			and I am | – – | withered • like | grass.

Psalm 102, continued

P. A. Tranchell

mf	12	But thou O Lord shalt en|dure for | ever :	
		and thy re|membrance · throughout | all · gene|rations.	
	13	Thou shalt arise and have | mercy · upon | Sion :	
		for it is time that thou have | mercy upon her * yea the | time is | come.	
	14	**2nd part** And why? * thy servants | think up·on her | stones :	
		and it | pitieth them · to | see her · in the | dust.	
Full f	15	The heathen shall | fear thy · Name O | Lord :	
		and all the | kings of · the | earth thy | majesty;	
Full	16 ‡	When the | Lord shall · build up | Sion :	
		and when his | – – | glory · shall ap|pear;	
mf	17	When he turneth him unto the | prayer of the · poor | destitute :	
		and de|spiseth · not | their de|sire.	
	18	This shall be written for | those · that come | after :	
		and the people which shall be | born shall | praise the | Lord.	
	19	For he hath looked | down · from his | sanctuary :	
		out of the | heaven · did the | Lord be·hold the | earth;	
	20	That he might hear the mournings of | such as are · in cap|tivity :	
		and deliver the | children · ap|pointed · unto | death;	
Full	21 ‡	That they may declare the | Name of the · Lord in | Sion :	
		– | – and his | worship · at Je|rusalem;	
Full	22	When the people are | gathered · to|gether :	
		and the kingdoms | also · to | serve the | Lord.	

Psalm 102, continued

P. A. Tranchell

mp   23 † He brought │ down my │ strength ‖ in my │ journey • and │ shortened • my │ days.

          24   But I said O my God take me not away in the │ midst • of mine │ age :
cresc.   as for thy years they en│dure through • out │ all • gene│rations.

mf   25   Thou Lord in the beginning hast laid the foun│dation • of the │ earth :
                   and the │ heavens • are the │ work of • thy │ hands.

          26   They shall perish but │ thou • shalt en│dure :
                   they │ all shall • wax │ old • as doth a │ garment;

cresc. 27   And as a vesture shalt thou change them and │ they shall • be │ changed :
                   but thou art the │ same • and thy │ years • shall not │ fail.

          28   The children of thy │ servants • shall con│tinue :
                   and their │ seed shall • stand │ fast • in thy │ sight.

Full **f**   Glory be to the Father │ and to • the │ Son :
                   and │ to the │ Holy │ Ghost.

Full   As it was in the beginning is │ now and • ever │ shall be :
                   world without │ end. A │ . . │ men.

PSALM 103

P. A. Tranchell

Benedic, anima mea

Full	*f*	1	Praise the | Lord • O my | soul :
			and all that is with|in me • praise his | holy | Name.
Full		2	Praise the | Lord • O my | soul :
			and for|get not | all his | benefits;
Full		3	Who for|giveth • all thy | sin :
			and | healeth | all • thine in|firmities;
Full		4	Who saveth thy | life • from de|struction :
			and crowneth thee with | mercy • and | loving-|kindness;
	mf	5	Who satisfieth thy | mouth with • good | things :
			making thee | young and | lusty • as an | eagle.
		6	The Lord executeth | righteousness • and | judgement :
			for all | them that • are op|pressed with | wrong.
		7	He shewed his | ways • unto | Moses :
			his | works • unto the | children • of | Israel.
	mp	8	The Lord is full of com|passion and | mercy :
			long | suffer•ing | and of • great | goodness.

Psalm 103, continued

P. A. Tranchell

9   He will not | alway · be | chiding :
       neither | keepeth · he his | anger · for | ever.

10   He hath not dealt with us | after · our | sins :
       nor re|warded us · ac|cording · to our | wickednesses.

cresc.   11   For look how high the heaven is in com|parison · of the | earth :
       so great is his | mercy · also to|ward · them that | fear him.

mf   12   Look how wide also the | east is · from the | west :
       so | far · hath he | set our | sins from us.

mp   13   Yea like as a father | pitieth · his own | children :
       even so is the Lord | merciful · unto | them that | fear him.

14   For he knoweth where|of · we are | made :
       he re|membereth · that | we are · but | dust.

cresc.   15   The days of | man are · but as | grass :
       for he | flourisheth · as a | flower · of the | field.

p   16   For as soon as the wind goeth | over it · it is | gone :
dim.   and the | place thereof · shall | know it · no | more.

Psalm 103, continued

P. A. Tranchell

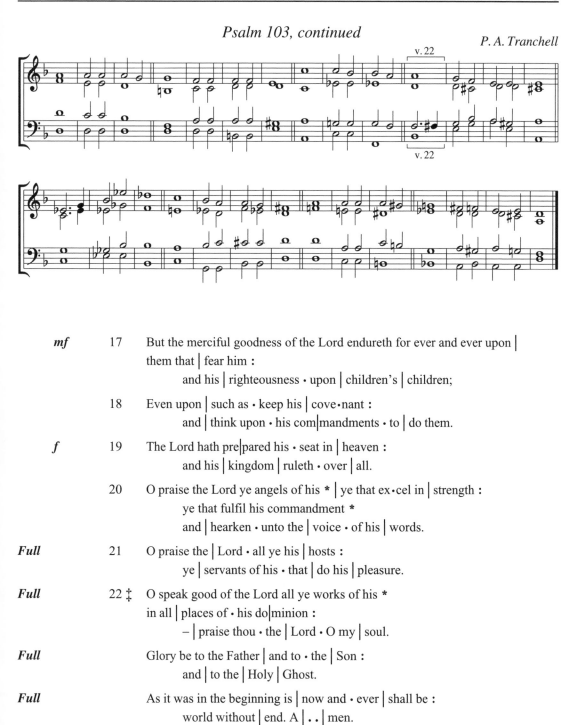

mf   17   But the merciful goodness of the Lord endureth for ever and ever upon |
            them that | fear him :
                  and his | righteousness • upon | children's | children;

      18   Even upon | such as • keep his | cove•nant :
                  and | think upon • his com|mandments • to | do them.

f   19   The Lord hath pre|pared his • seat in | heaven :
                  and his | kingdom | ruleth • over | all.

      20   O praise the Lord ye angels of his * | ye that ex•cel in | strength :
                  ye that fulfil his commandment *
                  and | hearken • unto the | voice • of his | words.

Full   21   O praise the | Lord • all ye his | hosts :
                  ye | servants of his • that | do his | pleasure.

Full   22 ‡   O speak good of the Lord all ye works of his *
            in all | places of • his do|minion :
                  – | praise thou • the | Lord • O my | soul.

Full   Glory be to the Father | and to • the | Son :
                  and | to the | Holy | Ghost.

Full   As it was in the beginning is | now and • ever | shall be :
                  world without | end. A | • • | men.

PSALM 104

"Trent" (Sydney Bevan)

Benedic, anima mea

Full *f*   1   Praise the | Lord • O my | soul :
     O Lord my God thou art become exceeding glorious *
     thou art | clothed with | majesty • and | honour.

Full   2   Thou deckest thyself with light as it | were • with a | garment :
     and | spreadest out • the | heavens • like a | curtain.

   3   Who layeth the beams of his | chambers • in the | waters :
     and maketh the clouds his chariot *
     and | walketh up•on the | wings • of the | wind.

   4   He maketh his | angels | spirits :
     and his | ministers • a | flaming | fire.

mf   5   He laid the foun|dations • of the | earth :
     that it | never • should | move at | any time.

   6   Thou coveredst it with the deep | like as • with a | garment :
     the | waters | stand • in the | hills.

   7   At thy re|buke they | flee :
     at the voice of thy | thunder | they are • a|fraid.

   8   They go up as high as the hills * and down to the | valleys • be|neath :
     even unto the | place which | thou • hast ap|pointed for them.

mp   9   Thou hast set them their bounds which they | shall not | pass :
     neither turn a|gain to | cover • the | earth.

10 †‡   He sendeth the | springs • into the | rivers ‖ – | – which | run a•mong the | hills.

Psalm 104, continued
"Trent" (Sydney Bevan)

mf	11	All | beasts of the • field | drink thereof :
		and the wild | asses | quench their | thirst.
	12 ‡	Beside them shall the fowls of the air have their | habi|tation :
		– | – and | sing a•mong the | branches.
	13	He watereth the | hills • from a|bove :
		the earth is | filled with • the | fruit • of thy | works.
	14	He bringeth forth | grass • for the | cattle :
		and green | herb • for the | service • of | men :
cresc.	15	That he may bring food out of the earth *
		and wine that maketh | glad the • heart of | man :
		and oil to make him a cheerful countenance *
		and | bread to | strengthen • man's | heart.
	16	The trees of the Lord | also are • full of | sap :
		even the cedars of | Liba•nus | which he • hath | planted;
mf	17	Wherein the | birds • make their | nests :
		and the | fir-trees • are a | dwelling • for the | stork.
	18	The high hills are a | refuge for the • wild | goats :
		and | so are the • stony | rocks • for the | conies.
mp	19	He appointed the | moon for • certain | seasons :
		and the | sun • knoweth his | going | down.
mf	20	Thou makest darkness that it | may be | night :
		wherein all the | beasts • of the | forest • do | move.
f	21 †	The lions | roaring • after their | prey ‖ do | seek their | meat from | God.
	22 ‡	The sun ariseth and they | get them a•way to|gether :
		– | – and lay them | down • in their | dens.
	23 †	2nd part Man goeth | forth • to his | work ‖ and to his |
		labour • un|til the | evening.

change chant (Full)

Psalm 104, continued

W. Parratt

Full *f*   24   O Lord how | manifold • are thy | works :
                          in wisdom hast thou made them all * the | earth is | full of • thy | riches.

Full   25   So is the | great and • wide sea | also :
                          wherein are things creeping in|numerable *
                          both | small and • great | beasts.

              26   There go the ships and | there is • that Le|viathan :
                          whom thou hast | made to • take his | pastime • there|in.

mf   27   These wait | all up•on | thee :
                          that thou mayest | give them | meat in • due | season.

              28   When thou | givest it • them they | gather it :
cresc.   and when thou openest thy | hand • they are | filled with | good.

mp   29   When thou hidest thy | face • they are | troubled :
dim.   when thou takest away their breath they die *
                          and are | turned a|gain • to their | dust.

cresc.   30   When thou lettest thy breath go | forth • they shall be | made :
                          and thou shalt re|new the | face • of the | earth.

f   31   The glorious majesty of the | Lord shall en•dure for | ever :
                          the | Lord • shall re|joice in • his | works.

              32   The earth shall | tremble • at the | look of him :
                          if he do but | touch the | hills • they shall | smoke.

              33   I will sing unto the Lord as | long as • I | live :
                          I will praise my | God • while I | have my | being.

              34   And so shall my | words | please him :
                          my | joy shall | be in • the | Lord.

mf   35   As for sinners they shall be consumed out of the earth *
                          and the ungodly shall | come • to an | end :
f   praise thou the Lord O my | soul * | praise the | Lord.

Full   Glory be to the Father | and to • the | Son :
                          and | to the | Holy | Ghost.

Full   As it was in the beginning is | now and • ever | shall be :
                          world without | end. A | . . | men.

PSALM 105

F. A. G. Ouseley

Confitemini Domino

Full *f*	1	O give thanks unto the Lord and | call up‧on his | Name :	
		tell the | people ‧ what | things ‧ he hath | done.	
Full	2	O let your | songs be of ‧ him and | praise him :	
		and let your | talking ‧ be of | all his ‧ wondrous | works.	
	3	Rejoice in his | holy | Name :	
		let the | heart of ‧ them re|joice that ‧ seek the | Lord.	
	4 ‡	Seek the | Lord ‧ and his | strength :	
		seek his | – – | face ‧ ever|more.	
	5	Remember the marvellous | works that ‧ he hath | done :	
		his | wonders ‧ and the | judgements ‧ of his | mouth,	
	6	O ye seed of | Abraham ‧ his | servant :	
		ye | children ‧ of | Jacob ‧ his | chosen.	
	7	He is the | Lord our | God :	
		his | judgements ‧ are in | all the | world.	
mf	8 †	He hath been alway mindful of his | covenant ‧ and | promise ‖ that he |	
		made ‧ to a | thousand ‧ gene|rations;	
	9	Even the | covenant that he ‧ made with | Abraham :	
		and the | oath ‧ that he | sware ‧ unto | Isaac;	
	10	And appointed the same unto | Jacob ‧ for a | law :	
		and to | Israel ‧ for an | ever‧lasting | testament;	
	11	Saying Unto thee will I give the | land of | Canaan :	
		the | lot of | your in|heritance;	
	12 ‡	When there were | yet ‧ but a | few of them :	
		and they | – – | strangers ‧ in the | land;	

Psalm 105, *continued*

F. A. G. Ouseley

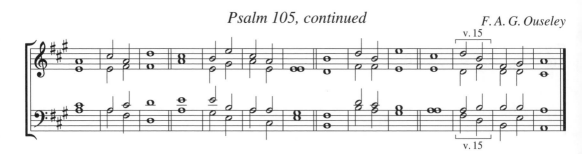

13   What time as they went from one | nation · to an|other :
        from one | kingdom · to an|other | people;

14   He suffered | no man to · do them | wrong :
        but re|proved · even | kings · for their | sakes;

15 ‡   **2nd part** Touch not | mine A|nointed :
        and do my | – – | prophets · no | harm.

change chant (Decani)

H. G. Ley

Dec. *mp*   16   Moreover he called for a | dearth up·on the | land :
        and de|stroyed · all the pro|vision · of | bread.

17   But he had sent a | man be|fore them :
        even | Joseph · who was | sold to · be a | bond-servant;

18   Whose feet they | hurt · in the | stocks :
        the | iron · entered | into · his | soul;

19 ‡   Until the time | came that his · cause was | known :
        the | – – | word of the · Lord | tried him.

Psalm 105, continued

H. G. Ley

mf   20   The king │ sent • and de│livered him :
     the prince of the │ people │ let him • go │ free.

   21   He made him lord │ also • of his │ house :
     and │ ruler • of │ all his │ substance;

   22   │**2nd part**│ That he might inform his │ princes • after his │ will :
     and │ teach his │ sena•tors │ wisdom.

                  change chant (Full)

H. G. Ley

Full   f   23   Israel also │ came • into │ Egypt :
     and Jacob was a │ stranger • in the │ land of │ Ham.

Full   24   And he increased his │ people • ex│ceedingly :
     and │ made them │ stronger • than their │ enemies;

Full   25   │**2nd part**│ Whose heart turned so that they │ hated • his │ people :
     and │ dealt un│truly • with his │ servants.

   26   Then sent he │ Moses • his │ servant :
     and │ Aaron │ whom he • had │ chosen.

   27   And these shewed his │ tokens • a│mong them :
     and │ wonders • in the │ land of │ Ham.

Psalm 105, *continued*

H. G. Ley

vv. 29, 31, 35

mf 28 He sent | darkness · and it was | dark :
and they were not o|bedient | unto · his | word.

29 ‡ He turned their | waters · into | blood :
– | – and | slew their | fish.

30 Their | land · brought forth | frogs :
yea | even · in their | kings' | chambers.

31 ‡ He spake the word and there came all | manner · of | flies :
– | – and | lice in · all their | quarters.

Full f 32 He gave them | hail-stones · for | rain :
and | flames of | fire · in their | land.

Full 33 He smote their | vines · also and | fig-trees :
and destroyed the | trees · that were | in their | coasts.

34 He spake the word and the grasshoppers came *
and | caterpillars · in|numerable :
and did eat up all the grass in their land *
and de|voured the | fruit · of their | ground.

35 ‡ He smote all the | first-born · in their | land :
– | – even the | chief of · all their | strength.

change chant (Decani)

Psalm 105, continued

F. A. G. Ouseley

vv. 37, 41, 44

vv. 37, 41, 44

Dec. *mf* 36 He brought them forth also with | silver • and | gold :
there was not one feeble | person • a|mong their | tribes.

37 †‡ Egypt was | glad at • their de|part‖ing * | – – | for they were • a|fraid of them.

38 He spread out a | cloud to • be a | covering :
and | fire to • give | light • in the | night-season.

39 At their de|sire he • brought | quails :
and he | filled them • with the | bread of | heaven.

40 He opened the rock of stone and the | waters • flowed | out :
so that | rivers | ran in the • dry | places.

41 ‡ For why? * he re|membered his • holy | promise :
and | – – | Abraham • his | servant.

f 42 † And he brought | forth his | people ‖ with | joy • and his |
chosen • with | gladness;

43 And gave them the | lands • of the | heathen :
and they took the | labours • of the | people • in pos|session;

Full 44 †‡ | **2nd part** | That they might | keep his | statutes ‖ and ob| – – |serve his | laws.

Full Glory be to the Father | and to • the | Son :
and | to the | Holy | Ghost.

Full As it was in the beginning is | now and • ever | shall be :
world without | end. A | . . | men.

Day 21: Evening

PSALM 106

C. Hylton Stewart

Confitemini Domino

Full *f* 1 O give thanks unto the | Lord for · he is | gracious :
and his | mercy · en|dureth · for | ever.

Full 2 ‡ Who can express the noble | acts · of the | Lord :
– | – or | shew forth · all his | praise?

mf 3 † Blessed are | they that | alway ‖ keep | judgement | and do | righteousness.

4 Remember me O Lord *
according to the favour that thou | bearest · unto thy | people :
O | visit me · with | thy sal|vation;

5 [2nd part] That I may see the fe|licity · of thy | chosen :
and rejoice in the gladness of thy |
people · and give | thanks with · thine in|heritance.

mp 6 We have | sinned · with our | fathers :
we have | done a|miss and · dealt | wickedly.

7 Our fathers regarded not thy wonders in Egypt *
neither kept they thy great | goodness · in re|membrance :
but were disobedient at the | sea · even | at the · Red | sea.

mf 8 Nevertheless he | helped them · for his | name's sake :
that he might | make his | power · to be | known.

9 He rebuked the Red sea also | and it was · dried | up :
so he | led them · through the | deep as · through a | wilderness.

10 And he saved them from the | adver·saries' | hand :
and de|livered them · from the | hand · of the | enemy.

11 ‡ As for those that troubled them the | waters · over|whelmed them :
– | – there was not | one of · them | left.

f 12 ‡ [2nd part] Then be|lieved they · his | words :
– | – and sang | praise · unto | him.

change chant (Decani)

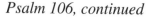

Psalm 106, continued

C. Hylton Stewart

Dec. *mp* 13 But within a | while they for‧gat his | works :
   and | would not ‧ a|bide his | counsel.

mf 14 But lust came up|on them ‧ in the | wilderness :
   and they | tempted | God ‧ in the | desert.

15 And he | gave them ‧ their de|sire :
   and sent | leanness ‧ with|al ‧ into their | soul.

16 They angered Moses | also ‧ in the | tents :
   and | Aaron ‧ the | saint ‧ of the | Lord.

f 17 So the earth opened and | swallowed ‧ up | Dathan :
   and | covered the ‧ congre|gation ‧ of A|biram.

18 And the fire was | kindled ‧ in their | company :
   the | flame burnt | up ‧ the un|godly.

mf 19 They made a | calf in | Horeb :
   and | worshipped ‧ the | molten | image.

20 † Thus they | turned their | glory ‖
   into the si|militude ‧ of a | calf that ‧ eateth | hay.

mp 21 And they forgat | God their | Saviour :
   who had done | so great | things in | Egypt;

22 Wondrous works in the | land of | Ham :
   and | fearful things ‧ by the | Red | sea.

23 **2nd part** So he said he would have destroyed them *
   had not Moses his chosen stood be|fore him ‧ in the | gap :
    to turn away his wrathful indig|nation |
    lest he ‧ should de|stroy them.

Psalm 106, continued

C. Hylton Stewart

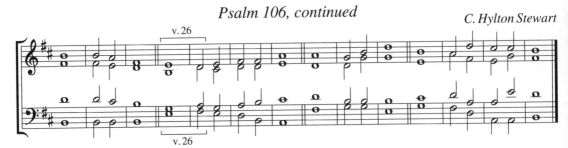

mf	24	Yea they thought │ scorn of that · pleasant │ land :
		and gave no │ credence │ unto · his │ word;

mp	25	But │ murmured · in their │ tents :
		and │ hearkened not · unto the │ voice · of the │ Lord.

mf	26 ‡	Then lift he │ up his · hand a│gainst them :
		– │ – to over│throw them · in the │ wilderness;

	27	To cast out their │ seed a·mong the │ nations :
		and to │ scatter · them │ in the │ lands.

change chant (Decani)

C. Hylton Stewart

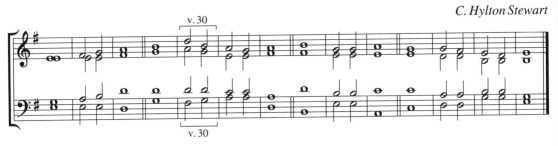

Dec. mf	28	They joined themselves unto │ Baal-│peor :
		and ate the │ offer·ings │ of the │ dead.

	29	Thus they provoked him to anger with their │ own in│ventions :
		and the │ plague was │ great a│mong them.

p	30 ‡	Then stood up │ Phinees · and │ prayed :
		and │ – – │ so the · plague │ ceased.

	31	And that was counted │ unto him · for │ righteousness :
		among all po│sterities · for │ ever│more.

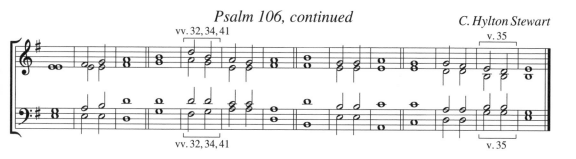

Psalm 106, continued

C. Hylton Stewart

mf   32 ‡   They angered him also at the | waters • of | strife :
                so that he punished | – – | Moses • for their | sakes;

         33   Because they pro|voked his | spirit :
                so that he spake unad|vised•ly | with his | lips.

         34 ‡   Neither de|stroyed they • the | heathen :
                as the | – – | Lord com|manded them;

         35 ‡   But were | mingled a•mong the | heathen :
                and | learned their | – – | works.

         36   Insomuch that they worshipped their idols *
         which turned to their | own de|cay :
                yea they offered their | sons • and their | daughters • unto | devils;

         37   And shed innocent blood *
         even the blood of their | sons and • of their | daughters :
                whom they offered unto the idols of Canaan *
                and the | land • was de|filed with | blood.

         38   **2nd part**   Thus were they | stained with their • own | works :
                and went a | whoring • with their | own in|ventions.

f   39   Therefore was the wrath of the Lord | kindled a•gainst his | people :
                insomuch that he ab|horred his | own in|heritance.

         40   And he gave them over into the | hand • of the | heathen :
                and they that | hated them • were | lords | over them.

         41 ‡   Their | enemies • op|pressed them :
                and | – – | had them • in sub|jection.

         42   Many a | time did • he de|liver them :
                but they rebelled against him with their own inventions * |
                and were • brought | down • in their | wickedness.

change chant (Decani)

Psalm 106, continued

C. Hylton Stewart

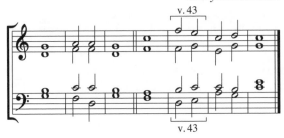

| Dec. | *mf* | 43 ‡ | Nevertheless when he \| saw • their ad\|versity : |
| | | | he \| – – \| heard • their com\|plaint. |

	mp	44	He thought upon his covenant and pitied them *
			according unto the | multitude • of his | mercies :
			yea he made all those that | led them a•way | captive • to | pity them.

	mf	45	Deliver us O Lord our God * and gather us from a|mong the | heathen :
			that we may give thanks unto thy holy Name *
			and | make our | boast • of thy | praise.

| *Full* | *f* | 46 | Blessed be the Lord God of Israel from everlasting and \| world with•out \| end : |
| | | | and let all the \| people \| say * A\|men. |

| *Full* | | | Glory be to the Father \| and to • the \| Son : |
| | | | and \| to the \| Holy \| Ghost. |

| *Full* | | | As it was in the beginning is \| now and • ever \| shall be : |
| | | | world without \| end. A \| . . \| men. |

PSALM 107

E. C. Bairstow

Confitemini Domino

Full *f* 1 O give thanks unto the | Lord for • he is | gracious :
and his | mercy • en|dureth • for | ever.

Full 2 Let them give thanks whom the | Lord • hath re|deemed :
and de|livered • from the | hand • of the | enemy;

Full 3 **2nd part** And gathered them out of the lands *
from the | east and • from the | west :
from the | north and | from the | south. ***change chant (Decani)***

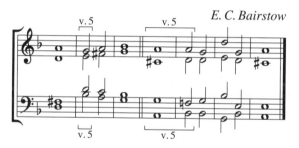

Dec. *mp* 4 They went astray in the wilderness | out of • the | way :
and | found no | city • to | dwell in;

5 ‡ Hungry | – and | thirsty :
– | – their | soul • fainted | in them. ***change chant (Decani)***

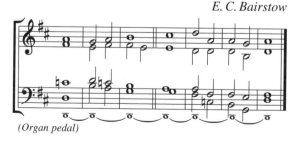

(Organ pedal)

Dec. *p* 6 So they cried unto the | Lord • in their | trouble :
and he de|livered • them | from their • di|stress.

Psalm 107, continued

E. C. Bairstow

(Organ pedal)

7   He led them │ forth • by the right │ way :

that they might │ go • to the │ city • where they │ dwelt.

change chant (Full)

E. C. Bairstow

Full   *f*   8   O that men would therefore praise the │ Lord • for his │ goodness :

and declare the wonders that he │ doeth • for the │ children • of │ men!

Full   9   For he │ satisfieth the • empty │ soul :

and │ filleth the • hungry │ soul with │ goodness.

change chant (Decani)

E. C. Bairstow

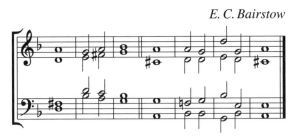

Dec.   *mp*   10   Such as sit in darkness and in the │ shadow • of │ death :

being fast │ bound in │ misery • and │ iron;

11   Because they rebelled against the │ words • of the │ Lord :

and lightly re│garded • the │ counsel • of the most │ Highest;

12   He also brought down their │ heart through │ heaviness :

they fell │ down and • there was │ none to │ help them.

change chant (Cantoris)

Psalm 107, continued

E. C. Bairstow

(Organ pedal)

Can. *p*   13   So when they cried unto the | Lord • in their | trouble
                    he de|livered • them | out of • their di|stress.

      cresc.   14   For he brought them out of darkness * and out of the | shadow • of | death :
                    and | brake their | bonds in | sunder.   *change chant (Full)*

E. C. Bairstow

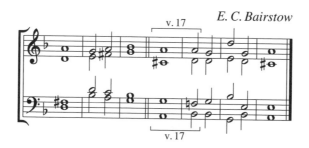

Full *f*   15   O that men would therefore praise the | Lord • for his | goodness :
                    and declare the wonders that he | doeth • for the | children • of | men!

Full   16   For he hath | broken the • gates of | brass :
                    and | smitten the • bars of | iron • in | sunder.   *change chant (Decani)*

E. C. Bairstow

Dec. *mp*   17 ‡   Foolish men are | plagued for • their of|fence :
                    – | – and be|cause of • their | wickedness.

              18   Their soul abhorred all | manner • of | meat :
                    and they were | even | hard at • death's | door.

                                                        change chant (Decani)

Psalm 107, continued

E. C. Bairstow

(Organ pedal)

Dec. p   19   So when they cried unto the | Lord · in their | trouble :
                          he de|livered · them | out of · their di|stress.

              20   He sent his | word and | healed them :
                          and they were | saved from | their de|struction.   ***change chant (Full)***

E. C. Bairstow

Full f   21   O that men would therefore praise the | Lord · for his | goodness :
                          and declare the wonders that he | doeth · for the | children · of | men!

Full   22   That they would offer unto him the | sacrifice · of | thanksgiving :
                          and | tell out · his | works with | gladness!   ***change chant (Decani)***

E. C. Bairstow

Dec. mf   23   They that go down to the | sea in | ships :
                          and occupy their | business · in | great | waters;

              24 ‡   These men see the | works · of the | Lord :
                          – | – and his | wonders · in the | deep.

              25 ‡   For at his word the stormy | wind a|riseth :
                          – | – which | lifteth up · the | waves thereof.

Psalm 107, continued

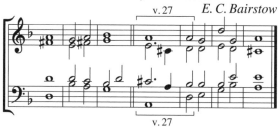

E. C. Bairstow

26   They are carried up to the heaven * and | down again • to the | deep :

dim.   their soul | melteth a•way be|cause of • the | trouble.

mf   27 ‡   They reel to and fro * and stagger like a | drunken | man :

                – | – and are | at their • wits' | end.   ***change chant (Cantoris)***

E. C. Bairstow

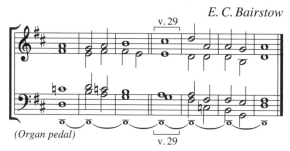

(Organ pedal)

Can. *p*   28   So when they cry unto the | Lord • in their | trouble :

                he de|livereth • them | out of • their di|stress.

        29 ‡   For he maketh the | storm to | cease :

                – | so that • the | waves there•of are | still.

pp   30   Then are they glad be|cause they • are at | rest :

                and so he bringeth them unto the | haven | where they | would be.

change chant (Full)

E. C. Bairstow

Full *f*   31   O that men would therefore praise the | Lord • for his | goodness :

                and declare the wonders that he | doeth • for the | children • of | men!

Full   32   That they would exalt him also in the congre|gation • of the | people :

                and | praise him • in the | seat • of the | elders!

Psalm 107, continued

E. C. Bairstow

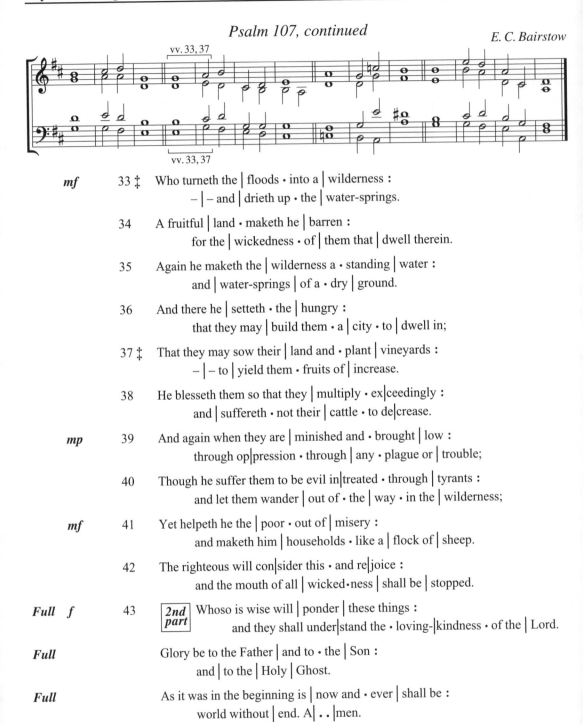

<table>
<tr><td>mf</td><td>33 ‡</td><td>Who turneth the | floods • into a | wilderness :
    – | – and | drieth up • the | water-springs.</td></tr>
<tr><td></td><td>34</td><td>A fruitful | land • maketh he | barren :
    for the | wickedness • of | them that | dwell therein.</td></tr>
<tr><td></td><td>35</td><td>Again he maketh the | wilderness a • standing | water :
    and | water-springs | of a • dry | ground.</td></tr>
<tr><td></td><td>36</td><td>And there he | setteth • the | hungry :
    that they may | build them • a | city • to | dwell in;</td></tr>
<tr><td></td><td>37 ‡</td><td>That they may sow their | land and • plant | vineyards :
    – | – to | yield them • fruits of | increase.</td></tr>
<tr><td></td><td>38</td><td>He blesseth them so that they | multiply • ex|ceedingly :
    and | suffereth • not their | cattle • to de|crease.</td></tr>
<tr><td>mp</td><td>39</td><td>And again when they are | minished and • brought | low :
    through op|pression • through | any • plague or | trouble;</td></tr>
<tr><td></td><td>40</td><td>Though he suffer them to be evil in|treated • through | tyrants :
    and let them wander | out of • the | way • in the | wilderness;</td></tr>
<tr><td>mf</td><td>41</td><td>Yet helpeth he the | poor • out of | misery :
    and maketh him | households • like a | flock of | sheep.</td></tr>
<tr><td></td><td>42</td><td>The righteous will con|sider this • and re|joice :
    and the mouth of all | wicked•ness | shall be | stopped.</td></tr>
<tr><td>Full f</td><td>43</td><td>**2nd part** Whoso is wise will | ponder | these things :
    and they shall under|stand the • loving-|kindness • of the | Lord.</td></tr>
<tr><td>Full</td><td></td><td>Glory be to the Father | and to • the | Son :
    and | to the | Holy | Ghost.</td></tr>
<tr><td>Full</td><td></td><td>As it was in the beginning is | now and • ever | shall be :
    world without | end. A | • • |men.</td></tr>
</table>

PSALM 108

Peter Hurford

Paratum cor meum

Full *f*   1   O God my heart is | ready my • heart is | ready :
    I will sing and give | praise • with the best | member • that I | have.

Full   2   A|wake thou • lute and | harp :
    I my|self • will a|wake right | early.

3   I will give thanks unto thee O | Lord a•mong the | people :
    I will sing praises unto | thee a|mong the | nations.

mf   4   For thy mercy is | greater • than the | heavens :
    and thy | truth • reacheth | unto • the | clouds.

f   5   Set up thyself O | God a•bove the | heavens :
    and thy | glory a•bove | all the | earth.

mf   6   That thy be|loved may • be de|livered :
    let thy | right hand | save them • and | hear thou me.

Change chant (Decani)

R. P. Stewart

Dec. *mf*   7   God hath | spoken • in his | holiness :
    I will rejoice therefore and divide Sichem *****
    and | mete out • the | valley • of | Succoth.

8   Gilead is mine and Ma|nasses • is | mine :
    Ephraim | also • is the | strength • of my | head.

Psalm 108, continued

R. P. Stewart

9 Judah is my law-giver * | Moab · is my | wash-pot :
   over Edom will I cast out my shoe * upon Phi|listi·a | will I | triumph.

10 Who will lead me into the | strong | city :
   and who will | bring me | into | Edom?

Change chant (Decani)

J. Harrison

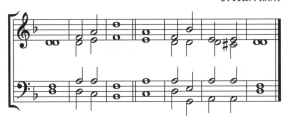

Dec. *mp*   11 Hast not thou for|saken us · O | God :
                  and wilt not thou O | God go | forth · with our | hosts?

                12 O help us a|gainst the | enemy :
                   for | vain · is the | help of | man.

       mf   13 Through God we shall | do great | acts :
                   and it is | he · that shall | tread down · our | enemies.

Change chant (Full)

J. Harrison

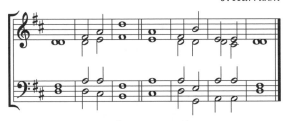

Full *f*   Glory be to the Father | and to · the | Son :
               and | to the | Holy | Ghost.

Full   As it was in the beginning is | now and · ever | shall be :
               world without | end. A | . . | men.

PSALM 109

J. Turle

Deus, laudem

Full *p*   1   Hold not thy tongue O | God of • my | praise :
                         for the mouth of the ungodly *
                         yea the mouth of the de|ceitful • is | opened • up|on me.

Full   2   And they have spoken a|gainst me • with | false tongues :
                         they compassed me about also with words of hatred *
                         and fought a|gainst me • with|out a | cause.

                  3   For the love that I had unto them * lo they take now my | contra•ry | part :
                         but I | give my•self | unto | prayer.

                  4   Thus have they rewarded me | evil • for | good :
                         and | hatred • for | my good|will.

mf   5 §   Set thou an ungodly man to be | ruler | over him :
                         and let | Satan | stand • at his | right hand.

                  6 §   When sentence is given upon him | let him • be con|demned;
                         and let his | prayer be | turned • into | sin.

                  7 §   Let his | days be | few :
                         and let an|other | take his | office.

                  8 §†‡ Let his | children • be | fatherless ‖ – | – and his | wife a | widow.

                  9 §   Let his children be | vagabonds and • beg their | bread :
                         let them seek it | also • out of | deso•late | places.

                 10 §   Let the extortioner con|sume • all that he | hath :
                         and let the | stranger | spoil his | labour.

                 11 §   Let there be | no man • to | pity him :
                         nor to have com|passion up•on his | father•less | children.

                 12 §   Let his po|sterity • be de|stroyed :
                         and in the next gene|ration • let his | name be • clean put | out.

§ Omitted in the St Paul's Cathedral use

Psalm 109, continued

J. Turle

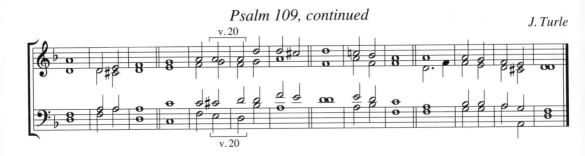

13 § Let the wickedness of his fathers be had in remembrance in the | sight • of the | Lord :
        and let not the sin of his | mother • be | done a|way.

14 § Let them alway be be|fore the | Lord :
        that he may root out the me|morial • of them from | off the | earth.

15 § And that because his mind was | not to • do | good :
        but persecuted the poor helpless man *
        that he might | slay • him that was | vexed • at the | heart.

16 § His delight was in cursing and it shall | happen | unto him :
        he loved not | blessing • therefore | it shall • be | far from him.

17 § He clothed himself with | cursing • like as with a | raiment :
        and it shall come into his bowels like | water *
        and like | oil • into his | bones.

18 § Let it be unto him as the cloke that he | hath up|on him :
        and as the girdle that he is | alway | girded • with|al.

19 § **2nd part** Let it thus happen from the | Lord • unto mine | enemies :
        and to those that speak | evil • a|gainst my | soul.

mp 20 ‡ But deal thou with me O Lord God according | unto • thy | Name :
        for | sweet is – | – thy | mercy.

21 O deliver me for I am | helpless • and | poor :
        and my | heart is | wounded • with|in me.

p 22 I go hence like the | shadow • that de|parteth :
        and am | driven • a|way • as the | grass•hopper.

23 My knees are | weak through | fasting :
        my flesh is dried | up for | want of | fatness.

24 **2nd part** I became | also • a re|proach unto them :
        they that | looked up•on me | shaked their | heads.

§ Omitted in the St Paul's Cathedral use

change chant (Decani)

Psalm 109, continued

J. Turle

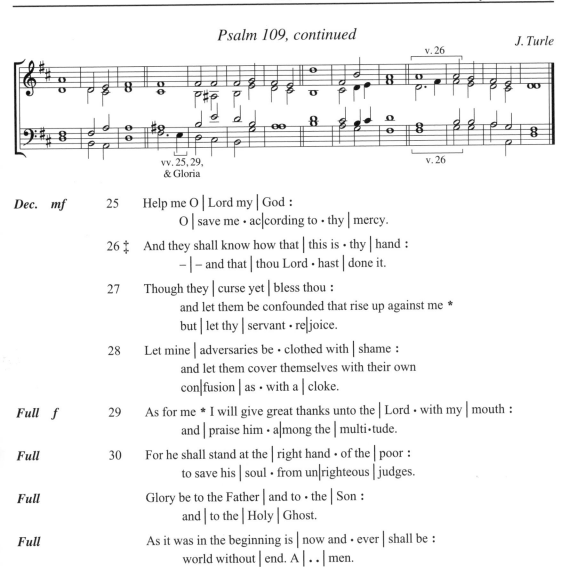

vv. 25, 29,
& Gloria

Dec.	*mf*	25	Help me O | Lord my | God : O | save me • ac|cording to • thy | mercy.
		26 ‡	And they shall know how that | this is • thy | hand : – | – and that | thou Lord • hast | done it.
		27	Though they | curse yet | bless thou : and let them be confounded that rise up against me * but | let thy | servant • re|joice.
		28	Let mine | adversaries be • clothed with | shame : and let them cover themselves with their own con|fusion | as • with a | cloke.
Full	*f*	29	As for me * I will give great thanks unto the | Lord • with my | mouth : and | praise him • a|mong the | multi•tude.
Full		30	For he shall stand at the | right hand • of the | poor : to save his | soul • from un|righteous | judges.
Full			Glory be to the Father | and to • the | Son : and | to the | Holy | Ghost.
Full			As it was in the beginning is | now and • ever | shall be : world without | end. A | . . | men.

PSALM 110

J. Turle

Dixit Dominus

Full	*f*	1	The Lord │ said • unto my │ Lord :
			Sit thou on my right hand un│til I • make thine │ enemies • thy │ footstool.
Full		2	The Lord shall send the rod of thy │ power • out of │ Sion :
			be thou ruler │ even • in the │ midst a•mong thine │ enemies.
	mf	3	In the day of thy power shall the people offer thee free-will offerings with an │ holy │ worship :
			the dew of thy │ birth is • of the │ womb • of the │ morning.
		4	The Lord sware and │ will not • re│pent :
			thou art a priest for ever │ after • the │ order • of Mel│chisedech.

---

f	5§†	The │ Lord up•on thy │ right hand ‖ shall wound even │ kings • in the │ day of • his │ wrath.
	6§	He shall judge among the heathen * he shall fill the │ places • with the dead │ bodies : and smite in sunder the │ heads • over │ divers │ countries.
mf	7§‡	**2nd part** He shall drink of the │ brook in • the │ way : – │ therefore • shall he │ lift up • his │ head.

Full	*f*	Glory be to the Father │ and to • the │ Son :
		and │ to the │ Holy │ Ghost.
Full		As it was in the beginning is │ now and • ever │ shall be :
		world without │ end. A │ . . │ men.

§ *Omitted in the St Paul's Cathedral use*

PSALM 111

R. Woodward

Confitebor tibi

Full	*f*	1	I will give thanks unto the | Lord with my · whole | heart : secretly among the | faithful | and in the · congre|gation.
Full		2	The works of the | Lord are | great : sought out of all | them · that have | pleasure · there|in.
	mf	3	His work is worthy to be | praised and · had in | honour : and his | righteousness · en|dureth · for | ever.
		4	The merciful and gracious Lord hath so done his | marvel·lous | works : that they | ought to · be | had · in re|membrance.
	mp	5	He hath given meat unto | them that | fear him : he shall | ever · be | mindful · of his | covenant.
		6	He hath shewed his people the | power · of his | works : that he may | give them · the | heritage · of the | heathen.
	mf	7 ‡	The works of his hands are | verity · and | judgement : – | all his · com|mandments · are | true.
		8 ‡	They stand fast for | ever · and | ever : and are | – – | done in · truth and | equity.
	mp	9	He sent re|demption · unto his | people : he hath commanded his covenant for ever * holy and | rever·end | is his | Name.
	mf	10	The fear of the Lord is the be|ginning · of | wisdom : a good understanding have all they that do thereafter * the | praise of it · en|dureth · for | ever.
Full	*f*		Glory be to the Father | and to · the | Son : and | to the | Holy | Ghost.
Full			As it was in the beginning is | now and · ever | shall be : world without | end. A | . . | men.

PSALM 112

W. Jacobs

Beatus vir

Full   *mp*   1   Blessed is the man that | feareth • the | Lord :
             he hath | great de|light in • his com|mandments.

Full   2   His seed shall be | mighty up•on | earth :
             the gene|ration • of the | faithful • shall be | blessed.

                3   Riches and plenteousness shall be | in his | house :
             and his | righteousness • en|dureth • for | ever.

      mf   4   Unto the godly there ariseth up | light • in the | darkness :
             he is | merci•ful | loving • and | righteous.

      p   5   A good man is | merciful • and | lendeth :
             and will | guide his | words • with dis|cretion.

                6   For he shall | never • be | moved :
             and the righteous shall be | had in • ever|lasting • re|membrance.

      mp   7   He will not be afraid of any | evil | tidings :
             for his heart standeth | fast • and be|lieveth • in the | Lord.

                8   His heart is e|stablished and • will not | shrink :
             until he | see his • de|sire up•on his | enemies.

      mf   9   He hath dispersed abroad and | given • to the | poor :
             and his righteousness remaineth for ever *
             his | horn shall • be ex|alted • with | honour.

              10   The ungodly shall | see it and • it shall | grieve him :
             he shall gnash with his teeth and consume away *
             the de|sire of • the un|godly • shall | perish.

Full   *mf*   Glory be to the Father | and to • the | Son :
             and | to the | Holy | Ghost.

Full   As it was in the beginning is | now and • ever | shall be :
             world without | end. A | . . | men.

PSALM 113

Stanley Vann

Laudate, pueri

Full *f*	1	Praise the | Lord ye | servants : O | praise the | Name • of the | Lord.
Full	2	Blessed be the | Name • of the | Lord : from this time | forth for | ever|more.
	3	The | Lord's • Name is | praised : from the rising up of the sun unto the | going | down • of the | same.
	4	The Lord is | high above • all | heathen : and his | glory • a|bove the | heavens.
mf	5	Who is like unto the Lord our God that hath his | dwelling • so | high : and yet humbleth himself to behold the | things that • are in | heaven and | earth?
mp	6	He taketh up the | simple • out of the | dust : and | lifteth • the | poor • out of the | mire;
mf	7 ‡	That he may | set him • with the | princes : even with the | – – | princes • of his | people.
	8	He maketh the barren | woman to • keep | house : and to be a | joyful | mother • of | children.
Full *f*		Glory be to the Father | and to • the | Son : and | to the | Holy | Ghost.
Full		As it was in the beginning is | now and • ever | shall be : world without | end. A | . . | men.

PSALM 114

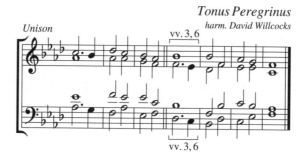

In exitu Israel

Full f	1	When Israel came │ out of │ Egypt :
		and the house of │ Jacob • from a│mong the • strange │ people.
Full	2	Judah │ was his │ sanctua•ry :
		and │ Isra•el │ his do│minion.
Dec.	3 ‡	The sea saw │ that and │ fled :
		– │ Jordan • was │ driven back.
Can.	4	The mountains │ skipped like │ rams :
		and the little │ hills like │ young │ sheep.
Trebles mf	5	What aileth thee O thou │ sea • that thou │ fleddest :
		and thou │ Jordan • that │ thou wast • driven │ back?
Tenors & Basses	6 ‡	Ye mountains that ye │ skipped like │ rams :
		– │ and ye • little │ hills like • young │ sheep?
Full f	7	Tremble thou earth at the │ presence • of the │ Lord :
		at the │ presence • of the │ God of │ Jacob;
Full	8	Who turned the hard rock into a │ standing │ water :
		and the │ flint-stone • into a │ springing │ well.
Full		Glory be to the Father │ and to • the │ Son :
		and │ to the │ Holy │ Ghost.
Full		As it was in the beginning is │ now and • ever │ shall be :
		world without │ end. A │ . . │ men.

PSALM 115

G. H. Knight

Non nobis, Domine

Full *f*   1   Not unto us O Lord not unto us * but unto │ thy Name • give the │ praise :
                          for thy loving │ mercy • and │ for thy │ truth's sake.

Full   2 † Wherefore │ shall the │ heathen ‖ say * │ Where is │ now their │ God?

       mf   3   As for │ our God • he is in │ heaven :
                          he hath │ done • whatso│ever │ pleased him.

                   4 ‡ Their idols are │ silver • and │ gold :
                          – │ – even the │ work of • men's │ hands.

                   5 ‡ They have │ mouths and │ speak not :
                          eyes have they │ – – │ – and │ see not.

                   6 † They have │ ears and │ hear ‖ not * │ noses • have │ they and │ smell not.

                   7   They have hands and handle not * │ feet have • they and │ walk not :
                          neither │ speak they │ through their │ throat.

                   8   They that │ make them • are │ like unto them :
                          and so are │ all • such as │ put their │ trust in them.

Full *f*   9   But thou house of Israel │ trust thou • in the │ Lord :
                          he is their │ succour │ and de│fence.

Full   10   Ye house of Aaron put your │ trust • in the │ Lord :
                          he is their │ helper │ and de│fender.

       mf   11   Ye that fear the Lord put your │ trust • in the │ Lord :
                          he is their │ helper │ and de│fender.

                  12   The Lord hath been mindful of │ us and • he shall │ bless us :
                          even he shall bless the house of Israel *
                          he shall │ bless the │ house of │ Aaron.

Psalm 115, continued   G. H. Knight

mp	13 ‡	He shall bless | them that · fear the | Lord : both | – – | small and | great.
cresc.	14 †‡	The Lord shall in|crease you | more and || more * | – – | you and · your | children.
mp	15 ‡	Ye are the | blessed · of the | Lord : who made | – – | heaven and | earth.
mf	16	All the whole | heavens · are the | Lord's : the earth hath he | given · to the | children · of | men.
mp	17	The dead | praise not · thee O | Lord : neither all | they that · go | down · into | silence.
Full f	18	But we will | praise the | Lord : from this time forth for evermore * | Praise . | . the | Lord.
Full		Glory be to the Father | and to · the | Son : and | to the | Holy | Ghost.
Full		As it was in the beginning is | now and · ever | shall be : world without | end. A | . . | men.

PSALM 116

J. Robinson

Dilexi, quoniam

Full	*mf*	1 †	I am | well | pleased ‖ that the Lord hath | heard the | voice • of my | prayer;
Full		2	That he hath in|clined his • ear | unto me :
			therefore will I | call upon • him as | long as • I | live.
	mp	3	The snares of death | compassed me • round a|bout :
			and the | pains of | hell gat | hold upon me.
		4	I shall find trouble and heaviness * and I will call upon the | Name • of the | Lord :
			O Lord I be|seech thee • de|liver my | soul.
	p	5 †	Gracious is the | Lord and | right‖eous * | yea our | God is | merciful.
		6	The Lord pre|serveth • the | simple :
			I was in | mise•ry | and he | helped me.
		7 ‡	Turn again then unto thy | rest • O my | soul :
			– | – for the | Lord • hath re|warded thee.
	cresc.	8	And why? * thou hast delivered my | soul from | death :
			mine eyes from | tears • and my | feet from | falling.
	mf	9 ††‡	I will | walk be•fore the | Lord ‖ – | – in the | land • of the | living.
		10	I believed and therefore will I speak * | but I was • sore | troubled :
			I said in my | haste * | All men • are | liars.
		11	What reward shall I | give • unto the | Lord :
			for all the | benefits • that | he hath • done | unto me?
		12	I will receive the | cup of • sal‖vation :
			and | call up•on the | Name • of the | Lord.
	mp	13	I will pay my vows now in the | presence of • all his | people :
			right dear in the sight of the | Lord • is the | death of • his | saints.
		14	Behold O Lord how that | I am • thy | servant :
	cresc.		I am thy servant and the son of thine hand-maid *
			thou hast | broken • my | bonds in | sunder.

Psalm 116, continued

J. Robinson

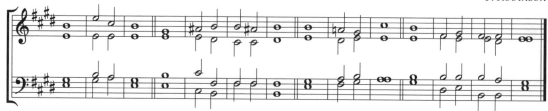

> *f*   15   I will offer to thee the | sacrifice · of | thanksgiving :
>   and will | call up·on the | Name · of the | Lord.

>   16   I will pay my vows unto the Lord in the | sight of · all his | people :
>   in the courts of the Lord's house *
>   even in the midst of thee O Je|rusa·lem * | Praise the | Lord.

> *Full*   Glory be to the Father | and to · the | Son :
>   and | to the | Holy | Ghost.

> *Full*   As it was in the beginning is | now and · ever | shall be :
>   world without | end. A | . . | men.

PSALM 117

Christopher Dearnley

Laudate Dominum

> *Full*   *f*   1 ‡   O praise the | Lord · all ye | heathen :
>   – | praise him · all ye | nations.

> *Full*   2   For his merciful kindness is ever | more and more · to|wards us :
>   and the truth of the Lord endureth for ever * | Praise the | Lord.

> *Full*   Glory be to the Father | and to · the | Son :
>   and to the | Holy | Ghost.

> *Full*   As it was in the beginning is | now and · ever | shall be :
>   world without | end. A|men.

PSALM 118

A. Gray

Confitemini Domino

Full *f*	1	O give thanks unto the | Lord for • he is | gracious :
		because his | mercy • en|dureth • for | ever.
Full	2	Let Israel now con|fess that • he is | gracious :
		and that his | mercy • en|dureth • for | ever.
Full	3 †	Let the house of | Aaron • now con|fess ‖ that his | mercy • en|dureth • for | ever.
Full	4 †	Yea let them now that fear the | Lord con|fess ‖ that his | mercy • en|dureth • for ever.
mp	5 ‡	I called upon the | Lord in | trouble :
		– | – and the | Lord • heard me at | large.
mf	6	The | Lord is • on my | side :
		I will not | fear what | man • doeth | unto me.
	7	**2nd part** The Lord taketh my | part with • them that | help me :
		therefore shall I | see • my de|sire up•on mine | enemies.
	8 †	It is better to | trust • in the | Lord ‖ than to | put • any | confidence • in | man.
	9 †	It is better to | trust • in the | Lord ‖ than to | put • any | confidence • in | princes.
Full *f*	10	All nations | compassed me • round a|bout :
		but in the | Name • of the | Lord • will I de|stroy them.
Full	11	They kept me in on every side * they kept me in I say on | every | side :
		but in the | Name • of the | Lord • will I de|stroy them.
Full	12	**2nd part** They came about me like bees *
		and are extinct even as the | fire a•mong the | thorns :
		for in the | Name • of the | Lord • I will de|stroy them.

Psalm 118, continued

A. Gray

mf   13 ‡   Thou hast thrust | sore at me • that I might | fall :
                  – | – but the | Lord • was my | help.

f   14 ‡   The Lord is my | strength • and my | song :
                  and is be| – – |come • my sal|vation.

        15   The voice of joy and health is in the | dwellings • of the | righteous :
                  the right hand of the | Lord • bringeth | mighty things • to | pass.

        16   The right hand of the | Lord • hath the pre-|emi•nence :
                  the right hand of the | Lord • bringeth | mighty things • to | pass.

        17   I shall not | die but | live :
                  and de|clare the | works • of the | Lord.

        18   The Lord hath | chastened • and cor|rected • me :
                  but he hath not | given • me | over • unto | death.

change chant (Decani)

S. Wesley

Dec. *mf*   19   Open me the | gates of | righteousness :
                  that I may go | into them • and give | thanks • unto the | Lord.

        20   This is the | gate • of the | Lord :
                  the | righteous • shall | enter | into it.

Psalm 118, continued

S. Wesley

21 ‡   I will thank thee for | thou hast | heard me :
      – | and art · be|come · my sal|vation.

22   The same stone which the | builders · re|fused :
      is be|come the | head-stone · in the | corner.

Full *f*   23   This is the | Lord's | doing :
      and it is | marvel·lous | in our | eyes.

Full   24 ‡   This is the day which the | Lord hath | made :
      – | – we will re|joice · and be | glad in it.

mp   25   Help me | now O | Lord :
      O | Lord · send us | now pro|sperity.

26   Blessed be he that cometh in the | Name · of the | Lord :
      we have wished you good luck * |
      ye that are · of the | house · of the | Lord.

cresc.   27 | **2nd part** | God is the | Lord who hath · shewed us | light :
      bind the sacrifice with cords *
      yea | even · unto the | horns · of the | altar.

Full *f*   28 ‡   Thou art my | God and · I will | thank thee :
      – | thou art · my | God and · I will | praise thee.

Full   29   O give thanks unto the | Lord for · he is | gracious :
      and his | mercy · en|dureth · for | ever.

Full   Glory be to the Father | and to · the | Son :
      and | to the | Holy | Ghost.

Full   As it was in the beginning is | now and · ever | shall be :
      world without | end. A | . . | men.

PSALM 119, *vv. 1 - 32*

K. J. Pye

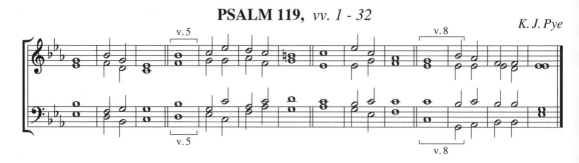

Beati immaculati

Full   *mf*   1   Blessed are those that are unde|filed · in the | way :
and | walk in · the | law · of the | Lord.

Full   2   Blessed are | they that · keep his | testimonies :
and | seek him · with their | whole | heart.

3 †   For | they who | do ‖ no | wicked·ness | walk in · his | ways.

4 †   Thou hast | charged that | we ‖ shall | diligent·ly |
keep thy · com|mandments.

5 ‡   O that my ways were | made · so di|rect :
– | that I · might | keep thy | statutes.

6   So shall I | not · be con|founded :
while I have re|spect · unto | all · thy com|mandments.

f   7   I will thank thee with an | unfeigned | heart :
when I shall have | learned the | judgements · of thy | righteousness.

8 ‡   I will | keep thy | ceremonies :
– | – O for|sake me · not | utterly.

change chant (Decani)

Psalm 119, continued

J. Nares

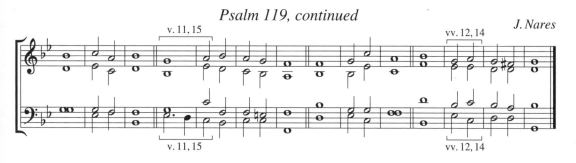

In quo corriget?

Dec. **mp**   9   Wherewithal shall a | young man • cleanse his | way :
                              even by | ruling him•self | after • thy | word.

          10   With my whole | heart • have I | sought thee :
                              O let me not go | wrong • out of | thy com|mandments.

p   11 ‡   Thy words have I | hid with•in my | heart :
                              – | – that I | should not • sin a|gainst thee.

mp   12 ‡   Blessed art | thou O | Lord :
                              O | – – | teach me • thy | statutes.

mf   13 †   With my | lips have • I been | telling ‖ of all the | judgements | of thy | mouth.

          14 ‡   I have had as great delight in the | way of • thy | testimonies :
                              as in all | – – | manner • of | riches.

mp   15 ‡   I will | talk of • thy com|mandments :
                              – | – and have re|spect • unto thy | ways.

mf   16   My de|light shall be • in thy | statutes :
                              and I | will not • for|get thy | word.

change chant (Decani)

Psalm 119, continued

G. M. Garrett

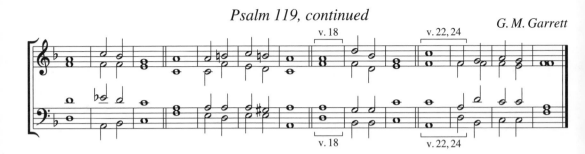

Retribue servo tuo

Dec. *mf* 17   O do | well • unto thy | servant :
       that I may | live and | keep thy | word.

      18 ‡   – | Open • thou mine | eyes :
       that I may | see the • wondrous | things • of thy | law.

p   19   I am a | stranger up•on | earth :
       O | hide not • thy com|mandments | from me.

cresc.   20 †   My soul breaketh out for the very | fervent • de|sire ‖
       that it hath | alway | unto • thy | judgements.

mf   21   Thou hast re|buked the | proud :
       and | cursed are • they that do | err from • thy com|mandments.

      22 ‡   O turn from me | shame • and re|buke :
       – | – for I have | kept thy | testimonies.

      23   Princes also did | sit and • speak a|gainst me :
       but thy | servant • is | occupied • in thy | statutes.

      24 †‡ For thy | testi•monies | are ‖ – | – my de|light • and my | counsellors.

change chant (Decani)

Psalm 119, continued

C. Hylton Stewart

Adhæsit pavimento

Dec.   *p*   25   My soul | cleaveth · to the | dust :
O | quicken thou me · ac|cording · to thy | word.

26 ‡   I have acknowledged my | ways · and thou | heardest me :
O | – – | teach me · thy | statutes.

27   Make me to understand the | way of · thy com|mandments :
and so shall I | talk of · thy | wondrous | works.

28   My soul melteth a|way for · very | heaviness :
comfort thou | me ac|cording · to thy | word.

mp   29   Take from me the | way of | lying :
and | cause thou me · to make | much · of thy | law.

mf   30   I have | chosen the · way of | truth :
and thy | judgements · have I | laid be|fore me.

31   I have | stuck · unto thy | testimonies :
O | Lord con|found me | not.

32   I will run the | way of · thy com|mandments :
dim.   when thou hast | set my | heart at | liberty.

Full   *p*   Glory be to the Father | and to · the | Son :
and | to the | Holy | Ghost.

Full   As it was in the beginning is | now and · ever | shall be :
world without | end. A | . . | men.

PSALM 119, *vv. 33 - 72*

G. Thalben-Ball

Legem pone

Full	**mf**	33	Teach me O Lord the | way of • thy | statutes :
			and I shall | keep it | unto • the | end.
Full		34	Give me understanding and I shall | keep thy | law :
			yea I shall | keep it • with my | whole | heart.
		35 ‡	Make me to go in the | path of • thy com|mandments :
			– | – for there|in is • my de|sire.
		36 †‡	Incline my | heart • unto thy | testimonies ‖
			– | – and | not to | covetousness.
	mp	37	O turn away mine eyes | lest they be•hold | vanity :
			and | quicken • thou | me • in thy | way.
		38 †‡	O stablish thy | word • in thy | servant ‖ – | – that | I may | fear thee.
	mf	39 ‡	Take away the rebuke that | I am • a|fraid of :
			– | – for thy | judgements • are | good.
		40	Behold my de|light is in • thy com|mandments :
			O | quicken • me | in thy | righteousness.

change chant (Decani)

Psalm 119, continued

H. West

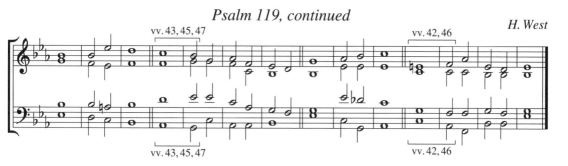

Et veniat super me

Dec. **mf** 41   Let thy loving mercy come also | unto me · O | Lord :
                       even thy salvation ac|cording | unto · thy | word.

         42 ‡   So shall I make answer | unto my · blas|phemers :
                       – | – for my | trust is · in thy | word.

         43 ‡   O take not the word of thy truth utterly | out of · my | mouth :
                       – | – for my | hope is · in thy | judgements.

         44 †   So shall I | alway | keep ‖ thy | law · yea for | ever · and | ever.

mp   45 ‡   And I will | walk at | liberty :
                       – | – for I | seek · thy com|mandments.

         46 ‡   I will speak of thy testimonies also | even be·fore | kings :
                       – | – and | will not · be a|shamed.

mf   47 †‡ And my delight shall | be in · thy com|mandments ‖ – | – which |
                 I have | loved.

         48   My hands also will I lift up unto thy com|mandments · which I have | loved :
                       and my | study · shall | be in · thy | statutes.

change chant (Decani)

Psalm 119, continued

J. Jones

Memor esto servi tui

Dec. *mp*   49   O think upon thy servant as con|cerning · thy | word :
wherein thou hast | caused me · to | put my | trust.

50 ‡   The same is my | comfort · in my | trouble :
– | – for thy | word hath | quickened me.

mf   51 ‡   The proud have had me ex|ceedingly · in de|rision :
– | yet have · I not | shrinked · from thy | law.

52 †   For I remembered thine ever|lasting | judgements ‖ O |
Lord · and re|ceived | comfort.

53 †   I am | horribly · a|fraid ‖ for the un|godly · that for|sake thy | law.

54 †   Thy | statutes · have | been ‖ my | songs · in the | house · of my | pilgrimage.

55 ‡   I have thought upon thy Name O | Lord · in the | night-season :
– | and have | kept thy | law.

56 †‡   This I | had be|cause ‖ – | – I | kept · thy com|mandments.

change chant (Decani)

Psalm 119, continued

T. Attwood

Portio mea, Domine

Dec. **mf** 57 Thou art my | portion · O | Lord :
I have | promised · to | keep thy | law.

58 I made my humble petition in thy presence with my | whole | heart :
O be merciful unto | me ac|cording · to thy | word.

mp 59 I called mine own | ways · to re|membrance :
and | turned my | feet unto · thy | testi·monies.

60 †‡ I made haste and pro|longed not · the | time ‖ – | – to |
keep · thy com|mandments.

mf 61 The congregations of the un|godly · have | robbed me :
but I | have not · for|gotten · thy | law.

62 At midnight I will rise to give | thanks · unto | thee :
be|cause of · thy | righteous | judgements.

63 † I am a com|panion · of all | them ‖ that | fear thee · and |
keep · thy com|mandments.

64 ‡ The earth O Lord is | full of · thy | mercy :
– | – O | teach me · thy | statutes.

change chant (Decani)

Psalm 119, continued

W. J. Mothersole

Bonitatem fecisti

Dec. *mp* 65 O Lord thou hast dealt | graciously • with thy | servant :
ac|cording | unto • thy | word.

66 O learn me true under|standing • and | knowledge :
for | I have • be|lieved • thy com|mandments.

67 Before I was | troubled • I went | wrong :
but | now • have I | kept thy | word.

68 ‡ Thou art | good and | gracious :
– | – O | teach me • thy | statutes.

mf 69 The proud have i|magined a • lie a|gainst me :
but I will keep thy com|mandments • with my | whole | heart.

70 Their | heart is as • fat as | brawn :
but my de|light hath | been in • thy | law.

mp 71 ‡ It is good for me that I have | been in | trouble :
– | that I • may | learn thy | statutes.

72 † The law of thy | mouth is • dearer | unto me ‖ than |
thousands • of | gold and | silver.

Full Glory be to the Father | and to • the | Son :
and | to the | Holy | Ghost.

Full As it was in the beginning is | now and • ever | shall be :
world without | end. A | . . | men.

PSALM 119, *vv. 73 - 104*

H. Skeats

Manus tuæ fecerunt me

Full **mf** 73 Thy hands have | made me • and | fashioned me :
O give me under|standing that • I may | learn • thy com|mandments.

Full 74 They that fear thee will be | glad • when they | see me :
be|cause I have • put my | trust • in thy | word.

mp 75 I know O Lord that thy | judgements • are | right :
and that thou of very | faithfulness • hast | caused me • to be | troubled.

76 O let thy merciful | kindness • be my | comfort :
ac|cording • to thy | word • unto thy | servant.

mf 77 ‡ O let thy loving mercies come unto | me that • I may | live :
for thy | – – | law is • my de|light.

78 Let the proud be confounded *
for they go wickedly a|bout • to de|stroy me :
but I will be | occupied • in | thy com|mandments.

79 ‡ Let such as fear thee and have | known thy | testimonies :
be | – – | turned • unto | me.

80 ‡ O let my heart be | sound • in thy | statutes :
– | – that I be | not a|shamed.

change chant (Decani)

Psalm 119, continued

H. J. Gauntlett

Defecit anima mea

Dec.	*mf*	81	My soul hath | longed for • thy sal|vation : and I have a good | hope be|cause of • thy | word.
		82 ‡	Mine eyes long | sore • for thy | word : saying | – O | when • wilt thou | comfort me?
	p	83	For I am become like a | bottle • in the | smoke : yet do I | not for|get thy | statutes.
	mp	84	How many are the | days • of thy | servant : when wilt thou be a|venged of | them that | persecute me?
	mf	85 ‡	The | proud have • digged | pits for me : which are not | – – | after • thy | law.
		86	All thy com|mandments • are | true : they persecute me | falsely * O be | thou my | help.
	mp	87 ‡	They had almost made an | end of me • upon | earth : but I for| – – |sook not • thy com|mandments.
		88	O quicken me | after thy • loving-|kindness : and so shall I | keep the | testimonies • of thy | mouth.

change chant (Decani)

Psalm 119, continued

P. Armes

In æternum, Domine

Dec. *mf*   89 †   O | Lord thy | word ‖ en|dureth · for | ever · in | heaven.

            90   Thy truth also remaineth from one gene|ration · to an|other :
                     thou hast laid the foun|dation · of the | earth and · it a|bideth.

            91 ‡   They continue this day ac|cording · to thine | ordinance :
                     for | – – | all things | serve thee.

            92 ‡   If my delight had | not been · in thy | law :
                     – | – I should have | perished · in my | trouble.

            93 ‡   I will never for|get · thy com|mandments :
                     for with | – – | them · thou hast | quickened me.

            94 ‡   I am | thine O | save me :
                     – | – for I have | sought · thy com|mandments.

            95 ‡   The ungodly laid | wait for me · to de|stroy me :
                     but I will con| – – |sider · thy | testimonies.

mp   96   I see that all things | come · to an | end :
mf   but thy com|mandment · is ex|ceeding | broad.

change chant (Decani)

Psalm 119, continued

S. Marchant

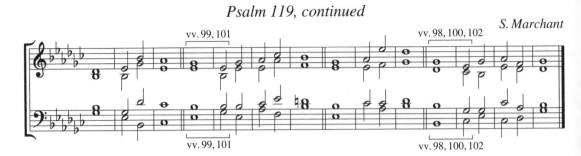

Quomodo dilexi!

Dec. *p* 97 Lord what love have I | unto • thy | law :
all the day | long • is my | study | in it.

98 ‡ Thou through thy commandments hast made me | wiser • than mine | enemies :
– | – for they are | ever | with me.

mp 99 ‡ I have more under|standing • than my | teachers :
– | – for thy | testimonies • are my | study.

100 ‡ I am | wiser • than the | aged :
– | – because I | keep • thy com|mandments.

101 ‡ I have refrained my feet from | every • evil | way :
– | – that I may | keep thy | word.

102 †‡ I have not | shrunk • from thy | judge‖ – | – ments * | for thou | teachest me.

p 103 O how sweet are thy | words • unto my | throat :
yea sweeter than | honey | unto • my | mouth.

mp 104 Through thy commandments I get | under|standing :
therefore I | hate all | evil | ways.

Full *p* Glory be to the Father | and to • the | Son :
and | to the | Holy | Ghost.

Full As it was in the beginning is | now and • ever | shall be :
world without | end. A | . . | men.

PSALM 119, *vv. 105 - 144*

F. A. G. Ouseley

Lucerna pedibus meis

Full   *mf*   105   Thy word is a | lantern • unto my | feet :
and a | light | unto • my | paths.

Full   106 †   I have sworn and am | stedfast•ly | purposed ‖ to | keep thy |
righteous | judgements.

mp   107   I am | troubled a•bove | measure :
quicken me O | Lord ac|cording • to thy | word.

mf   108 ‡   Let the free-will offerings of my mouth | please thee • O | Lord :
– | – and | teach me • thy | judgements.

mp   109   My soul is | alway • in my | hand :
yet do I | not for|get thy | law.

mf   110   The un|godly have • laid a | snare for me :
but yet I | swerved not • from | thy com|mandments.

111   Thy testimonies have I claimed as mine | heritage • for | ever :
and why? * they are the | very | joy of • my | heart.

112 †   I have applied my heart to ful|fil thy | statutes ‖ alway * |
even | unto • the | end.

change chant (Decani)

Psalm 119, continued

H. S. Oakeley

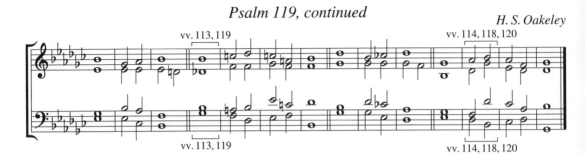

Iniquos odio habui

Dec.	**mf**	113 ‡ I hate them that i|magine • evil | things : − | but thy | law • do I | love.
		114 ‡ Thou art my de|fence and | shield : and my | − − | trust is • in thy | word.
	f	115 A|way from me • ye | wicked : I will | keep • the com|mandments • of my | God.
		116 O stablish me according to thy | word that • I may | live : and let me | not be • disap|pointed • of my | hope.
	mf	117 Hold thou me | up and • I shall be | safe : yea my de|light • shall be | ever • in thy | statutes.
		118 ‡ Thou hast trodden down all them that de|part from • thy | statutes : for they i| − − |magine • but de|ceit.
	mp	119 ‡ Thou puttest away all the ungodly of the | earth like | dross : − | therefore • I | love thy | testimonies.
	p	120 ‡ My flesh | trembleth • for | fear of thee : and I am a| − − |fraid of • thy | judgements.

change chant (Decani)

Psalm 119, continued

J. Goss

Feci judicium

Dec. *mf* 121 I deal with the thing that is | lawful • and | right :
O give me not | over • unto | mine op|pressors.

122 ‡ Make thou thy servant to delight in | that • which is | good :
– | – that the | proud • do me no | wrong.

mp 123 ‡ Mine eyes are wasted away with | looking • for thy | health :
– | – and for the | word • of thy | righteousness.

124 ‡ O deal with thy servant according unto thy | loving | mercy :
– | – and | teach me • thy | statutes.

mf 125 ‡ I am thy servant O | grant me • under|standing :
– | – that I may | know thy | testimonies.

126 It is time for thee Lord to | lay to • thine | hand :
for | they have • de|stroyed thy | law.

p 127 †‡ For I | love • thy com|mandments ‖ – | – above | gold and • precious | stone.

mp 128 Therefore hold I straight | all • thy com|mandments :
and all | false ways • I | utterly • ab|hor.

change chant (Decani)

Psalm 119, continued

J. Coward

Mirabilia

Dec. *mf*   129 ‡ Thy | testimonies • are | wonderful :
therefore | doth my – | – soul | keep them.

130   When thy | word • goeth | forth :
it giveth light and under|standing | unto • the | simple.

131   I opened my mouth and | drew in • my | breath :
for my de||light • was in | thy com|mandments.

mp   132   O look thou upon me and be | merci•ful | unto me :
as thou usest to do unto | those that | love thy | Name.

mf   133   Order my | steps • in thy | word :
and so shall no | wickedness • have do|minion | over me.

134   O deliver me from the wrongful | dealings • of | men :
and | so shall • I | keep • thy com|mandments.

mp   135 ‡ Shew the light of thy | countenance up•on thy | servant :
and | teach me – | – thy | statutes.

136   Mine eyes gush | out with | water :
be|cause men | keep not • thy | law.

__change chant (Decani)__

Psalm 119, *continued*

E. J. Hopkins

Justus es, Domine

Dec. *mf*　137 ‡ Righteous art | thou O | Lord :
　　　　　　　　　　　　　and | true is – | – thy | judgement.

　　　　　　138 † The testimonies that | thou hast · com|manded ‖ are ex|ceeding |
　　　　　　　　　　righteous · and | true.

　　　　　　139 　My zeal hath | even · con|sumed me :
　　　　　　　　　　　　　because mine | enemies · have for|gotten · thy | words.

　　　　　　140 ‡ Thy word is | tried · to the | uttermost :
　　　　　　　　　　　　　– | – and thy | servant | loveth it.

mp　　141 　I am small and of | no · repu|tation :
　　　　　　　　　　　　　yet do I | not for|get · thy com|mandments.

mf　　142 ‡ Thy righteousness is an ever|lasting | righteousness :
　　　　　　　　　　　　　– | – and thy | law · is the | truth.

mp　　143 ‡ Trouble and heaviness have taken | hold up|on me :
mf　　　　　　　　　　　　　yet is my de|light in – | – thy com|mandments.

　　　　　　144 　The righteousness of thy | testimonies is · ever|lasting :
cresc.　　　　　　　　　　　O grant me under|standing · and | I shall | live.

Full *f*　　Glory be to the Father | and to · the | Son :
　　　　　　　　　　　　　and | to the | Holy | Ghost.

Full　　As it was in the beginning is | now and · ever | shall be :
　　　　　　　　　　　　　world without | end. A | . . | men.

PSALM 119, *vv. 145 - 176*

Alan Hemmings

Clamavi in toto corde meo

Full	*mf*	145	I call with my | whole | heart : hear me O | Lord • I will | keep thy | statutes.
Full		146	Yea even unto | thee • do I | call : help me and | I shall | keep thy | testimonies.
		147	Early in the morning do I | cry • unto | thee : for in | thy word | is my | trust.
		148	Mine eyes pre|vent the | night-watches : that I might be | occu•pied | in thy | words.
	mp	149	Hear my voice O Lord according | unto thy • loving-|kindness : quicken me ac|cording • as | thou art | wont.
		150	They draw nigh that of | malice | perse•cute me : and are | far | from thy | law.
	mf	151	Be thou nigh at | hand O | Lord : for | all • thy com|mandments • are | true.
		152	As concerning thy testimonies I have | known long | since : that thou hast | grounded | them for | ever.

change chant (Decani)

Psalm 119, continued

T. A. Walmisley

Vide humilitatem

Dec.	*mp*	153	O consider mine ad|versity • and de|liver me :
			for I │ do not • for|get thy │ law.

mf 154 ‡ Avenge thou my │ cause • and de|liver me :
– │ quicken me • ac|cording • to thy │ word.

155 ‡ Health is │ far • from the un|godly :
– │ for they • re|gard not • thy │ statutes.

mp 156 ‡ Great is thy │ mercy • O │ Lord :
– │ quicken me • as │ thou art │ wont.

mf 157 Many there are that │ trouble me • and │ persecute me :
yet │ do I • not │ swerve • from thy │ testimonies.

158 It grieveth me when I │ see the • trans|gressors :
be|cause they │ keep not • thy │ law.

mp 159 Consider O Lord how I │ love • thy com|mandments :
O quicken me ac|cording • to thy │ loving-|kindness.

mf 160 Thy word is │ true from • ever|lasting :
all the judgements of thy │ righteousness • en|dure for • ever │ more.

__change chant (Decani)__

Psalm 119, continued

Lord Mornington

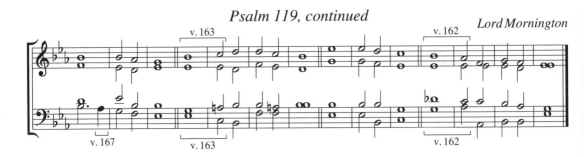

Principes persecuti sunt

Dec. *f*   161   Princes have persecuted me with|out a | cause :
   but my | heart • standeth in | awe • of thy | word.

162†‡   I am as | glad of • thy | word ‖ – | – as one that | findeth • great | spoils.

mf   163 ‡   As for lies I | hate • and ab|hor them :
   – | – but thy | law • do I | love.

164   Seven times a | day • do I | praise thee :
   be|cause of • thy | righteous | judgements.

p   165   Great is the peace that | they have who • love thy | law :
   and | they are | not of|fended at it.

166   Lord I have | looked for thy • saving | health :
   and | done • after | thy com|mandments.

mp   167 †   My | soul hath | kept ‖ thy | testimonies • and | loved them • ex|ceedingly.

mf   168   I have kept thy com|mandments • and | testimonies :
   for | all my | ways • are be|fore thee.

change chant (Decani)

Psalm 119, continued

J. Goss *(from J. Clarke)*

Appropinquet deprecatio

Dec. *p*   169   Let my complaint come be|fore thee • O | Lord :
                      give me under|standing • ac|cording • to thy | word.

          170   Let my suppli|cation • come be|fore thee :
                      de|liver me • ac|cording • to thy | word.

mf   171 ‡ My lips shall | speak of • thy | praise :
                      – | when thou • hast | taught me • thy | statutes.

          172   Yea my tongue shall | sing of • thy | word :
                      for | all • thy com|mandments • are | righteous.

mp   173 ‡ Let thine | hand | help me :
                      – | for I • have | chosen • thy com|mandments.

          174 ‡ I have longed for thy saving | health O | Lord :
                      – | – and in thy | law is • my de|light.

mf   175 ‡ O let my soul | live and • it shall | praise thee;
                      – | and thy | judgements • shall | help me.

p   176   I have gone astray like a | sheep • that is | lost :
                      O seek thy servant * for I | do not • for|get • thy com|mandments.

Full *p*   Glory be to the Father | and to • the | Son :
                      and | to the | Holy | Ghost.

Full   As it was in the beginning is | now and • ever | shall be :
                      world without | end. A | . . | men.

PSALM 120

C. Hylton Stewart

Ad Dominum

Full	*mp*	1 †	When I │ was in │ trouble ‖ I │ called up•on the │ Lord • and he │ heard me.
Full		2	Deliver my soul O │ Lord from • lying │ lips :
			and │ from a • de│ceitful │ tongue.
	mf	3	What reward shall be given or done unto │ thee thou • false │ tongue :
			even mighty and sharp │ arrows • with │ hot • burning │ coals.
	p	4	Woe is me that I am con│strained to • dwell with │ Mesech :
			and to have my habi│tation a•mong the │ tents of │ Kedar.
		5 †	My soul hath long │ dwelt a•mong │ them ‖ that are │ ene•mies │ unto │ peace.
	cresc.	6	I labour for peace * but when I │ speak unto • them there│of :
			they │ make them │ ready • to │ battle.
Full	*mp*		Glory be to the Father │ and to • the │ Son :
			and │ to the │ Holy │ Ghost.
Full			As it was in the beginning is │ now and • ever │ shall be :
			world without │ end. A │ . . │ men.

PSALM 121

H. Walford Davies

Levavi oculos

Solo *p*   1   I will lift up mine | eyes · unto the | hills :
Full   from | whence | cometh · my | help.

Solo   2 ‡   My help cometh | even · from the | Lord :
Full   – | who hath · made | heaven · and | earth.

[sim.]   3   He will not suffer thy | foot · to be | moved :
                and he that | keepeth · thee | will not | sleep.

             4 †   Behold | he that · keepeth | Isra·el ‖ shall | neither | slumber · nor | sleep.

     mp   5   The Lord him|self · is thy | keeper :
                the Lord is thy de|fence up·on thy | right | hand.

             6 ‡   So that the sun shall not | burn thee · by | day :
                – | neither · the | moon by | night.

             7   The Lord shall pre|serve thee · from all | evil :
                yea it is even | he · that shall | keep thy | soul.

             8   The Lord shall preserve thy going | out and thy · coming | in :
     dim.   from this time | forth for | ever | more.

Solo *p*   Glory be to the Father | and to · the | Son :
Full   and | to the | Holy | Ghost.

Solo   As it was in the beginning is | now and · ever | shall be :
Full   world without | end. A | . . | men.

PSALM 122

G. C. Martin

Lætatus sum

Full *f*	1	I was │ glad • when they │ said unto me :
		we will │ go • into the │ house of • the │ Lord.
Full	2 †	Our │ feet shall │ stand ‖ in thy │ gates │ O Je│rusalem.
mf	3 †	Jerusalem is │ built • as a │ city ‖ that is at │ uni•ty │ in it│self.
	4	For thither the tribes go up * even the │ tribes • of the │ Lord :
		to testify unto Israel * to give │ thanks • unto the │ Name • of the │ Lord.
	5	**2nd part** For there is the │ seat of │ judgement :
		even the │ seat of • the │ house of │ David.
p	6 †	O pray for the │ peace • of Je│rusa‖lem * │ they shall │ prosper • that │ love thee.
	7	Peace be with│in thy │ walls :
		and │ plenteousness • with│in thy │ palaces.
mp	8 ‡	For my brethren and com│panions' │ sakes :
		– │ I will │ wish thee • pro│sperity.
mf	9	Yea because of the house of the │ Lord our │ God :
		I will │ seek to │ do thee │ good.
Full *f*		Glory be to the Father │ and to • the │ Son :
		and │ to the │ Holy │ Ghost.
Full		As it was in the beginning is │ now and • ever │ shall be :
		world without │ end. A │ . . │ men.

PSALM 123

C. C. Palmer

Ad te levavi oculos meos

Full *mp* 1   Unto thee | lift I up • mine | eyes :
    O | thou that | dwellest • in the | heavens.

Full 2   Behold even as the eyes of servants look unto the hand of their masters *
and as the eyes of a maiden unto the | hand • of her | mistress :
    even so our eyes wait upon the Lord our God *
un|til he • have | mercy • up|on us.

p 3 ‡   Have mercy upon us O Lord have | mercy • up|on us :
    – | for we • are | utterly • de|spised.

mf 4   Our soul is filled with the scornful re|proof • of the | wealthy :
    and with the de|spiteful•ness | of the | proud.

Full *mp*   Glory be to the Father | and to • the | Son :
    and | to the | Holy | Ghost.

Full   As it was in the beginning is | now and • ever | shall be :
    world without | end. A | . . | men.

PSALM 124

G. M. Garrett

Nisi quia Dominus

Full *f*   1   If the Lord himself had not been on our side * now may | Isra·el | say :
                          if the Lord himself had not been on | our side · when |
                          men rose · up a|gainst us;

Full   2 ‡   They had | swallowed us · up | quick :
                          when they were | – so | wrathfully · dis|pleased at us.

        mf   3   Yea the | waters · had | drowned us :
                          and the | stream · had gone | over · our | soul.

                  4 †   The deep | waters · of the | proud ‖ had gone | even | over · our | soul.

        f   5   But | praised · be the | Lord :
                          who hath not given us | over · for a | prey · unto their | teeth.

                  6   Our soul is escaped * even as a bird out of the | snare · of the | fowler :
                          the snare is | broken · and | we are · de|livered.

                  7   **2nd part** Our help standeth in the | Name · of the | Lord :
                          who hath | made | heaven · and | earth.

Full *f*   Glory be to the Father | and to · the | Son :
                          and | to the | Holy | Ghost.

Full   As it was in the beginning is | now and · ever | shall be :
                          world without | end. A | · · | men.

PSALM 125

C. H. Lloyd

Qui confidunt

Full	*mf*	1	They that put their trust in the Lord shall be even as the | mount | Sion :
			which may not be re|moved but | standeth · fast for | ever.
Full		2 ‡	The hills | stand about · Je|rusalem :
			even so standeth the Lord round about his people *
			from this time | – – | forth for · ever|more.
		3	For the rod of the ungodly cometh not into the | lot · of the | righteous :
			lest the | righteous · put their | hand · unto | wicked·ness.
		4 †	Do | well O | Lord ‖ unto | those · that are | good and · true of | heart.
		5	As for such as turn | back · unto their own | wickedness :
			the Lord shall lead them forth with the evil doers *
	dim.		but | peace shall | be up·on | Isra·el.
Full	*mp*		Glory be to the Father | and to · the | Son :
			and | to the | Holy | Ghost.
Full			As it was in the beginning is | now and · ever | shall be :
			world without | end. A | . . | men.

PSALM 126

G. M. Garrett

In convertendo

Full *f*	1	When the Lord turned again the cap|tivity • of | Sion :
			then were we | like • unto | them that | dream.
Full	2 ‡	Then was our | mouth • filled with | laughter :
			and our | tongue – | – with | joy.
mf	3	Then | said they a•mong the | heathen :
			The | Lord • hath done | great things | for them.
	4 ‡	Yea the Lord hath done | great things for • us al|ready :
			where|of – | – we re|joice.
mp	5 †‡	Turn our cap|tivity • O | Lord ‖ as the | – – | rivers • in the | south.
cresc.	6 †‡	They that | sow in | tears ‖ shall | reap – | – in | joy.
mp	7	**2nd part** He that now goeth on his way weeping *
			and | beareth forth • good | seed :
cresc.			shall doubtless come again with | joy and | bring his |
			sheaves with him.
Full *f*		Glory be to the Father | and to • the | Son :
			and | to the | Holy | Ghost.
Full		As it was in the beginning is | now and • ever | shall be :
			world without | end. A | • • | men.

PSALM 127

J. Goss

Nisi Dominus

Full *f*   1   Except the | Lord · build the | house :
> their | labour · is but | lost that | build it.

Full   2   Except the | Lord · keep the | city :
> the | watchman | waketh · but in | vain.

    mf   3   It is but lost labour that ye haste to rise up early and so late take rest *
and | eat the · bread of | carefulness :
> for so he | giveth · his be|loved | sleep.

     4 †   Lo children and the | fruit · of the | womb ‖ are an heritage and |
gift that | cometh · of the | Lord.

    f   5   Like as the arrows in the | hand · of the | giant :
> even | so · are the | young | children.

     6   Happy is the man that hath his | quiver | full of them :
> they shall not be ashamed when they speak with their |
> ene·mies | in the | gate.

Full   Glory be to the Father | and to · the | Son :
> and | to the | Holy | Ghost.

Full   As it was in the beginning is | now and · ever | shall be :
> world without | end. A | · · | men.

PSALM 128

J. Goss

Beati omnes

Full	*p*	1 †‡	Blessed are all | they that • fear the | Lord ‖ – | – and | walk in • his | ways.
Full		2	For thou shalt eat the | labours • of thine | hands :
			O | well is thee • and | happy • shalt thou | be.
	mp	3 †‡	Thy wife shall be as the | fruitful | vine ‖ – | – upon the | walls • of thine | house.
		4 †	Thy | children • like the | olive-‖branches | round a|bout thy | table.
		5 †	Lo | thus • shall the | man ‖ be | blessed • that | feareth • the | Lord.
	mf	6	The Lord from out of | Sion • shall so | bless thee :
			that thou shalt see Jerusalem in pro|speri•ty | all thy • life | long.
		7 ‡	**2nd part** Yea that thou shalt | see thy • children's | children :
	dim.		– | – and | peace up•on | Israel.
Full	*p*		Glory be to the Father | and to • the | Son :
			and | to the | Holy | Ghost.
Full			As it was in the beginning is | now and • ever | shall be :
			world without | end. A | . . | men.

PSALM 129

T. A. Walmisley

Sæpe expugnaverunt

Full   *f*   1 ‡   Many a time have they fought a|gainst me • from my youth | up :
                 may | – – | Israel • now | say.

Full   2   Yea many a time have they | vexed me • from my youth | up :
                 but they | have not • pre|vailed a|gainst me.

        mf   3 ‡   The plowers | plowed up•on my | back :
                 and | – – | made long | furrows.

               4 †   But the | righteous | Lord ‖ hath hewn the | snares of • the un|godly • in | pieces.

               5 ‡   Let them be con|founded • and turned | backward :
                 as many as have | – – | evil • will at | Sion.

               6   Let them be even as the grass | growing up•on the | house-tops :
                 which | withereth • a|fore it • be plucked | up.

               7   Whereof the mower | filleth • not his | hand :
                 neither he that | bindeth • up the | sheaves his | bosom.

               8   So that they who go by say not so much as The | Lord | prosper you :
                 we wish you good | luck • in the | Name • of the | Lord.

Full   *f*   Glory be to the Father | and to • the | Son :
                 and | to the | Holy | Ghost.

Full   As it was in the beginning is | now and • ever | shall be :
                 world without | end. A | . . | men.

PSALM 130

C. Macpherson

De profundis

Full *p* 1 ‡ Out of the deep have I | called unto · thee O | Lord :
– | – Lord | hear my | voice.

Full 2 † O let thine | ears con·sider | well ‖ the | voice of | my com|plaint.

3 If thou Lord wilt be extreme to | mark what is · done a|miss :
O | Lord | who may · a|bide it?

4 ‡ For there is | mercy · with | thee :
– | therefore | shalt thou · be | feared.

mp 5 ‡ I look for the Lord * my | soul doth | wait for him :
– | – in his | word · is my | trust.

6 My soul | fleeth · unto the | Lord :
before the morning watch I | say be|fore the · morning | watch.

mf 7 O Israel trust in the Lord * for with the | Lord · there is | mercy :
and with | him is | plenteous · re|demption.

dim. 8 † And he shall re|deem | Israel ‖ from | all | his | sins.

Full *p* Glory be to the Father | and to · the | Son :
and | to the | Holy | Ghost.

Full As it was in the beginning is | now and · ever | shall be :
world without | end. A | . . | men.

PSALM 131

J. L. Rogers

Domine, non est

Full *p* 1 ‡   Lord I am │ not high │ minded :
              – │ – I │ have no · proud │ looks.

Full   2 †   I do not │ exercise · my│self in ‖ great │ matters │ which are · too │ high for me.

          3   But I refrain my soul and keep it low *
              like as a child that is │ weaned · from his │ mother :
              yea my │ soul is · even │ as a · weaned │ child.

      mf   4 †   O Israel │ trust · in the │ Lord ‖ from this time │ forth for │ ever│more.

Full *mp*   Glory be to the Father │ and to · the │ Son :
              and │ to the │ Holy │ Ghost.

Full   As it was in the beginning is │ now and · ever │ shall be :
              world without │ end. A │ . . │ men.

PSALM 132

J. H. Maunder

Memento, Domine

Full *mf*   1 †‡   Lord re|member | David ‖ – | – and | all his | trouble;

Full   2   How he | sware • unto the | Lord :
             and vowed a | vow • unto the Al|mighty • God of | Jacob;

             3   I will not come within the | tabernacle • of mine | house :
             nor | climb up | into • my | bed;

             4   I will not suffer mine eyes to sleep nor mine | eyelids • to | slumber :
             neither the temples of my | head to | take • any | rest;

             5   ⟦**2nd part**⟧ Until I find out a place for the | temple • of the | Lord :
             an habi|tation • for the | mighty • God of | Jacob.

             6 ‡   Lo we heard of the | same at | Ephrata :
             – | – and | found it • in the | wood.

             7   We will | go • into his | tabernacle :
             and fall | low • on our | knees be•fore his | footstool.

change chant (Full)

E. Edwards

Full *f*   8 ‡   Arise O | Lord • into thy | resting-place :
             – | thou • and the | ark • of thy | strength.

Full   9 ‡   Let thy | priests be • clothed with | righteousness :
             – | – and let thy | saints • sing with | joyfulness.

Psalm 132, continued

E. Edwards

mf   10   For thy | servant | David's sake :
                turn not away the | presence · of | thine a|nointed.

          11 ‡ The Lord hath made a faithful | oath · unto | David :
                – | – and he | shall not | shrink from it;

          12 †‡ Of the | fruit · of thy | body ‖ – | – shall I | set up·on thy | seat.

          13   If thy children will keep my covenant *
                and my | testimonies that · I shall | learn them :
                their children also shall | sit up·on thy | seat for · ever|more.

mp   14 ‡ For the Lord hath chosen Sion to be an habi|tation · for him|self :
                – | – he hath | longed for | her.

          15   This shall be my | rest for | ever :
                here will I | dwell for · I | have a · de|light therein.

mf   16   I will bless her | victuals · with | increase :
                and will | satisfy · her | poor with | bread.

          17   I will deck her | priests with | health :
                and her | saints shall · re|joice and | sing.

f   18   There shall I make the horn of | David · to | flourish :
                I have ordained a | lantern · for | mine A|nointed.

          19   As for his enemies I shall | clothe them · with | shame :
                but upon him|self shall · his | crown | flourish.

Full f   Glory be to the Father | and to · the | Son :
               and | to the | Holy | Ghost.

Full   As it was in the beginning is | now and · ever | shall be :
               world without | end. A | . . | men.

PSALM 133

Donald Mossman

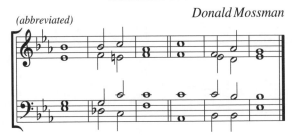

Ecce, quam bonum!

Full   *mf*   1   Behold how good and | joyful · a | thing it is :
                 brethren to dwell to|gether · in | unity!

Full   2   It is like the precious ointment upon the head *
                 that ran | down · unto the | beard :
                     even unto Aaron's beard * and went down to the |
                     skirts · of his | clothing.

             3   Like as the | dew of | Hermon :
                 which fell upon the | hill of | Sion.

       mp   4   For there the Lord | promised · his | blessing :
                 and | life for · ever|more.

Full   *mf*   Glory be to the Father | and to · the | Son :
                 and to the | Holy | Ghost.

Full   As it was in the beginning is | now and · ever | shall be :
                 world without | end. A|men.

PSALM 134

J. Turle

Ecce nunc

Full *f*   1 ‡   Be|hold now · praise the | Lord :
                         all ye | – – | servants · of the | Lord.

Full   2   Ye that by night stand in the | house · of the | Lord :
                         even in the | courts of · the | house · of our | God.

Full   3 ‡   Lift up your | hands · in the | sanctuary :
                         and | – – | praise the | Lord.

Full   4   The Lord that made | heaven · and | earth :
                         give thee | blessing | out of | Sion.

Full   Glory be to the Father | and to · the | Son :
                         and | to the | Holy | Ghost.

Full   As it was in the beginning is | now and · ever | shall be :
                         world without | end. A | . . | men.

PSALM 135

G. J. Elvey

Laudate Nomen

Full *f*   1 ‡   O praise the Lord * laud ye the | Name · of the | Lord :
      – | praise it · O ye | servants · of the | Lord;

Full   2   Ye that stand in the | house · of the | Lord :
      in the | courts of · the | house · of our | God.

   3   O praise the Lord for the | Lord is | gracious :
      O sing | praises · unto his | Name for · it is | lovely.

   4   For why? * the Lord hath chosen | Jacob · unto him|self :
      and | Israel · for his | own pos|session.

mf   5   For I know that the | Lord is | great :
      and that our | Lord · is a|bove | all gods.

   6   Whatsoever the Lord pleased * that did he in | heaven · and in | earth :
      and in the | sea · and in | all deep | places.

f   7   He bringeth forth the clouds from the | ends · of the | world :
      and sendeth forth lightnings with the rain * |
      bringing the · winds | out of · his | treasures.

   8 ‡   He smote the | first-born · of | Egypt :
      both of | – – | man and | beast.

mf   9   He hath sent tokens and wonders into the midst of thee O thou | land of | Egypt :
      upon | Pharaoh · and | all his | servants.

   10 †‡   He smote | divers | nations ‖ and | – – | slew · mighty | kings;

   11 ‡   Sehon king of the Amorites * and | Og the · king of | Basan :
      – | and all · the | kingdoms · of | Canaan;

   12   And gave their | land to · be an | heritage :
      even an | heritage · unto | Israel · his | people.

Psalm 135, continued

G. J. Elvey

_f_ 13   Thy Name O Lord en|dureth · for | ever :
              so doth thy memorial O Lord from | one · gene|ration · to an|other.

     14   For the Lord will a|venge his | people :
              and be | gracious | unto · his | servants.

_mf_ 15 ‡ As for the images of the heathen * they are but | silver · and | gold :
              – | – the | work of · men's | hands.

     16 † They have | mouths and | speak ‖ not * | eyes · have they | but they | see not.

     17   They have | ears and · yet they | hear not :
              neither is there | any | breath · in their | mouths.

     18   They that | make them · are | like unto them :
              and so are | all · they that | put their | trust in them.

Full f 19   Praise the | Lord ye · house of | Israel :
              praise the | Lord ye | house of | Aaron.

Full 20   Praise the | Lord ye · house of | Levi :
              ye that | fear the · Lord | praise the | Lord.

Full 21 ‡ **2nd part** Praised be the | Lord · out of | Sion :
              who | – – | dwelleth · at Je|rusalem.

Full   Glory be to the Father | and to · the | Son :
              and | to the | Holy | Ghost.

Full   As it was in the beginning is | now and · ever | shall be :
              world without | end. A | . . | men.

PSALM 136

Jonathan Bielby

Confitemini

Full *f*	1	O give thanks unto the | Lord for • he is | gracious :
		and his | mercy • en|dureth • for | ever.
Full	2	O give thanks unto the | God of | all gods :
		for his | mercy • en|dureth • for | ever.
Full	3	O thank the | Lord of | all lords :
		for his | mercy • en|dureth • for | ever.
mf	4	Who only | doeth • great | wonders :
		for his | mercy • en|dureth • for | ever.
	5	Who by his excellent | wisdom • made the | heavens :
		for his | mercy • en|dureth • for | ever.
	6	Who laid out the | earth a•bove the | waters :
		for his | mercy • en|dureth • for | ever.
mp	7	Who hath | made great | lights :
		for his | mercy • en|dureth • for | ever.
	8	The | sun to • rule the | day :
		for his | mercy • en|dureth • for | ever;
	9	The moon and the stars to | govern • the | night :
		for his | mercy • en|dureth • for | ever.

Psalm 136, continued

Jonathan Bielby

mf   10   Who smote | Egypt · with their | first-born :
for his | mercy · en|dureth · for | ever;

11   And brought out | Israel · from a|mong them :
for his | mercy · en|dureth · for | ever;

12   With a mighty | hand and · stretched out | arm :
for his | mercy · en|dureth · for | ever.

f   13   Who divided the Red | sea in · two | parts :
for his | mercy · en|dureth · for | ever;

14   And made Israel to | go · through the | midst of it :
for his | mercy · en|dureth · for | ever.

15   But as for Pharaoh and his host * he over|threw them · in the Red | sea :
for his | mercy · en|dureth · for | ever.

mf   16   Who led his | people · through the | wilderness :
for his | mercy · en|dureth · for | ever.

17   Who | smote great | kings :
for his | mercy · en|dureth · for | ever;

18   Yea and | slew · mighty | kings :
for his | mercy · en|dureth · for | ever;

Psalm 136, *continued*

Jonathan Bielby

19   Sehon | king • of the | Amorites :
              for his | mercy • en|dureth • for | ever;

20   And | Og the • king of | Basan :
              for his | mercy • en|dureth • for | ever;

21   And gave away their | land • for an | heritage :
              for his | mercy • en|dureth • for | ever;

mp   22   Even for an heritage unto | Israel • his | servant :
              for his | mercy • en|dureth • for | ever.

23   Who remembered us | when we • were in | trouble :
              for his | mercy • en|dureth • for | ever;

cresc.   24   And hath de|livered us • from our | enemies :
              for his | mercy • en|dureth • for | ever.

f   25   Who giveth | food to • all | flesh :
              for his | mercy • en|dureth • for | ever.

26   O give thanks unto the | God of | heaven :
              for his | mercy • en|dureth • for | ever.

27   O give thanks unto the | Lord of | lords :
              for his | mercy • en|dureth • for | ever.

Psalm 136, continued

Jonathan Bielby

Full *f*

Glory be to the Father | and to · the | Son :
and | to the | Holy | Ghost.

Full

As it was in the beginning is | now and · ever | shall be :
world without | end. A | . . | men.

PSALM 137

C. S. Lang

Super flumina

Full *p*   1   By the waters of Babylon we sat | down and | wept :
            when we re|membered | thee O | Sion.

Full   2 †   As for our | harps we | hanged ‖ them | up up·on the | trees that · are there|in.

       3   For they that led us away captive required of us then a song *
          and | melody · in our | heavi·ness :
            Sing us | one of · the | songs of | Sion.

       4 †‡   How shall we | – – | sing the ‖ Lord's | song · in a | strange | land?

mp   5   If I for|get thee · O Je|rusa·lem :
          let my | right hand · for|get her | cunning.

       6   If I do not remember thee * let my tongue cleave to the | roof · of my | mouth :
          yea if I pre|fer not · Je|rusalem · in my | mirth.

Psalm 137, continued

C. S. Lang

7 §   Remember the children of Edom O Lord in the | day of · Je|rusa·lem :
       how they said Down with it | down with · it | even · to the | ground.

8 §   O daughter of Babylon | wasted · with | misery :
       yea happy shall he be that re|wardeth thee · as | thou hast | served us.

9 §†   **2nd part** Blessed shall he be that | taketh · thy | children ‖
       and | throweth them · a|gainst the | stones.

Full   p   Glory be to the Father | and to · the | Son :
               and | to the | Holy | Ghost.

Full   As it was in the beginning is | now and · ever | shall be :
               world without | end. A | . . | men.

PSALM 138

J. Turle

Confitebor tibi

Full   f   1   I will give thanks unto thee O | Lord with my · whole | heart :
                    even before the | gods will · I sing | praise · unto | thee.

Full   2   I will worship toward thy holy temple and praise thy Name *
                    because of thy loving | kindness · and | truth :
                        for thou hast magnified thy | Name · and thy | Word a·bove | all things.

§ Omitted in the St Paul's Cathedral use

Psalm 138, continued

J. Turle

v. 5 & Gloria

mf 3 When I | called upon • thee thou | heardest me :
and en|duedst • my | soul with • much | strength.

4 All the kings of the earth shall | praise thee • O | Lord :
for they have | heard the | words • of thy | mouth.

f 5 Yea they shall sing in the | ways • of the | Lord :
that | great is • the | glory • of the | Lord.

mf 6 For though the Lord be high * yet hath he re|spect • unto the | lowly :
as for the proud he be|holdeth | them a•far | off.

mp cresc. 7 Though I walk in the midst of trouble * | yet shalt • thou re|fresh me :
thou shalt stretch forth thy hand upon the furiousness of mine |
enemies * and thy | right hand • shall | save me.

Full mf 8 The Lord shall make good his loving-|kindness • to|ward me :
yea thy mercy O Lord endureth for ever *
despise not then the | works • of thine | own | hands.

Full f Glory be to the Father | and to • the | Son :
and | to the | Holy | Ghost.

Full As it was in the beginning is | now and • ever | shall be :
world without | end. A | • • | men.

PSALM 139

E. F. Day

Domine, probasti

Full *mp* 1 O Lord thou hast │ searched me out • and │ known me :
　　　　　　　　thou knowest my down-sitting and mine up-rising *
　　　　　　　　thou under│standest • my │ thoughts • long be│fore.

Full 2 ‡ Thou art about my │ path and a•bout my │ bed :
　　　　　　　　– │ – and │ spiest out • all my │ ways.

3 For lo there is not a │ word • in my │ tongue :
　　　　　　　　but │ thou O • Lord │ knowest it • alto│gether.

4 ‡ Thou hast fashioned me be│hind • and be│fore :
　　　　　　　　– │ – and laid thine │ hand up│on me.

5 │2nd part│ Such knowledge is too wonderful and │ excel•lent │ for me :
　　　　　　　　I │ cannot • at│tain │ unto it.

p 6 Whither shall I │ go then • from thy │ Spirit :
　　　　　　　　or │ whither • shall I │ go then • from thy │ presence?

7 If I climb up into │ heaven • thou art │ there :
　　　　　　　　if I go down to │ hell • thou art │ there │ also.

mp 8 If I take the │ wings • of the │ morning :
　　　　　　　　and remain in the │ utter•most │ parts • of the │ sea;

9 ‡ Even there │ also shall • thy hand │ lead me :
　　　　　　　　– │ – and thy │ right hand • shall │ hold me.

10 ‡ If I say Peradventure the │ darkness • shall │ cover me :
cresc.　　　　　　– │ then shall • my │ night be • turned to │ day.

mf 11 Yea the darkness is no darkness with thee *
　　　　but the night is as │ clear • as the │ day :
　　　　　　　the darkness and │ light to │ thee are • both a│like.

Psalm 139, *continued*

E. F. Day

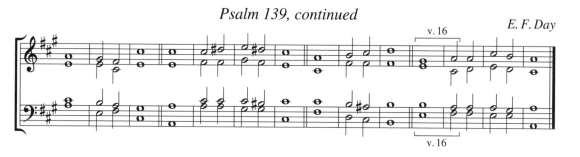

mp	12	For my | reins are | thine :
		thou hast | covered me • in my | mother's | womb.
mf	13	I will give thanks unto thee * for I am fearfully and | wonderful•ly | made :
		marvellous are thy works * and | that my | soul • knoweth right | well.
mp	14	My | bones • are not | hid from thee :
		though I be made secretly and | fashioned • be|neath • in the | earth.
	15	Thine eyes did see my substance yet | being • un|perfect :
		and in thy | book were | all my • members | written;
	16 ‡	**2nd part** Which | day by day • were | fashioned :
		– | – when as | yet • there was | none of them.

change chant (Decani)

J. Soaper

Dec.	*mf*	17 ‡	How dear are thy counsels | unto me • O | God :
			– | – O how | great • is the | sum of them!
		18	If I tell them * they are more in | number • than the | sand :
			when I wake | up • I am | present • with | thee.

	19 §	Wilt thou not slay the | wicked • O | God :
		de|part from me • ye | blood•thirsty | men.
	20 §	For they speak un|righteously • a|gainst thee :
		and thine | enemies • take thy | Name in | vain.

§ *Omitted in the St Paul's Cathedral use*

Psalm 139, continued

J. Soaper

21 §   Do not I hate them O │ Lord that • hate │ thee :
         and am not I grieved with │ those that │ rise up • a│gainst thee?

22 §‡   Yea I │ hate them • right │ sore :
         – │ – even as │ though they • were mine │ enemies.

23 ‡   Try me O God and seek the │ ground • of my │ heart.
         – │ prove me • and ex│amine • my │ thoughts.

24   Look well if there be any way of │ wicked•ness │ in me :
         and │ lead me • in the │ way • ever│lasting.

Full   f   Glory be to the Father │ and to • the │ Son :
         and │ to the │ Holy │ Ghost.

Full   As it was in the beginning is │ now and • ever │ shall be :
         world without │ end. A │ . . │ men.

PSALM 140

M. Camidge

Eripe me, Domine

Full   mf   1 ‡   Deliver me O │ Lord • from the │ evil man :
                 – │ – and pre│serve me • from the │ wicked man.

Full   2 ‡   Who imagine │ mischief • in their │ hearts :
                 and stir up │ – – │ strife • all the day │ long.

§ *Omitted in the St Paul's Cathedral use*

Psalm 140, *continued*

M. Camidge

mp   3   They have sharpened their | tongues • like a | serpent :
                    adder's | poison • is | under • their | lips.

        4   Keep me O Lord from the | hands of the • un|godly :
                    preserve me from the wicked men who are | purposed • to |
                    over•throw my | goings.

mf   5 ‡   The proud have laid a snare for me and spread a | net abroad • with | cords :
                    – | yea and • set | traps • in my | way.

        6   I said unto the Lord | Thou art • my | God :
                    hear the | voice • of my | prayers O | Lord.

        7   O Lord God thou | strength • of my | health :
                    thou hast covered my | head • in the | day of | battle.

        8   Let not the ungodly have his de|sire O | Lord :
                    let not his mischievous imagination | prosper • lest they | be too | proud.

        9 §†   Let the | mischief • of their own | lips ‖ fall upon the | head of • them that |
                    compass me • a|bout.

      10 §   Let hot burning | coals • fall up|on them :
                    let them be cast into the fire and into the pit that they |
                    never | rise up • a|gain.

      11   **2nd part**   A man full of words shall not | prosper up•on the | earth :
                    evil shall hunt the wicked | person • to | over|throw him.

change chant (Decani)

§ Omitted in the St Paul's Cathedral use

Psalm 140, continued

G. J. Elvey (after M. Camidge)

Dec.   *mf*   12   Sure I am that the | Lord will a‧venge the | poor :
                     and main|tain the | cause ‧ of the | helpless.

                 13   The righteous also shall give | thanks ‧ unto thy | Name :
                     and the | just ‧ shall con|tinue ‧ in thy | sight.

Full   *f*   Glory be to the Father | and to ‧ the | Son :
                     and | to the | Holy | Ghost.

Full   As it was in the beginning is | now and ‧ ever | shall be :
                     world without | end. A | ‧‧ | men.

PSALM 141

John Bertalot

Domine, clamavi

Full   *mp*   1   Lord I call upon thee | haste thee | unto me :
                     and con|sider ‧ my | voice ‧ when I | cry unto thee.

Full   2   Let my prayer be set forth in thy | sight ‧ as the | incense :
                     and let the lifting up of my | hands ‧ be an | evening | sacrifice.

                 3 ‡   Set a watch O | Lord be‧fore my | mouth :
                     – | – and keep the | door ‧ of my | lips.

                 4   O let not mine heart be in|clined to ‧ any | evil thing :
                     let me not be occupied in ungodly works with the men that work
                     wickedness * lest I | eat of ‧ such | things as | please them.

Psalm 141, continued

John Bertalot

mf   5 †‡   Let the righteous rather │ smite me │ friendly ‖ – │ – – │ and re│prove me.

      6   But let not their precious │ balms • break my │ head :
                  yea I will │ pray yet • a│gainst their │ wickedness.

      7 §   Let their judges be over│thrown in • stony │ places :
                  that they may │ hear my │ words for • they are │ sweet.

      8 §   Our bones lie │ scattered be•fore the │ pit :
                  like as when one │ breaketh and • heweth │ wood up•on the │ earth.

      9   But mine eyes look unto │ thee O • Lord │ God :
                  in thee is my │ trust * O │ cast not • out my │ soul.

     10   Keep me from the │ snare that • they have │ laid for me :
                  and from the │ traps • of the │ wicked │ doers.

     11   **2nd** Let the ungodly fall into their │ own • nets to│gether :
           part and │ let me │ ever • es│cape them.

Full   *mp*   Glory be to the Father │ and to • the │ Son :
                  and │ to the │ Holy │ Ghost.

Full   As it was in the beginning is │ now and • ever │ shall be :
                  world without │ end. A │ • • │ men.

§ Omitted in the St Paul's Cathedral use

PSALM 142

C. Hylton Stewart

Voce mea ad Dominum

Full *p*   1   I cried unto the | Lord • with my | voice :
     yea even unto the | Lord • did I | make my • suppli|cation.

Full   2 ‡   I poured out my com|plaints be|fore him :
     and | – – | shewed him • of my | trouble.

   3   When my spirit was in heaviness thou | knewest • my | path :
     in the way wherein I walked have they | privi•ly | laid a | snare for me.

   4 ‡   I looked also up|on my | right hand :
     and saw there was | – – | no man • that would | know me.

pp   5   I had | no place • to | flee unto :
     and | no man | cared • for my | soul.

mp   6   I cried unto | thee O • Lord and | said :
     Thou art my hope and my | portion • in the | land • of the | living.

p   7 ‡   **2nd part** Con|sider • my com|plaint :
     for I am | – – | brought • very | low.

mp   8 ‡   O de|liver me • from my | persecutors :
     – | – for | they are • too | strong for me.

mf   9   Bring my soul out of prison * that I may give | thanks • unto thy | Name :
     which thing if thou wilt grant me *
     then shall the | righteous • re|sort • unto my | company.

Full *mp*   Glory be to the Father | and to • the | Son :
     and | to the | Holy | Ghost.

Full   As it was in the beginning is | now and • ever | shall be :
     world without | end. A | . . | men.

PSALM 143

F. A. J. Hervey

Domine, exaudi

Full *p* 1 Hear my prayer O Lord and con|sider • my de|sire :
    hearken unto me for thy | truth and | righteous•ness' | sake.

Full 2 And enter not into | judgement • with thy | servant :
    for in thy sight shall | no man | living • be | justified.

pp 3 For the enemy hath persecuted my soul *
he hath smitten my life | down • to the | ground :
    he hath laid me in the darkness as the | men that • have been | long | dead.

4 Therefore is my | spirit • vexed with|in me :
    and my | heart with|in me • is | desolate.

p 5 Yet do I remember the time past * I | muse upon • all thy | works :
    yea I exercise my|self • in the | works • of thy | hands.

mp 6 I stretch forth my | hands • unto | thee :
    my soul gaspeth unto | thee • as a | thirsty | land.

p 7 Hear me O Lord and that soon * for my | spirit • waxeth | faint :
hide not thy face from me *
lest I be like unto | them • that go | down • into the | pit.

mp 8 O let me hear thy loving-kindness betimes in the morning *
for in | thee • is my | trust :
shew thou me the way that I should walk in *
for I | lift up • my | soul • unto | thee.

mf 9 Deliver me O | Lord • from mine | enemies :
for I | flee • unto | thee to | hide me.

10 Teach me to do the thing that pleaseth thee * for | thou • art my | God :
    let thy loving Spirit lead me | forth • into the | land of | righteousness.

Psalm 143, continued

F. A. J. Hervey

f   11   **2nd part**   Quicken me O | Lord · for thy | Name's sake :
                            and for thy righteousness' sake | bring my | soul · out of | trouble.

       12 §   And of thy | goodness · slay mine | enemies :
                            and destroy all them that vex my | soul for | I am · thy | servant.

Full f   Glory be to the Father | and to · the | Son :
                            and | to the | Holy | Ghost.

Full   As it was in the beginning is | now and · ever | shall be :
                            world without | end. A | . . | men.

When v.12 is sung, v.11 should be sung to the first part of the chant, and v.12 to the second part.

§ Omitted in the St Paul's Cathedral use

PSALM 144

E. G. Monk

Benedictus Dominus

Full *f*   1   Blessed be the | Lord my | strength :
      who teacheth my hands to | war • and my | fingers • to | fight;

Full   2   My hope and my fortress my castle and deliverer *
      my de|fender in • whom I | trust :
      who sub|dueth • my | people • that is | under me.

mf   3   Lord what is man that | thou hast • such re|spect unto him :
      or the | son of man • that thou | so re|gardest him?

mp   4   Man is like a | thing of | nought :
      his time | passeth • a|way • like a | shadow.

mf   5   Bow thy heavens O | Lord • and come | down :
      touch the | mountains • and | they shall | smoke.

   6 ‡   Cast forth thy | lightning • and | tear them :
      shoot out thine | arrows – | – and con|sume them.

   7   Send down thine | hand • from a|bove :
      deliver me and take me out of the great waters * |
      from the | hand of • strange | children;

   8   Whose mouth | talketh • of | vanity :
      and their | right hand • is a | right hand • of | wickedness.

f   9   I will sing a new song unto | thee O | God :
      and sing praises unto | thee up•on a | ten-stringed | lute.

   10   Thou hast given | victory • unto | kings :
      and hast delivered David thy | servant • from the | peril • of the | sword.

Psalm 144, *continued*

E. G. Monk

mf   11 Save me and deliver me from the | hand of · strange | children :
              whose mouth talketh of vanity *
              and their | right hand · is a | right hand · of in|iquity.

      12 That our sons may grow up | as the · young | plants :
              and that our daughters may be as the | polished | corners · of the | temple.

      13 That our garners may be full and plenteous with all | manner · of | store :
              that our sheep may bring forth | thousands · and ten |
              thousands · in our | streets.

      14 That our oxen may be strong to labour * that there be | no de|cay :
              no leading into captivity * and no com|plaining | in our | streets.

f   15 2nd part Happy are the | people that · are in | such a case :
                  yea blessed are the | people who · have the | Lord · for their | God.

Full   Glory be to the Father | and to · the | Son :
              and | to the | Holy | Ghost.

Full   As it was in the beginning is | now and · ever | shall be :
              world without | end. A | . . | men.

PSALM 145

T. Hanforth

Exaltabo te, Deus

Full	*f*	1	I will magnify thee O │ God my │ King :
			and I will praise thy │ Name for │ ever • and │ ever.
Full		2	Every day will I give │ thanks • unto │ thee :
			and praise thy │ Name for │ ever • and │ ever.
	mf	3 ‡	Great is the Lord * and marvellous │ worthy • to be │ praised :
			– │ there is • no │ end • of his │ greatness.
		4 ‡	One generation shall praise thy │ works • unto an│other :
			– │ – and de│clare thy │ power.
	f	5	As for me I will be │ talking of • thy │ worship :
			thy │ glory • thy │ praise and • wondrous │ works;
		6	So that men shall speak of the might of thy │ marvel•lous │ acts :
			and I will │ also │ tell of • thy │ greatness.
	mf	7	**2nd part** The memorial of thine abundant │ kindness • shall be │ shewed :
			and │ men shall │ sing of • thy │ righteousness.
	mp	8	The Lord is │ gracious • and │ merciful :
			long-│suffer•ing │ and of • great │ goodness.
		9	The Lord is │ loving • unto │ every man :
			and his │ mercy • is │ over • all his │ works.
	mf	10	All thy works │ praise thee • O │ Lord :
			and thy │ saints give │ thanks • unto │ thee.
		11 ‡	They shew the │ glory • of thy │ kingdom :
			– │ – and │ talk of • thy │ power;
	f	12 ‡	That thy power thy glory and │ mightiness • of thy │ kingdom :
			– │ might be │ known • unto │ men.

Psalm 145, continued

T. Hanforth

		13	Thy kingdom is an ever|lasting | kingdom :
			and thy do|minion • en|dureth through•out all | ages.
		14	**2nd part** The Lord upholdeth | all • such as | fall :
			and lifteth | up all | those • that are | down.
mp		15	The eyes of all | wait upon • thee O | Lord :
			and thou | givest them • their | meat in • due | season.
mf		16	Thou | openest • thine | hand :
			and | fillest • all things | living • with | plenteousness.
p		17	The Lord is | righteous in • all his | ways :
			and | holy • in | all his | works.
		18	The Lord is nigh unto | all them • that | call upon him :
			yea | all • such as | call up•on him | faithfully.
mp		19	He will fulfil the de|sire of • them that | fear him :
			he also will | hear their | cry • and will | help them.
		20	The Lord pre|serveth • all them that | love him :
mf			but | scattereth • a|broad • all the un|godly.
Full	*f*	21	**2nd part** My mouth shall speak the | praise • of the | Lord :
			and let all flesh give thanks unto his holy | Name for |
			ever • and | ever.
Full	*f*		Glory be to the Father | and to • the | Son :
			and | to the | Holy | Ghost.
Full			As it was in the beginning is | now and • ever | shall be :
			world without | end. A | . . | men.

PSALM 146

E. G. Monk

Lauda, anima mea

Full *f*   1   Praise the Lord O my soul * while I | live will I · praise the | Lord :
                  yea as long as I have any being I will sing | praises | unto · my | God.

Full   2 ‡   O put not your trust in princes * nor in | any · child of | man :
                  – | – for there | is no | help in them.

     mf   3   For when the breath of man goeth forth he shall turn a|gain · to his | earth :
                  and | then · all his | thoughts | perish.

              4   Blessed is he that hath the God of | Jacob · for his | help :
                  and whose | hope is · in the | Lord his | God;

              5   Who made heaven and earth * the sea and | all that · therein | is :
                  who | keepeth · his | promise · for | ever;

              6 ‡   Who helpeth them to | right that · suffer | wrong :
                  – | – who | feedeth · the | hungry.

     mp   7   The Lord looseth | men · out of | prison :
                  the | Lord · giveth | sight · to the | blind.

              8 ‡   The Lord helpeth | them · that are | fallen :
                  – | – the Lord | careth · for the | righteous.

              9   The Lord careth for the strangers * he defendeth the | fatherless · and | widow :
     mf   as for the way of the un|godly · he | turneth it · upside | down.

     f   10 ‡   The Lord thy God O Sion shall be | King for · ever|more :
                  – | – and through|out all · gene|rations.

Full *f*   Glory be to the Father | and to · the | Son :
                  and | to the | Holy | Ghost.

Full   As it was in the beginning is | now and · ever | shall be :
                  world without | end. A | . . | men.

Day 30: Evening

PSALM 147

C. V. Stanford

Laudate Dominum

Full	*f*	1	O praise the Lord * for it is a good thing to sing │ praises • unto our │ God :
			yea a joyful and pleasant │ thing it │ is • to be │ thankful.
Full		2	The Lord doth │ build up • Je│rusalem :
			and gather to│gether • the │ outcasts • of │ Israel.
	mf	3	He healeth those that are │ broken • in │ heart :
			and giveth │ medicine • to │ heal their │ sickness.
		4	He telleth the │ number • of the │ stars :
			and │ calleth • them │ all • by their │ names.
	f	5 ‡	Great is our Lord and │ great • is his │ power :
			yea and his │ – – │ wisdom • is │ infinite.
		6	The Lord │ setteth up • the │ meek :
			and bringeth the un│godly │ down • to the │ ground.
		7 ‡	O sing unto the │ Lord with │ thanksgiving :
			sing praises upon the │ – – │ harp • unto our │ God;
	mf	8	Who covereth the heaven with clouds * and prepareth │ rain • for the │ earth :
			and maketh the grass to grow upon the mountains *
			and │ herb • for the │ use of │ men;
		9	Who giveth │ fodder • unto the │ cattle :
			and feedeth the young │ ravens • that │ call up│on him.
	mp	10	He hath no pleasure in the │ strength • of an │ horse :
			neither de│lighteth • he in │ any • man's │ legs.

Psalm 147, continued

C. V. Stanford

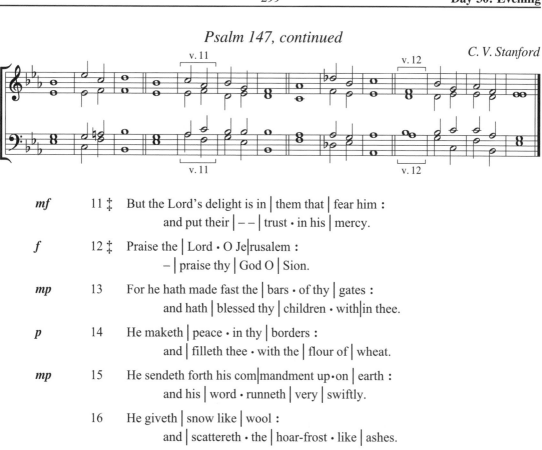

11 ‡   But the Lord's delight is in │ them that │ fear him :
        and put their │ – – │ trust • in his │ mercy.

f   12 ‡   Praise the │ Lord • O Je│rusalem :
        – │ praise thy │ God O │ Sion.

mp   13   For he hath made fast the │ bars • of thy │ gates :
        and hath │ blessed thy │ children • with│in thee.

p   14   He maketh │ peace • in thy │ borders :
        and │ filleth thee • with the │ flour of │ wheat.

mp   15   He sendeth forth his com│mandment up•on │ earth :
        and his │ word • runneth │ very │ swiftly.

16   He giveth │ snow like │ wool :
        and │ scattereth • the │ hoar-frost • like │ ashes.

17   He casteth forth his │ ice like │ morsels :
        who is │ able • to a│bide his │ frost?

mf   18   He sendeth out his │ word and │ melteth them :
        he bloweth with his │ wind • and the │ waters │ flow.

f   19   He sheweth his │ word • unto │ Jacob :
        his │ statutes • and │ ordinances • unto │ Israel.

20   He hath not dealt │ so with • any │ nation :
        neither have the │ heathen │ knowledge • of his │ laws.

Full   Glory be to the Father │ and to • the │ Son :
        and │ to the │ Holy │ Ghost.

Full   As it was in the beginning is │ now and • ever │ shall be :
        world without │ end. A │ . . │ men.

PSALM 148

David Willcocks

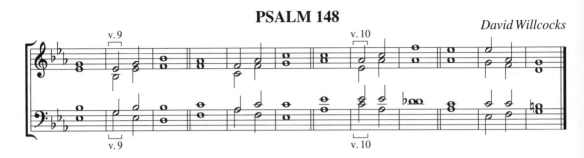

Laudate Dominum

Full   *f*   1   O praise the | Lord of | heaven :
          praise him | in the | height.

Full   2   Praise him all ye | angels • of | his :
          praise him | all his | host.

        3   Praise him | sun and | moon :
          praise him | all ye • stars and | light.

        4   Praise him | all ye | heavens :
          and ye waters that | are a•bove the | heavens.

        5   Let them praise the | Name • of the | Lord :
          for he spake the word and they were made *
          he commanded and | they were • cre|ated.

        6   He hath made them fast for | ever • and | ever :
          he hath given them a law which | shall not • be | broken.

        7   Praise the | Lord up•on | earth :
          ye | dragons and • all | deeps;

        8   Fire and | hail • snow and | vapours :
          wind and storm ful|filling • his | word;

mf   9 ‡   Mountains and | – all | hills :
          fruitful | trees and • all | cedars;

     10 ‡   Beasts and | – all | cattle :
          worms and | feathered | fowls;

Psalm 148, continued

David Willcocks

f   11   Kings of the | earth and · all | people :
                    princes and all | judges · of the | world;

           12   Young men and maidens *
                    old men and children praise the | Name · of the | Lord :
                    for his Name only is excellent *
                    and his praise above | heaven and | earth.

Full   13   **2nd part**   He shall exalt the horn of his people * | all his · saints shall | praise him :
                        even the children of Israel * even the | people · that | serveth him.

David Willcocks

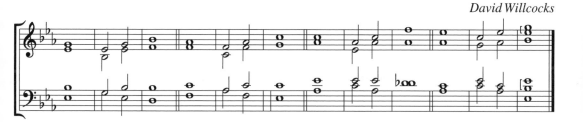

Full   Glory be to the Father | and to · the | Son :
                     and to the | Holy | Ghost.

Full   As it was in the beginning is | now and · ever | shall be :
                     world without | end. A|men.

PSALM 149

C. V. Stanford

Cantate Domino

Full	*f*	1	O sing unto the | Lord a · new | song : let the congre|gation · of | saints | praise him.
Full		2	Let Israel re|joice in · him that | made him : and let the children of | Sion · be | joyful · in their | King.
	mf	3	Let them praise his | Name · in the | dance : let them sing praises | unto him · with | tabret · and | harp.
		4 ‡	For the Lord hath | pleasure · in his | people : – | – and | helpeth the · meek-|hearted.
	f	5 ‡	Let the saints be | joyful · with | glory : – | let them · re|joice · in their | beds.
		6	Let the praises of | God be · in their | mouth : and a | two-edged | sword · in their | hands;
	mf	7 ‡	To be a|venged · of the | heathen : – | and to · re|buke the | people;
		8	To bind their | kings in | chains : and their | nobles · with | links of | iron.
		9	**2nd part** That they may be avenged of them | as it · is | written : Such | honour · have | all his | saints.
Full	*f*		Glory be to the Father | and to · the | Son : and | to the | Holy | Ghost.
Full			As it was in the beginning is | now and · ever | shall be : world without | end. A | . . | men.

PSALM 150

Laudate Dominum

C. V. Stanford

6. Let every thing that hath breath : _ praise _____ the Lord. _____

Glory be to the Father and to the Son : ___ and to the Ho - ly Ghost :

As it was in the beginning is now and ever shall be : world without end __ A - - - men.

PSALM 150

G. S. Talbot

Laudate Dominum

Full *f* 1 O praise | God · in his | holiness :
　　　　　　praise him in the | firma·ment | of his | power.

Full 2 Praise him in his | noble | acts :
　　　　　　praise him ac|cording · to his | excel·lent | greatness.

3 Praise him in the | sound · of the | trumpet :
　　　　　　praise him up|on the | lute and | harp.

4 Praise him in the | cymbals · and | dances :
　　　　　　praise him up|on the | strings and | pipe.

5 Praise him upon the | well-tuned | cymbals :
　　　　　　praise him up|on the | loud | cymbals.

Full 6 Let | everything · that hath | breath :
　　　　　　praise | . . | . the | Lord.

Full Glory be to the Father | and to · the | Son :
　　　　　　and | to the | Holy | Ghost.

Full As it was in the beginning is | now and · ever | shall be :
　　　　　　world without | end. A | . . | men.

Morning Canticles

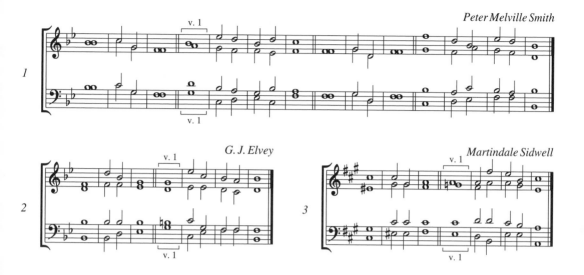

Peter Melville Smith

G. J. Elvey

Martindale Sidwell

Easter Anthems

Full *f* 1 ‡ Christ our passover is | sacri·ficed | for us :
– | therefore · let us | keep the | feast;

Full 2 Not with the old leaven * nor with the leaven of | malice · and | wickedness :
but with the unleavened | bread · of sin|cerity · and | truth.

3 Christ being raised from the dead | dieth · no | more :
death hath no | more do|min·ion | over him.

mf 4 For in that he died he died unto | sin | once :
f but in that he | liveth · he | liveth · unto | God.

mf 5 Likewise reckon ye also yourselves to be dead in|deed · unto | sin :
f but alive unto God through | Jesus | Christ our | Lord.

Full 6 Christ is | risen · from the | dead :
and become the | first-fruits · of | them that | slept.

mp 7 For since by | man came | death :
cresc. by man came also the resur|rection | of the | dead.

mp 8 For as in | Adam · all | die :
cresc. even so in | Christ shall · all be | made a|live.

Full *f* Glory be to the Father | and to · the | Son :
and | to the | Holy | Ghost.

Full As it was in the beginning is | now and · ever | shall be :
world without | end. A | . . | men.

Easter Anthems, continued

John Scott

f Christ our passover is sacri - ficed for us : therefore let us keep the feast;

Not with the old leaven * nor with the leaven of malice and wicked - ness :

but with the unleavened bread of sin - ce - ri - ty and truth. ____

ff Christ being raised from the dead dieth no more : death hath no more do - mi - nion over him.

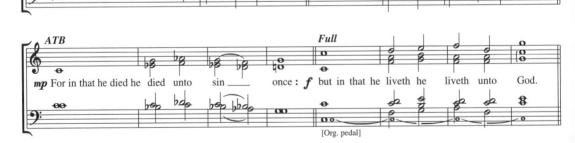

ATB *mp* For in that he died he died unto sin ____ once : *f* but in that he liveth he liveth unto God.

[Org. pedal]

ATB *mp* Likewise reckon ye also yourselves to be dead ____ in - deed un - to sin : ____

Venite, exultemus Domino

Full *f*   1   O come let us | sing • unto the | Lord :
  let us heartily re|joice • in the | strength of • our sal|vation.

Full   2   Let us come before his | presence • with | thanksgiving :
  and | shew our•selves | glad in him • with | psalms.

mf   3   For the | Lord is • a | great God :
  and a | great | King a•bove | all gods.

4   In his hand are all the | corners • of the | earth :
  and the | strength of • the | hills • is his | also.

5   The sea is | his and • he | made it :
  and his | hands pre|pared the • dry | land.

mp   6   O come let us | worship • and fall | down :
  and | kneel before • the | Lord our | Maker.

7   For | he is the • Lord our | God :
  and we are the people of his | pasture • and the | sheep • of his | hand.

mf   8 §   Today if ye will hear his voice * | harden • not your | hearts :
  as in the provocation *
  and as in the | day of • temp|tation • in the | wilderness;

9 §†   When your | fathers | tempted ‖ me * |
  proved me • and | saw my | works.

10 §   Forty years long was I grieved with this gene|ration • and | said :
  It is a people that do err in their hearts * |
  for they • have not | known my | ways;

11 §   Unto whom I | sware • in my | wrath :
  that they should not | enter | into • my | rest.

Full *f*   Glory be to the Father | and to • the | Son :
  and | to the | Holy | Ghost.

Full   As it was in the beginning is | now and • ever | shall be :
  world without | end. A | . . | men.

§ *Omitted in the St Paul's Cathedral use*

Maurice Bevan

Set 8

Te Deum laudamus

Full   *f*   1   We | praise thee · O | God :
                       we ack|nowledge thee · to | be the | Lord.

Full   2 †   All the | earth doth | worship thee ‖ the | Father | ever|lasting.

       mf   3   To thee all | Angels · cry a|loud :
                       the | heavens and · all the | powers · there|in.

                 4 †   To thee | Cherubin · and | Seraphin ‖ con|tinual|ly do | cry,

Full   *f*   5   Holy | Holy | Holy :
                       Lord | God of | Saba|oth;

Full   6 †   Heaven and | earth are | full ‖ of the | Majes·ty | of thy | glory.

       mf   7   The glorious company of the A|postles | praise thee :
                       the goodly | fellowship · of the | Prophets | praise thee.

                 8   The noble army of | Martyrs | praise thee :
                       the holy church throughout | all the | world · doth ack|nowledge thee :

                 9 | **2nd part** | The Father of an | infi·nite | majesty :
                       thine honourable true and only Son * |
                       also the · Holy | Ghost the | Comforter.

                                          change chant (Decani)

Set 1 — G. M. Garrett
(small notes for organ only)

Set 2 — T. Attwood

Set 3 — H. G. Ley

Set 4 — G. J. Elvey

Set 5 — A. Gray

Set 6 — Francis Jackson

Set 7 — John Barnard

Maurice Bevan

Set 8

f 10 Thou art the king of | Glory • O | Christ :
            thou art the | ever•lasting | Son • of the | Father.

11 When thou tookest upon thee to de|liver | man :
            thou | didst not ab•hor the | Virgin's | womb.

12 **2nd part** When thou hadst overcome the | sharpness • of | death :
            thou didst open the kingdom of | heaven to | all be|lievers.

Full 13 † Thou sittest at the | right hand • of | God ‖ in the | Glory | of the | Father.

Full 14 † We be|lieve that | thou ‖ shalt | come to | be our | Judge.

mf 15 We therefore | pray thee • help thy | servants :
            whom thou hast re|deemed • with thy | precious | blood.

16 † Make them to be | numbered • with thy | saints ‖ in | glory | ever|lasting.

change chant (Decani)

Set 1 — J. Turle

Set 2 — T. Attwood

Set 3 — G. Cooper

Set 4 — W. Parratt

Set 5 — A. Gray

Set 6 — John Joubert

Set 7 — John Barnard

Maurice Bevan

Set 8

mf   17   O Lord save thy people and | bless thine | heritage :
              govern them and | lift them | up for | ever.

      18   Day by | day we | magnify thee :
              and we worship thy | Name • ever | world with•out | end.

mp   19   Vouchsafe O Lord to keep us this | day with•out | sin :
              O Lord have mercy up|on us • have | mercy • up|on us.

cresc. 20   O Lord let thy mercy | lighten • up|on us :
              as our | trust | is in | thee.

Full f   21   2nd part O Lord in | thee • have I | trusted :
              let me | never | be con|founded.

Chant A (vv. 1–12)

Benedicite, omnia opera

Full *f*   1   O all ye works of the Lord | bless ye • the | Lord :
                            praise him and | magni•fy | him for | ever.

Full   2   O ye angels of the Lord | bless ye • the | Lord :
                            praise him and | magni•fy | him for | ever.

Full   3   O ye Heavens | bless ye • the | Lord :
                            praise him and | magni•fy | him for | ever.

[Full]   4   O ye Waters that be above the Firmament | bless ye • the | Lord :
                            praise him and | magni•fy | him for | ever.

                  5   O all ye Powers of the Lord | bless ye • the | Lord :
                            praise him and | magni•fy | him for | ever.

                  6   O ye Sun and Moon | bless ye • the | Lord :
                            praise him and | magni•fy | him for | ever.

                  7   O ye Stars of Heaven | bless ye • the | Lord :
                            praise him and | magni•fy | him for | ever.

                  8   O ye Showers and Dew | bless ye • the | Lord :
                            praise him and | magni•fy | him for | ever.

                  9   O ye Winds of God | bless ye • the | Lord :
                            praise him and | magni•fy | him for | ever.

                  10   O ye Fire and Heat | bless ye • the | Lord :
                            praise him and | magni•fy | him for | ever.

                  11   O ye Winter and Summer | bless ye • the | Lord :
                            praise him and | magni•fy | him for | ever.

                  12   O ye Dews and Frosts | bless ye • the | Lord :
                            praise him and | magni•fy | him for | ever.

change chant (Full)

When Set 1 chants are used, only the first three verses are to be sung Full.

Chant B (vv. 13–24)

J. Naylor

Set 1

Maurice Bevan

Set 2

C. H. Lloyd

Set 3

Full   13   O ye Frost and Cold │ bless ye • the │ Lord :
                        praise him and │ magni•fy │ him for │ ever.

Full   14   O ye Ice and Snow │ bless ye • the │ Lord :
                        praise him and │ magni•fy │ him for │ ever.

[Full]   15   O ye Nights and Days │ bless ye • the │ Lord :
                        praise him and │ magni•fy │ him for │ ever.

[Full]   16   O ye Light and Darkness │ bless ye • the │ Lord :
                        praise him and │ magni•fy │ him for │ ever.

                  17   O ye Lightnings and Clouds │ bless ye • the │ Lord :
                        praise him and │ magni•fy │ him for │ ever.

                  18   O Let the Earth │ bless ye • the │ Lord :
                        yea let it praise him and │ magni•fy │ him for │ ever.

                  19   O ye Mountains and Hills │ bless ye • the │ Lord :
                        praise him and │ magni•fy │ him for │ ever.

                  20   O all ye Green Things upon the earth │ bless ye • the │ Lord :
                        praise him and │ magni•fy │ him for │ ever.

                  21   O ye Wells │ bless ye • the │ Lord :
                        praise him and │ magni•fy │ him for │ ever.

                  22   O ye Seas and Floods │ bless ye • the │ Lord :
                        praise him and │ magni•fy │ him for │ ever.

                  23   O ye Whales and all that move in the Waters │ bless ye • the │ Lord :
                        praise him and │ magni•fy │ him for │ ever.

                  24   O all ye Fowls of the Air │ bless ye • the │ Lord :
                        praise him and │ magni•fy │ him for │ ever.

change chant (Full)

When Set 1 chants are used, verses 13 to 15 are to be sung Full;
when Set 2 chants are used, verses 13 to 16 are to be sung Full.

Chant C (vv. 25–32)

C. Hylton Stewart

Maurice Bevan

Christopher Brown

N.B. *In the Gloria, both halves of this chant are sung simultaneously. Decani = A; Cantoris = B*

Full   25   O all ye Beasts and Cattle | bless ye · the | Lord :
                             praise him and | magni·fy | him for | ever.

Full   26   O ye Children of Men | bless ye · the | Lord :
                             praise him and | magni·fy | him for | ever.

Full   27   O let Israel | bless · the | Lord :
                             praise him and | magni·fy | him for | ever.

[Full]   28   O ye Priests of the Lord | bless ye · the | Lord :
                             praise him and | magni·fy | him for | ever.

                  29   O ye Servants of the Lord | bless ye · the | Lord :
                             praise him and | magni·fy | him for | ever.

                  30   O ye Spirits and Souls of the righteous | bless ye · the | Lord :
                             praise him and | magni·fy | him for | ever.

                  31   O ye holy and humble Men of heart | bless ye · the | Lord :
                             praise him and | magni·fy | him for | ever.

                  32   O Ananias Azarias and Misael | bless ye · the | Lord :
                             praise him and | magni·fy | him for | ever.

Full *f*   Glory be to the Father | and to · the | Son :
                             and | to the | Holy | Ghost.

Full   As it was in the beginning is | now and · ever | shall be :
                             world without | end. A | . . | men.

When Set 1 chants are used, verses 25 to 27 are to be sung Full, and the portion of the chant omitted in the Gloria is to be omitted in verses 31 and 32 also.

E. C. Bairstow

W. Fitzherbert

H. Murrill

R. Cooke

G. C. Martin

M. M. Bridges

Malcolm Archer

Martin How

Benedictus

Full *mf* 1 Blessed be the | Lord • God of | Israel :
                       for he hath | visited • and re|deemed his | people;

Full   2 And hath raised up a mighty sal|vation | for us :
                       in the | house of • his | servant | David;

               3 As he spake by the mouth of his | holy | prophets :
                       which have | been • since the | world be|gan;

               4 That we should be | saved • from our | enemies :
                       and from the | hands of | all that | hate us;

               5 To perform the mercy | promised • to our | forefathers :
                       and to re|member • his | holy | Covenant;

            6 † To per|form the | oath ‖ which he | sware to • our | fore•father | Abraham;

    mp   7 That he would give us *
                   that we being delivered out of the | hands • of our | enemies :
                       might | serve him | without | fear;

               8 In holiness and | righteousness • be|fore him :
                       all the | days | of our | life.

    mf   9 And thou child shalt be called the | Prophet • of the | Highest :
                       for thou shalt go before the face of the | Lord • to pre|pare his | ways;

              10 To give knowledge of sal|vation • unto his | people :
                       for the re|mission | of their | sins;

    mp   11 Through the tender | mercy • of our | God :
                       whereby the | day-spring • from on | high hath | visited us;

              12 To give light to them that sit in darkness and in the | shadow • of | death :
    dim.   and to guide our | feet • into the | way of | peace.

Full *mf*   Glory be to the Father | and to • the | Son :
                       and | to the | Holy | Ghost.

Full   As it was in the beginning is | now and • ever | shall be :
                       world without | end. A | • • | men.

J. Randall

1

Stephen Darlington

2

E. Poston

3

H. C. Stewart

4

"St Anne" — John Bertalot

5

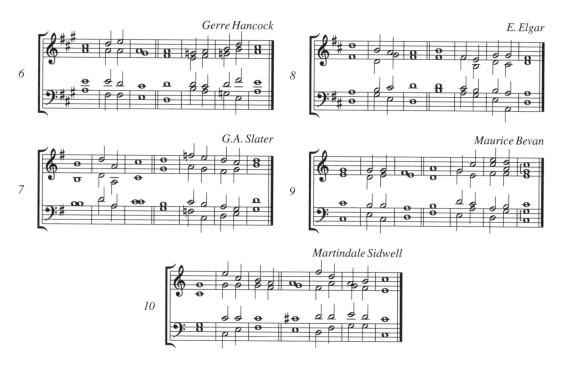

Gerre Hancock

E. Elgar

G.A. Slater

Maurice Bevan

Martindale Sidwell

Jubilate Deo

Full *f* 1 O be joyful in the | Lord · all ye | lands :
serve the Lord with gladness *
and | come before · his | presence · with a | song.

Full 2 Be ye sure that the | Lord · he is | God :
it is he that hath made us and not we ourselves *
we are his | people · and the | sheep · of his | pasture.

3 O go your way into his gates with thanksgiving *
and into his | courts with | praise :
be thankful unto | him and · speak | good · of his | Name.

mf 4 For the Lord is gracious * his | mercy is · ever|lasting :
and his truth endureth from gene|ration · to | gene|ration.

Full *f* Glory be to the Father | and to · the | Son :
and | to the | Holy | Ghost.

Full As it was in the beginning is | now and · ever | shall be :
world without | end. A | . . | men.

John Barnard

Paul Edwards

Magnificat

Full	*mf*	1	My soul doth | magnify · the | Lord :
			and my | spirit · hath re|joiced in · God my | Saviour.
Full		2 †	For | he · hath re|garded ‖ the | lowli·ness | of his | handmaiden.
		3	For be|hold from | henceforth :
			all gene|rations · shall | call me | blessed.
		4	For he that is | mighty · hath | magnified me :
	dim.		and | holy | is his | Name.
	p	5	[2nd part] And his mercy is on | them that | fear him :
			through|out all | gene|rations.
	f	6	He hath shewed | strength · with his | arm :
			he hath scattered the proud in the imagi|nation | of their | hearts.
		7	He hath put down the | mighty · from their | seat :
			and hath ex|alted · the | humble · and | meek.
	mf	8	He hath filled the | hungry · with good | things :
			and the | rich he · hath sent | empty · a|way.
		9	He remembering his mercy hath holpen his | servant | Israel :
			as he promised to our forefathers * | Abraham · and his | seed for | ever.
Full	*f*		Glory be to the Father | and to · the | Son :
			and | to the | Holy | Ghost.
Full			As it was in the beginning is | now and · ever | shall be :
			world without | end. A | . . | men.

Nunc dimittis

mp 1 Lord now lettest thou thy | servant de•part in | peace :
        ac|cording | to thy | word.

      2 For mine eyes have | seen • thy sal|vation :
         which thou hast pre|pared be•fore the | face of • all | people;

mf 3 To be a light to | lighten • the | Gentiles :
         and to be the | glory • of thy | people | Israel.

mp   Glory be to the Father | and to • the | Son :
         and | to the | Holy | Ghost.

         As it was in the beginning is | now and • ever | shall be :
         world without | end. A | • • | men.

Alternative Settings

PSALM 114

In exitu Israel

E.C. Bairstow

1 When Israel came out of Egypt * and the house of Jacob from a - mong the strange people :

2 Judah was his sanctuary * and Isra - el his do - minion.

3 The sea saw that and fled * Jor - dan was dri - ven back :

4 The mountains skipped like rams * and the little hills like young sheep.

5 What aileth thee O thou sea that thou fleddest * and thou Jordan that thou wast dri - ven back :

6 Ye mountains that ye skipped like rams * and ye little hills like young sheep?

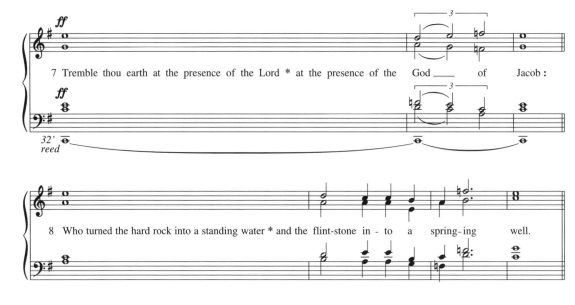

7 Tremble thou earth at the presence of the Lord * at the presence of the God ___ of Jacob :

32' reed

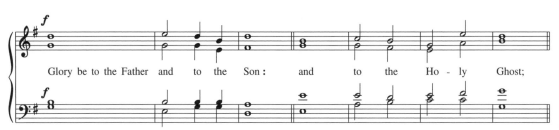

8 Who turned the hard rock into a standing water * and the flint-stone in - to a spring-ing well.

Glory be to the Father and to the Son : and to the Ho - ly Ghost;

As it was in the beginning is now and ev - er shall be : world without end. A - - men.

PSALM 121

Levavi oculos

Barry Rose

1 I will lift up mine eyes unto the hills : from whence ‿ cometh my help.

Organ Pedal   *Ped.*

2 My help cometh even from the Lord : ‿ who hath made ‿ heav'n and earth.

Ped.

3 He will not suffer thy foot to be moved : and he that keepeth thee will not sleep.

* *may also be Alto*   *senza Ped.*

4 Behold he that keepeth Isra - el : shall nei - ther slumber nor sleep.

* *may also be Alto*   *senza Ped.*

5 The Lord him - self is thy keeper : the Lord is thy de - fence up - on thy right ‿ hand.

Ped.

6 So that the sun shall not burn thee by day : ___ neither the moon by night.

Ped.

mp

7 The Lord shall pre - serve thee from all evil : yea it is even he that shall keep thy soul.

senza Ped.

8 The Lord shall preserve thy going out and thy com - ing in : ___ from this time forth for ev - er - more.

senza Ped.

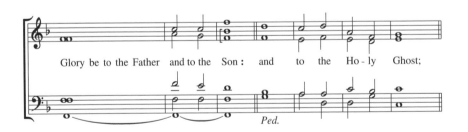

Glory be to the Father and to the Son : and to the Ho - ly Ghost;

Ped.

As it was in the beginning, is now and ever shall be : world without end. A - - men.

Ped.

PSALM 150

Laudate Dominum

Noel Rawsthorne

1 O praise God in his holiness : praise him in the fir - ma - ment of his power.

2 Praise him in his no - ble acts : praise him ac - cording to his ex - cel - lent greatness.

3 Praise him in the sound of the trumpet : praise him up - on the lute and harp.

4 Praise him in the cym - bals and dances : praise him up - on the strings and pipe.

Tenors and Basses

5 Praise him upon the well-tuned cymbals: Praise him up-on the loud ___ cymbals.

Full Swell

Ped.

(Optional descant)

poco rall.

f

praise _____ the Lord.

Choir and Organ

f

S.
A.

6 Let everything that hath breath: praise _____ the Lord.

poco rall.

f

T.
B.

Ped.

Full Unison

f

Glory be to the Father and to the Son: and to the Ho - ly Ghost;

3

Great 8' 4' 2'
+ Full Swell

Ped.

3

As it was in the beginning is now and ever shall be:

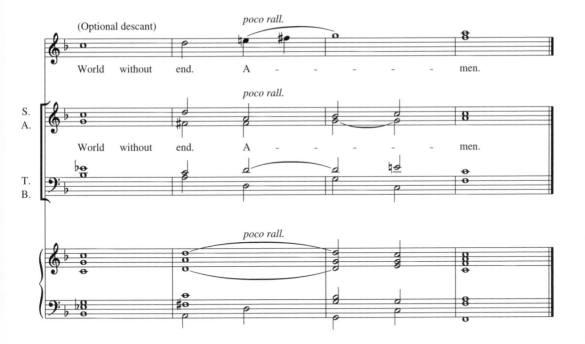

Composers of Chants and Settings

ALCOCK, Sir Walter Galpin (1861-1947)
DMus (Dunelm), FRCO, MVO; Organist of Holy Trinity, Sloane Street, 1895-1902; Assistant Organist, Westminster Abbey, 1896-1916; Organist of the Chapel Royal, 1902-16; Organist of Salisbury Cathedral, 1917-47.
Te Deum 1st Set

ALDRICH, Henry (1647-1710)
DD (Oxon); Dean of Christ Church, Oxford, 1681-1710; Vice-Chancellor, Oxford University, 1692-95.
Psalm 70

ANONYMOUS
"Cambridge Chant". First appearing in Walmisley's *A Cambridge Collection of Chants* [1845], this may have had customary usage for University services in Gt St Mary's church.
Psalm 44

ANONYMOUS
"Parisian Tone". In the 1840s there was a fondness for basing church compositions on music from the French Roman Catholic liturgy, as with Walmisley's imports from the Sanctus of Dumont's *Missa Regia* into his Evening Service in D minor. This chant may have had a similar origin, although it is not in Walmisley's collection.
Nunc Dimittis 1

ANONYMOUS
"Tonus Peregrinus". Derived from the plainchant which, unlike the eight regular psalm tones, had two different reciting notes, one for each half of the chant. For this reason it was described as 'foreign', and reserved for Psalm 114.
Psalm 114

ARCHER, Malcolm David (b.1952)
MA (Cantab), FRCO; Assistant Organist, Norwich Cathedral, 1978-83; Organist of Bristol Cathedral, 1983-89; Freelance composer, conductor and organist 1989-96; Organist of Wells Cathedral, 1996-2004; Organist of St Paul's Cathedral, 2004-07; Director of Music, Winchester College, from 2007.
Te Deum 6th Set, Benedictus 7

ARMES, Philip (1836-1908)
DMus (Oxon), HonFRCO; Organist of Chichester Cathedral, 1861-63; Organist of Durham Cathedral, 1863-1907.
Psalm 119 (vv. 89-96)

ARMSTRONG, Sir Thomas Henry Wait (1898-1994)
MA, DMus (Oxon), HonDMus (Edinburgh), FRCO; Organist of Exeter Cathedral, 1928-33; Organist of Christ Church Cathedral, Oxford, 1933-55; University Choragus, Oxford, 1937-55; Principal of the Royal Academy of Music, 1955-68.
Benedicite 1st Set

ASHFIELD, Robert (1911-2006)
DMus (London), FRCO; Organist of Southwell Minster, 1946-56; Organist of Rochester Cathedral, 1956-77.
Psalm 2

ATKINS, Sir Ivor Algernon (1869-1953)
DMus (Oxon), FRCO; Organist of Worcester Cathedral, 1897-1950.
Psalms 39, 63, 66, 78, 80

ATTWOOD, Thomas (1765-1838)
Pupil of Mozart, Organist of St Paul's Cathedral, 1796-1838.
Psalms 9, 10, 14, 53, 69, 100, 119 (vv. 57-64), Te Deum 2nd Set

AYRTON, Edmund (1734-1808)
MusD (Cantab); Organist of Southwell Minster, 1755-64; Gentleman of the Chapel Royal, 1764-1808; Vicar Choral of St Paul's Cathedral, 1767-1808; Lay Vicar of Westminster Abbey, 1780-1808; Master of the Children of the Chapel Royal, 1780-1805.
Venite 3

BAIRSTOW, Sir Edward Cuthbert (1874-1946)
DMus (Dunelm), HonDMus (Oxon), FRCO; Organist of Wigan Parish Church, 1899-1906; Organist of Leeds Parish Church, 1906-1913; Organist of York Minster, 1913-46; Professor of Music, Durham University, 1929-46.
Psalms 51, 107, 114 (alternative setting), Benedictus 1

BARNARD, John (b.1948)
MA (Cantab), FRCO; John Lyon School, Harrow, teaching Modern Languages 1974-2002, latterly Second Master; part-time teaching Aldenham and Godolphin & Latymer Schools from 2002; Director of Music at various West London high-profile churches, including St Alban's Church, North Harrow and John Keble Church, Mill Hill.
Te Deum 7th Set, Magnificat 7

BARNBY, Sir Joseph (1838-1896)
Precentor of Eton College, 1875-92; Principal of the Guildhall School of Music, 1892-96.
Psalms 24, 38, 44, 69, 78

BATTISHILL, Jonathan (1738-1801)
Organist of Christ Church, Newgate Street, London, 1767-1801. In 1763 he married a Miss Davies, one of the original singers in Arne's *'Love in a Village'*. In 1777 she eloped to Dublin with an actor named Webster. Battishill is buried in the crypt of St Paul's Cathedral.
Psalms 87, 89

BAYLEY, William (1810-1858)
Composer of songs. Vicar Choral St Paul's Cathedral,
sometime Master of Choristers St Paul's Cathedral.
Organist of St John's Horsleydown, Southwark.
Psalm 56

BENNETT, George John (1863-1930)
MusD (Cantab), FRCO; Organist of Lincoln
Cathedral, 1895-1930.
Psalm 64

BERTALOT, John (b.1931)
MA (Cantab), FRCO; Organist of St Matthew's,
Northampton, 1958-64; Organist of Blackburn
Cathedral, 1964-83; Organist of Trinity Church,
Princeton, New Jersey, USA, 1983-1998.
Psalm 141, Jubilate 5

BEVAN, Maurice (1921-2006)
BMus (Cantuar), Vicar Choral of St Paul's Cathedral,
1949-84; Concert singer (Baritone). Editor of 17th-
and 18th-century English music, sacred and secular.
Psalm 71, Te Deum 8th Set, Benedicite 2nd Set, Jubilate 9

BEVAN, Sydney (1838-1901)
see under 'TRENT'

BEXFIELD, William Richard (1824-1853)
DMus, (Oxon); Organist of St Helen's Church,
Bishopgate Street, London. Composed an oratorio
"Israel Restored" which was performed at the Norwich
Music Festival in 1852.
Nunc Dimittis 6

BIELBY, Jonathan Leonard (b.1944)
MA, MusB (Cantab), FRCO; Organist of Wakefield
Cathedral, from 1970.
Psalm 136

BOYCE, William (1711-1779)
MusD (Cantab); Organist of the Chapel Royal,
1758-79; Master of the King's Music, 1755-79.
Conductor of the Three Choirs Festival and the
Festival of the Sons of the Clergy. Buried in the crypt
of St Paul's Cathedral.
Psalms 62, 72

BRIDGES, Mary Monica (1863-1949)
Wife of Robert Bridges, Poet Laureate
Benedictus 6

BROWN, Christopher (b.1943)
MA (Cantab); Studied at the Royal Academy of Music
under Lennox Berkeley, and in Berlin under Boris
Blacher; Professor at the Royal Academy of Music
from 1969; Conductor, Huntingdonshire Philharmonic,
1976-91; Composer-in-Residence, Nene College,
Northampton, 1986-88; Conductor, Dorset Bach
Cantata Club from 1988; Musical Director, New
Cambridge Singers, from 1997. Freelance composer.
Benedicite 3rd Set

CAMIDGE, John (1790-1859)
MusD (Cantab et Cantuar); Organist of York Minster,
1842-59.
Magnificat 1

CAMIDGE, Matthew (1764-1844)
Organist of York Minster, 1799-1842.
Psalm 140, Magnificat 4

CARTER, Andrew (b.1939)
BA (Hons Music), Leeds; Bass Songman, York
Minster, 1962-69; Founder and director of York
Minster Chapter House Choir, 1965-82. Freelance
composer.
Psalm 6

**CHAMPNEYS, Sir Frank Henry, Bart
(1848-1930)**
DM (Oxon), Physician at St Bartholomew's Hospital.
Venite 4

CLARK, Richard (1780-1856)
Lay Clerk, St George's Chapel, Windsor, and Eton
College, 1802-11; Lay Vicar of Westminster Abbey
and Vicar Choral of St Paul's Cathedral, 1811-56;
Gentleman of the Chapel Royal, 1820-56.
Psalm 94

COOKE, Robert (1768-1814)
Organist of Westminster Abbey, 1802-14. He met his
death by drowning in the Thames.
Psalms 7, 45, Benedictus 4

COOPER, George (1820-1876)
Organist of the Chapel Royal, 1856-76; Assistant
Organist of St Paul's Cathedral, 1838-76.
Psalm 78, Te Deum 3rd Set

CORFE, Joseph (1740-1820)
Gentleman of the Chapel Royal, 1781-92;
Organist of Salisbury Cathedral, 1792-1804.
Psalm 8

COWARD, James (1824-1880)
Organist of St George's, Bloomsbury; Organist of the
Crystal Palace, Sydenham, 1857-80.
Psalm 119 (vv. 129-36)

CROFT, William (1678-1727)
DMus (Oxon); Organist of the Chapel Royal, 1704-27;
Organist of Westminster Abbey, 1708-27.
Psalm 13

CROTCH, William (1775-1847)
DMus (Oxon); Organist of Christ Church Cathedral,
Oxford, 1790-1807; Professor of Music, Oxford
University, 1797-1847; First Principal of the Royal
Academy of Music, 1822-32. Crotch also achieved
considerable fame as a child prodigy, as well as being
accomplished in drawing and painting.
Psalms 68, 73, 92, 95

DAKERS, Lionel Frederick, (1924-2000)
DMus (Cantuar), BMus (Dunelm), FRCO, HonDMus Exeter, CBE; Assistant Organist, St George's Chapel, Windsor Castle, 1950-54; Organist of Ripon Cathedral, 1954-57; Organist of Exeter Cathedral, 1957-73; Director of the Royal School of Church Music, 1973-89.
Nunc Dimittis 8

DARLINGTON, Stephen (b.1952)
MA (Oxon), FRCO, DMus (Cantuar); Assistant Organist, Canterbury Cathedral, 1974-78; Organist of St Alban's Abbey, 1978-85; Organist of Christ Church Cathedral, Oxford and University Lecturer in Music, Oxford University, from 1985.
Jubilate 2

DAVIES, Sir Henry Walford (1869-1941)
MusD (Cantab), HonDMus (Oxon), HonMusD (Dublin), HonFRCO, KCVO, OBE; Organist of the Temple Church, 1898-1923; Organist of St George's Chapel, Windsor, 1927-32; Master of the King's Music, 1934-41; Professor of Music, Aberystwyth (University College of Wales) 1919-26; Gresham Professor of Music, London, 1924-41.
Psalms 5, 91, 121, Venite 10

DAVY, John (1763-1824)
Articled to William Jackson, Organist of Exeter Cathedral, 1777; Composer of many works for the stage, mostly produced at Covent Garden between 1800 and 1821. Perhaps he is best known for his song, *'The Bay of Biscay'*.
Psalm 47

DAY, Edgar Frederick (1891-1983)
Sub-organist of Worcester Cathedral, 1912-1962.
Psalms 71, 99, 139

DEARNLEY, Christopher Hugh (1930-2000)
DMus (Cantuar), MA, BMus(Oxon), FRCO, LVO; Organist of Salisbury Cathedral, 1957-1968; Organist of St Paul's Cathedral, 1968-1990.
Psalm 117

EDWARDS, Edwin (1830-1907)
Organist and Choirmaster of Rugby School.
Psalm 132

EDWARDS, Paul (b.1955)
ARCO; Chorister at St Paul's Cathedral, 1964-68; Lay Clerk (alto), Peterborough Cathedral, 1978-82; Organist, Weston Favell, Northamptonshire, 1987-92; Organist, St Paul's Church, Bedford, 1992-2001; Organist, All Saints', Kempston, from 2001.
Magnificat 8

ELGAR, Sir Edward, Bart. (1857-1934)
HonMusD (Cantab), HonDMus (Oxon), (Dunelm), (Yale), OM, GCVO; Professor of Music, Birmingham University, 1905-8; Master of the King's Music, 1924-34.
Psalm 1, Jubilate 8

ELVEY, Sir George Job (1816-1893)
DMus (Oxon); Organist of St George's Chapel, Windsor, 1835-1882.
Psalms 4, 135, 140, E.Anth. 2, Venite 12, Te Deum 4th Set

ELVEY, Stephen (1805-1860)
DMus (Oxon); Organist of New College, Oxford. 1830-60; University Choragus, 1848-60. Brother of the preceding.
Psalm 11

FITZHERBERT, William (c.1713-1797)
MA; Sometime Minor Canon of St Paul's Cathedral; Buried in the crypt of St Paul's Cathedral.
Benedictus 2

FLINTOFT, The Revd Luke (d.1727)
Priest Vicar of Lincoln Cathedral, 1704-14; Gentleman of the Chapel Royal, 1715; Reader in the Whitehall Chapel, 1719-27; Minor Canon of Westminster Abbey, 1719-27. It is possible that he was only the arranger of this chant, which has its origins in Allison's Psalter (1599) and John Playford's *Whole Booke of Psalms* (1677), where it appears under the name 'Salisbury'. It seems to be the earliest known example of a double chant.
Psalm 88

FOSTER, John (1827-1915)
Organist of St Andrew's, Well Street, 1847-56; Lay Vicar of Westminster Abbey, from 1856. Gentleman of the Chapel Royal.
Psalm 55

GARRETT, George Mursell (1834-1897)
MusD (Cantab); Organist of Madras Cathedral, 1854-56; Organist of St John's College, Cambridge, 1856-97.
Psalms 119 (vv. 17-24), 124, 126, Te Deum 1st Set

GAUNTLETT, Henry John (1805-1876)
DMus (Cantuar). Lawyer and Musician. Organist of various London churches. In about 1842 he gave up his law practice and devoted himself to music. He was largely responsible for the introduction of the C organ in England, in place of the old F and G instruments.
Psalms 78, 119 (vv. 81-88)

GIBBONS, Christopher (1615-1676)
DMus (Oxon); Organist of Winchester Cathedral, 1628-61; Organist of Westminster Abbey, 1660-66; Organist of the Chapel Royal, 1660-76. Son of Orlando Gibbons.
Psalm 15

GOODENOUGH, The Revd Robert Philip (c.1776-1826)

MA (Oxon); Son of Samuel Goodenough, Bishop of Carlisle, to whom he was at one time Chaplain. Prebendary of York, Southwell and Carlisle; Rector of Carlton-in-Lyndricks, Notts, 1806; Rector of Beesby, Lincs, 1819. A Manuscript collection of 25 chants by Goodenough is in the library of Christ Church, Oxford, where he was for many years Tutor and Censor.
Psalm 81

GOODSON, Richard (1655-1718)

BMus (Oxon); Organist of New College, Oxford, 1682-92; Organist of Christ Church Cathedral, Oxford, 1692-1718; Professor of Music, Oxford University, 1682-1718.
Venite 7

GOSS, Sir John (1800-1880)

HonMusD (Cantab), FRCO; Organist of St Paul's Cathedral, 1833-72; Composer to the Chapel Royal, 1856-80.
Psalms 21, 48, 60, 78, 119 (vv. 121-8, 169-76), 127, 128

GRAY, Alan (1855-1935)

MusD (Cantab), Director of Music, Wellington College, 1883-93; Organist of Trinity College, Cambridge, 1893-1930.
Psalms 96, 118, Te Deum 5th Set

HANCOCK, Gerre (b.1934)

DMus (Nashotah House Seminary), BMus(Texas), MSacredMus (Union Theological Seminary, New York), FAGO, HonFRCO; Assistant Organist, St Bartholomew's, New York; Organist and Choirmaster, Christ Episcopal Church, Cincinatti; Organist and Choirmaster, St Thomas's Church, Fifth Avenue, New York to 2004; Professor of Organ & Sacred Music, University of Texas, Austin.
Jubilate 6

HANFORTH, Thomas William (1867-1948)

BMus (Dunelm), FRCO; Organist of Sheffield Cathedral, 1892-1937.
Psalm 145

HARRIS, Sir William Henry (1883-1973)

MA, DMus (Oxon), FRCO, KCVO; Organist of New College, Oxford, 1919-29; Organist of Christ Church Cathedral, Oxford, 1929-33; Organist of St George's Chapel, Windsor Castle, 1933-61.
Te Deum 4th Set

HARRISON, J.

Identity uncertain; either John Harrison (1808-1871), organist of St Andrew's, Deal, or John Harrison, organist of St Botolph's, Aldgate, 1867-80.
Psalms 60, 108

HARWOOD, Basil (1859-1949)

MA, DMus (Oxon), FRCO; Organist of Ely Cathedral, 1887-92; Organist of Christ Church Cathedral, Oxford, 1892-1909; University Choragus, Oxford, 1900-09.
Psalm 40

HAVERGAL, The Revd William Henry (1793-1870)

MA (Oxon); Honorary Canon of Worcester Cathedral.
Psalm 16

HEMMINGS, Alan Stephen (b.1934)

MA (Cantab); Organ Student of St John's College, Cambridge 1953-56; taught for a while at Clifton College, Bristol.
Psalm 119 (vv. 145-52)

HERVEY, The Revd Frederick Alfred John (1846-1910)

MA (Cantab), CVO; Rector of Sandringham, 1878-1907; Canon of Norwich Cathedral, 1907-10. Domestic Chaplain to Edward VII.
Psalm 143

HESFORD, Bryan (1930-1996)

MA, PhD, DMus (Geneva Theological College, USA); Organist of Wymondham Abbey, 1960-63; Organist of Brecon Cathedral, 1963-66; Organist of St Margaret's Church, King's Lynn, 1966-70; Organist of Lancaster Priory, 1970-72; Organist of Melton Mowbray Parish Church, 1973-78; Organist of St Nicholas's Collegiate Church, Galway, Eire, 1990-96.
Nunc Dimittis 7

HEWITT-JONES, Tony (1926-1989)

MA (Oxon), ARCO; Director of Music, Dean Close Junior School, Cheltenham, 1953-58; Assistant Music Adviser, Gloucestershire, 1958-63; Music Organizer, Gloucester Community Council, 1963-69; Conductor of the Gloucester County Youth Orchestra and various Gloucestershire choral societies. Studied composition with Nadia Boulanger.
Te Deum 7th Set

HINE, William (1687-1730)

Chorister, Magdalen College, Oxford, 1694-1705; Organist of Gloucester Cathedral, 1713-30; (acting organist from 1707).
Psalm 70

HOPKINS, Edward John (1818-1901)

DMus (Cantuar), FRCO; Organist of the Temple Church, London, 1843-98.
Psalms 3, 28, 36, 57, 65, 119 (vv. 137-144)

HOPKINS, John Larkin (1819-1873)

MusD (Cantab); Organist of Rochester Cathedral, 1841-56; Organist of Trinity College, Cambridge, 1856-73. Cousin of the preceding.
Psalm 27

HOW, Martin, (b.1931)
MA (Cantab), FRCO, MBE; Organist of Grimsby Parish Church, 1961-64; Commissioner, Royal School of Church Music, 1955-91; Special Adviser to the Royal School of Church Music (part-time), from 1991.
Benedictus 8

HOWELLS, Herbert Norman (1892-1983)
DMus (Oxon), HonMusD (Cantab), HonDMus (RCM), CH, CBE; Director of Music, St Paul's Girls' School, 1936-45; Acting organist of St John's College, Cambridge, 1939-45; King Edward Professor of Music, London University.
Psalm 37

HURFORD, Peter (b.1930)
MA, MusB (Cantab), FRCO, OBE; Organist of Holy Trinity, Leamington Spa, 1956-57; Organist of St Alban's Abbey, 1957-78. From 1978 has been a freelance organ recitalist.
Psalm 108

JACKSON, Francis Alan (b.1917)
DMus (Dunelm), FRCO, OBE; Organist of Malton Parish Church, 1933-40; Assistant Organist, York Minster, 1946; Organist of York Minster, 1946-82.
Te Deum 6th Set

JACOBS, The Revd William (c.1800-1873)
MA (Oxon); Chaplain of New College, Oxford, 1862-1866.
Psalm 112

JONES, John (1728-1796)
Organist of the Temple Church, 1749-96; Organist of the Charterhouse, 1753-96; Organist of St Paul's Cathedral, 1755-96. From 1755 until his death he held the three posts simultaneously.
Psalm 119 (vv. 49-56)

JOUBERT, John (b.1927)
BMus (Dunelm), HonDMus (Dunelm), HonDMus (Birmingham); Lecturer in Music, Hull University, 1950-62; Senior Lecturer in Music, Birmingham University, 1962-87. British composer of South African origin.
Te Deum 6th Set

KELWAY, Thomas (1695-1744)
Organist of Chichester Cathedral, 1720-44.
Nunc Dimittis 4

KEYS, Ivor (1919-1993)
MA, DMus (Oxon), HonDMus Belfast, FRCO, FRCM, CBE; Lecturer, Queen's University, Belfast, 1947-54, (Professor, 1950-54); Professor of Music, Nottingham University, 1954-68; Professor of Music, Birmingham University, 1968-86.
Nunc Dimittis 2

KNIGHT, Gerald Hocken (1908-1979)
DMus (Cantuar), MA, MusB (Cantab), FRCO, CBE; Organist of Canterbury Cathedral, 1937-52; Director of the Royal School of Church Music, 1952-72; Overseas Commissioner, Royal School of Church Music, 1973-78.
Psalm 115

LANG, Craig Sellar (1891-1971)
DMus (Dunelm); Assistant Music Master, Royal Naval College, Osborne, 1913-20; Assistant Music Master, Clifton College, 1920-29; Director of Music, Christ's Hospital, 1929-45. Studied composition with Stanford.
Psalm 137

LEMON, Lt-Col. J. (1754-1814)
Lord Commissioner of the Admiralty, MP for Truro and other Cornish boroughs, distinguished amateur musician.
Magnificat 6

LEY, Henry George (1887-1962)
MA, DMus (Oxon), HonFRCO; Organist of Christ Church Cathedral, Oxford, 1909-26; University Choragus, Oxford, 1923-26; Precentor of Eton College, 1926-45.
Psalms 29, 105, Te Deum 3rd Set

LLOYD, Charles Harford (1849-1919)
MA, DMus (Oxon), FRCO; Organist of Gloucester Cathedral, 1876-82; Organist of Christ Church Cathedral, Oxford, 1882-92; Precentor of Eton College, 1892-1917; Organist of the Chapel Royal, 1917-1919.
Psalms 30, 31, 75, 125, Benedicite 3rd Set

LUARD-SELBY, Bertram (1853-1918)
Organist of Salisbury Cathedral, 1881-83; Organist of Rochester Cathedral, 1900-16; Director of Music, Bradfield College, 1916-18. Music Editor of the 1904 edition of *Hymns Ancient & Modern*.
Psalm 67

LUTHER, Martin (1483-1546)
Chant adapted from the chorale *'Ein feste Burg'*.
Psalm 46

MACFARREN, Sir George Alexander (1813-1887)
DMus (Oxon), MusD (Cantab), Professor of Music, Cambridge University, 1875-87; Principal of the Royal Academy of Music, 1876-87; At a comparatively early age his sight became impaired, resulting eventually in total blindness. He pursued, nevertheless, an active career as composer and teacher.
Psalm 93, Venite 6

MACPHERSON, Charles (1870-1927)
HonDMus (Dunelm); Chorister at St Paul's Cathedral; Sub-Organist of St Paul's Cathedral 1895-1916; Organist of St Paul's Cathedral 1916-27. Buried in the crypt of St Paul's Cathedral.
Psalm 130

MANN, Arthur Henry (1850-1929)
DMus (Oxon), HonMA (Cantab), FRCO; Organist of Beverley Minster, 1875-76; Organist of King's College, Cambridge, 1876-1929.
Psalms 78, 90

MARCHANT, Sir Stanley Robert (1883-1949)
MA, DMus (Oxon), FRCO, CVO; Sub-Organist of St Paul's Cathedral, 1916-27; Organist of St Paul's Cathedral, 1927-36; Principal of the Royal Academy of Music, 1936-49; King Edward Professor of Music, London University, 1937-48.
Psalm 119 (vv. 97-104)

MARTIN, Sir George Clement (1844-1916)
DMus (Cantuar), BMus (Oxon), HonDMus (Oxon), FRCO, MVO; Sub-Organist of St Paul's Cathedral, 1876-88; Organist of St Paul's Cathedral, 1888-1916. Buried in the crypt of St Paul's Cathedral.
Psalms 55, 122, Benedictus 5

MAUNDER, John Henry (1858-1920)
Organist of various churches in Forest Hill, Sydenham, Blackheath and Sutton. Choir trainer of the Lyceum Theatre. Composer of the sacred cantata *'Olivet to Calvary'* and other church music with a strong sentimental appeal, and also of operettas.
Psalm 132

MILLER, Charles Edward (1856-1933)
Solicitor; Organist of St Augustine's with St Faith's Church, Watling Street, and Lambeth Parish Church.
Magnificat 5

MONK, Edwin George (1819-1900)
DMus (Oxon), FRCO; Organist and Music Master, St Peter's College, Reading, 1848-59; Organist of York Minster, 1859-83.
Psalms 144, 146, Venite 2, 5

MORNINGTON, Earl of
(Garrett Colly Wellesley) (1735-1781)
MA, HonMusD (Dublin); Professor of Music, Trinity College, Dublin, 1764-74. He was a prolific composer of glees. He was the father of the first Duke of Wellington.
Psalm 119 (vv. 161-8)

MOSSMAN, Donald Wyndham Cremer
(1913-2003)
OBE; Rector of St James, Garlickhythe, 1971-84; Prebendary of St Paul's Cathedral, 1960-86; HonCanon Brussels Cathedral from 1981-84.
Psalm 133 (abbreviated)

MOTHERSOLE, Wilfred John (1898-1992)
Assistant Organist of St Edmundsbury Cathedral, 1923-78.
Psalm 119 (vv. 65-72)

MURRILL, Herbert (1909-1952)
MA, BMus (Oxon); Composer of choral, orchestral and chamber music. He worked for most of his life at the BBC, where he eventually became Head of Music, 1950-52.
Benedictus 3

NARES, James (1715-1783)
MusD (Cantab); Organist of York Minster, 1735-56; Organist of the Chapel Royal, 1756-83.
Psalm 119 (vv. 9-16), Venite 11

NAYLOR, John (1838-1897)
DMus (Oxon); Organist of St Mary's Church, Scarborough, 1856-73; Organist of All Saints' Church, Scarborough, 1873-83; Organist of York Minster, 1883-97. He died at sea during a voyage to Australia. His son, E.W. Naylor, and his grandson, Bernard Naylor, were both distinguished as organists, conductors and composers.
Benedicite 1st Set

NICHOLSON, Sir Sydney Hugo (1875-1947)
DMus (Cantuar), MA BMus (Oxon), FRCO, MVO; Acting Organist, Carlisle Cathedral, 1904-8; Organist of Manchester Cathedral, 1908-18; Organist of Westminster Abbey, 1919-28; Founder and first Director of the Royal School of Church Music, 1927-47.
Psalms 76, 101

NOBLE, Thomas Tertius (1867-1953)
DMus (Cantuar), HonDMus (Trinity College, Hartford, CT USA), HonFRCO; Organist of Ely Cathedral, 1892-98; Organist of York Minster, 1898-1913; Organist of St Thomas's Church, New York, USA, 1913-47.
Psalm 74

NORRIS, Thomas (1741-1790)
BMus (Oxon); Organist of Christ Church Cathedral, Oxford, 1776-90. He was an accomplished tenor singer, and held the posts of Lay Clerk at Christ Church, Oxford (1767) and Magdalen College, Oxford (1771), though he only attended the latter institution once every quarter to receive his salary. He was a frequent soloist at the Three Choirs Festival.
Psalm 89

OAKELEY, Sir Herbert Stanley (1830-1903)
MusD (Cantuar), MA, HonDMus (Oxon), HonMusD Dublin; Professor of Music, Edinburgh University, 1865-91; Composer of music to Her Majesty in Scotland, 1881-1903.
Psalm 119 (vv. 113-120), Benedicite 3rd Set

OUSELEY, The Revd Sir Frederick Arthur Gore, Bart (1825-1889)
MA, DMus (Oxon), HonDMus (Dunelm.), HonMusD (Dublin); Precentor of Hereford Cathedral, 1855-89; Professor of Music, Oxford University, 1855-89. Founder (1856) and first Warden of St Michael's College, Tenbury.
Psalms 73, 105, 119 (vv. 105-112), Venite 8

PALMER, Clement Charlton (1871-1944)
DMus (Oxon), FRCO; Organist of Canterbury Cathedral, 1908-36.
Psalm 123

PARRATT, Sir Walter (1841-1924)
HonMA, HonDMus (Oxon), HonMusD (Cantab), HonDMus (Dunelm), KCVO; Organist of Magdalen College, Oxford. 1872-82; Organist of St George's Chapel, Windsor, 1882-1924; Professor of Music, Oxford University, 1908-1918; Master of the Queen's Music 1893-1901; Master of the King's Music, 1901-1924.
Psalms 82, 85, 104, Te Deum 4th Set

PARRY, Sir Charles Hubert Hastings, Bart (1848-1918)
HonDMus (Oxon), HonMusD (Cantab), HonMusD (Dublin), BMus (Oxon); University Choragus, Oxford, 1883-1900; Professor of Music, Oxford University, 1900-08; Director of the Royal College of Music, 1894-1918. He took his Oxford BMus while still a boy at Eton. Buried in the crypt of St Paul's Cathedral.
Psalm 84

POSTON, Elizabeth (1905-1987)
Pianist and composer; Director of Music, BBC European Service, 1940-45; Musical editor of the *Cambridge Hymnal*, 1967.
Jubilate 3

PRING, Joseph (1776-1842)
DMus (Oxon); Organist of Bangor Cathedral, N Wales, 1793-1842.
Psalm 78

PYE, Kellow John (1812-1901)
BMus (Oxon). Pianist and composer. As a student at the Royal Academy of Music in 1823 he received the first piano lesson ever to be given within its walls.
Psalm 119 (vv. 1-8)

RANDALL, John (1715-1799)
MusD (Cantab); Organist of King's College, Cambridge, 1743-99; Organist of Trinity College, Cambridge, 1777-99; Professor of Music, Cambridge University, 1755-99.
Psalm 98, Jubilate 1

RAWSTHORNE, Christopher Noel (b.1929)
Assistant Organist Liverpool Cathedral 1949, Organist, 1955-1980; Liverpool City Organist, 1980-84.
Psalm 150 (Alternative Setting)

RIMBAULT, Edward Francis (1816-1876)
PhD (Stockholm), FSA, HonDCL (Oxon); Organist of Swiss Church, Soho, London; lecturer and writer on music; antiquarian.
Venite 9

ROBINSON, John (1682-1762)
Organist of Westminster Abbey, 1727-62 (according to William Boyce *"a most excellent performer on the organ"*).
Psalms 18, 116

ROGERS, Sir John Leman, Bart (1780-1847)
Composer and amateur enthusiast. As an ardent admirer of Tallis, he instituted an annual service in Westminster Abbey in which the music was wholly by Tallis.
Psalm 131

ROSE, Barry Michael (b.1934)
OBE; Organist Guildford Cathedral, 1960-1974; Sub-Organist, St Paul's Cathedral 1974, Master of the Choir 1977-1984; Master of Choirs, King's School Canterbury, 1984-1988; Organist St Albans Abbey, 1988-1997.
Psalm 114 (Alternative Setting)

ROSEINGRAVE, Ralph (c.1695-1747)
Organist of Christ Church and St Patrick's Cathedrals, Dublin, 1727-47.
Psalm 20

RUSSELL, William (177?-1813)
BMus (Oxon); Organist of St Ann's, Limehouse, 1798-1805; Organist of the Foundling Hospital, 1805-13.
Psalms 32, 89, Venite 1

SCAIFE, George Arthur (1874-1960)
Master of the Song School, York Minster, 1903-1957.
Psalm 52

SCOTT, John Gavin (b.1956)
MA, MusB (Cantab), FRCO; Assistant Organist of St Paul's and Southwark Cathedrals, 1978-85; Sub-Organist, St Paul's Cathedral, 1985-90; Director of Music of St Paul's Cathedral, 1990-2004; Organist, St Thomas's New York, from 2004.
Psalm 30, Easter Anthems

SIDWELL, John William Martindale (1916-1998)

FRCO; Organist of Hampstead Parish Church, 1946-92; Organist of St Clement Danes Church, London, 1957-92; Professor of Organ, Royal Academy of Music, 1963-81.

Easter Anthems 3, Jubilate 10

SINCLAIR, George Robertson (1863-1917)

DMus (Cantuar), HonFRCO; Organist of Truro Cathedral, 1880-89; Organist of Hereford Cathedral, 1889-1917. He was a friend of Elgar, who dedicated his *Pomp and Circumstance March No. 4* to him. The initials "GRS" on Variation 9 of the *Enigma Variations* refer to Sinclair.

Psalm 26

SKEATS, Highmore (d.1831)

Organist of Ely Cathedral, 1778-1803; Organist of Canterbury Cathedral, 1803-31. Or possibly his son, Highmore Skeats (1785-1835): Organist of Ely Cathedral, 1803-30; Organist of St George's Chapel Windsor, 1830-35.

Psalm 119 (vv. 73-80)

SLATER, Gordon Archibald (1896-1979)

DMus (Dunelm), FRCO, OBE; Organist of St Botolph's Church, Boston, 1919-27; Organist of Leicester Cathedral, 1927-31; Organist of Lincoln Cathedral, 1931-66.

Jubilate 7, Nunc Dimittis 5

SMART, Henry (1813-1879)

Organist of St Philip's, Regent Street, 1836-44; Organist of St Luke's, Old Street, 1844-64; Organist of St Pancras Church, 1864-79.

Psalms 18, 22, 68, 74, Te Deum 3rd Set

SMITH, Peter Melville (b.1943)

Assistant Director of Music, Eastbourne College, 1966-69; Assistant Music Master and Organist, Marlborough College, 1969-73; Senior piano teacher and Organist in Lower Chapel, Eton College, from 1973.

Easter Anthems 1

SOAPER, John (1743-1794)

Lay Vicar of Westminster Abbey; Gentleman of the Chapels Royal; Vicar Choral of St Paul's Cathedral, where buried. Composer and singer.

Psalm 139

SOUTH, Charles Frederick (1850-1916)

Organist of St Augustine & St Faith, Watling St, City of London, 1868-83; Organist of Salisbury Cathedral, 1883-1916.

Psalm 34

STAINER, Sir John (1840-1901)

MA, DMus (Oxon), HonDMus (Dunelm), FRCO; Organist of St Michael's College, Tenbury, 1857-60; Organist of Magdalen College, Oxford, 1860-72.; Organist of St Paul's Cathedral, 1872-88; Professor of Music, Oxford University, 1889-99; H.M. Inspector of Music in Training Colleges, 1883-1901.

Psalms 9, 10, 41, 77, 97

STANFORD, Sir Charles Villiers (1852-1924)

MA, MusD (Cantab), HonDMus (Oxon); Organist of Trinity College, Cambridge, 1874-92; Professor of Music, Cambridge University, 1887-1924; Professor of Composition, Royal College of Music, 1883-1923; Conductor of the London Bach Choir, 1885-1902. Buried in Westminster Abbey.

Psalms 59, 78, 147, 149, 150

STEWART, Charles Hylton (1884-1932)

MA, MusB (Cantab); Organist of Rochester Cathedral, 1916-30; Organist of Chester Cathedral, 1920-32; Organist of St George's Chapel, Windsor, 1932 (appointed in September, died in November 1932).

Psalms 23, 36, 61, 79, 106, 119 (vv. 25-32), 120, 142, Benedicite 1st Set

STEWART, Haldane Campbell (1868-1942)

MA, DMus (Oxon); Director of Music, Tonbridge School, 1898-1919; Organist of Magdalen College, Oxford, 1919-38; Acting Organist of Magdalen in 1941 during the absence of the organist (William McKie) on active service. Dr Stewart died as a result of a fall at his home in Oxford.

Jubilate 4

STEWART, Sir Robert Prescott (1825-1894)

MusD (Dublin); Organist of Christ Church Cathedral, Dublin, 1844-94; Organist of St Patrick's Cathedral, Dublin, 1852-61; Professor of Music, Trinity College, Dublin, 1862-94.

Psalms 60, 108

STONEX, Henry (1823-1897).

Assistant Organist, Norwich Cathedral. Organist of Great Yarmouth Parish Church, 1850-94.

Psalm 35

TALBOT, The Revd George Thomas Surtees (d.1918)

MA (Oxon); Vicar Choral (Minor Canon) of York Minster, 1903-18; Vicar of Huntington, York, 1915-18.

Psalm 150

THALBEN-BALL, Sir George (1896-1987)

DMus (Cantuar), HonDMus (Birmingham), HonFRCO, CBE; Organist of the Temple Church, 1923-82; Organist to the City of Birmingham, 1949-82.

Psalms 50, 56, 119 (vv. 33-40), Magnificat 2

TOMKINS, Thomas (1572-1656)
BMus (Oxon); Organist of Worcester Cathedral,
1596-1656; Organist of the Chapel Royal, 1621-56.
Psalm 13

TRANCHELL, Peter Andrew (1922-1993)
MA, MusB (Cantab); Music Master, Eastbourne
College, 1947-50; Lecturer in the Faculty of Music,
Cambridge, 1950-89; Fellow, 1960-93 and Precentor,
Gonville and Caius College, Cambridge, 1962-89.
Psalms 102, 103

TRENT
Chant composed by Sydney Bevan, 1838-1901, and
named after his home, Trent Park, Middlesex.
Psalm 104

TURLE, James (1802-1882)
Organist of Westminster Abbey, 1831-82.
**Psalms 17, 25, 33, 86, 109, 110, 134, 138, Te Deum 1st Set,
Magnificat 3**

VANN, William Stanley (b.1910)
DMus (Cantuar), BMus (London), FRCO; Organist of
Chelmsford Cathedral, 1949-53; Master of the Music,
Peterborough Cathedral, 1953-77.
Psalm 113

WALMISLEY, Thomas Attwood (1814-1856)
MA, MusD (Cantab); Organist of Trinity and St
John's Colleges, Cambridge, 1833-56; Professor of
Music, Cambridge University, 1836-56.
Psalms 18, 19, 49, 119 (vv. 153-160), 129

WESLEY, Samuel (1766-1837)
Son of Charles Wesley, the hymn writer; Nephew of
John Wesley, founder of Methodism; Natural father
of S.S. Wesley; Pupil of William Boyce. A prolific
composer in all areas of music and an enthusiastic
promoter of the music of J.S. Bach.
Psalms 22, 42, 43, 118

WESLEY, Samuel Sebastian (1810-1876)
Natural son of the preceding. DMus (Oxon); Organist
of Hereford Cathedral, 1832-35; Organist of Exeter
Cathedral, 1835-42; Organist of Leeds Parish Church,
1842-49; Organist of Winchester Cathedral, 1849-65;
Organist of Gloucester Cathedral, 1865-76.
Psalms 18, 58, Nunc Dimittis 3

WEST, Hezekiah (d.1826)
He was a chorister at New College, Oxford, and later
'Bible Clerk' at the same establishment. In 1824 he
published a collection of chants '... *for the use of New
College Chapel, Oxford.'*
Psalm 119 (vv. 41-48)

WILLCOCKS, Sir David Valentine (b.1919)
MA, MusB (Cantab), HonDMus (Exeter), (Leicester),
(Princeton), (Bristol), FRCO, CBE, MC; Organist of
Salisbury Cathedral, 1947-50; Organist of Worcester
Cathedral, 1950-57; Director of Music, King's
College, Cambridge, 1958-73; Director of the Royal
College of Music, 1974-84; Conductor of the London
Bach Choir, 1960-98.
Psalms 81, 83, 148

WILTON, Charles H. (fl.1795)
English violinist, conductor and composer of works for
violin, harpsichord, piano, as well as psalms, hymns
and chants. Resident in Liverpool in 1790s. Studied
violin in Italy with Nardini.
Psalm 12

WISE, Michael (c.1648-1687)
Organist of Salisbury Cathedral, 1668-87; Gentleman
of the Chapel Royal, 1676-87; Almoner and Master of
the Choristers, St Paul's Cathedral, 1687. In the
course of an altercation with the night watchman in
Salisbury, he received a blow on the head *"which
broke his skull, of the consequence whereof he died".*
Psalm 54

WOLSTENHOLME, William (1865-1931)
BMus (Oxon); Blind organist and composer; Organist
successively (from 1902) of The King's Weigh House
Church; All Saints', Norfolk Square and All Saints',
St John's Wood.
Psalm 27

WOODWARD, Richard (1744-1777)
MusD (Dublin); Organist of Christ Church Cathedral,
Dublin, 1765-77; Master of Choristers, St Patrick's
and Christ Church Cathedrals.
Psalms 94, 111

Thematic Index of Chants

This thematic index brings together chants whose melodic profile for the first quarter is similar. The four figures in the first columns represent the number of semitones, with reference to the starting note (always taken to be "0", and, therefore, not listed), from which subsequent notes are distant. In order to avoid confusion when a version of the chant might have passing notes or other melodic decoration, the initial pitches are taken with reference to the chant, had it been notated in a "plain" fashion, *i.e.* just with semibreves and minims, and without any passing notes. The table thus provides the pitches of the melody for the first quarter and the reciting chord of the second quarter. The example gives the first half of two chants, one without passing notes, and one with, showing, above the stave, the pitch figures which would represent their melodic "fingerprint" in this index.

The scheme is similar to that employed in Bryden and Hughes: *An index to Gregorian Chant.*

Andrew Parker

G.W. Chard

W. Crotch

Abbreviations
Type: S = Single; D = Double; T = Triple; Q = Quadruple; X = Short or Condensed
Keys: *a*F = Flat; *a*S = Sharp; mode = major unless otherwise indicated
Ref: Ben = Benedictus; BenOm = Benedicite; Mag = Magnificat; Nunc = Nunc Dimittis; TD = Te Deum; Ven = Venite

Fingerprint	Type	Key	Reference	Composer
-8 -10 -12 -10	D	D	Ps 68	Crotch, W
-8 -7 -5 -3	S	D	Ven 2	Monk, EG
-7 -5 -5 -12	D	F	TD 8	Bevan, M
-7 -5 -4 -2	D	D*mi*	Ps 109	Turle, J
-7 -5 -4 -2	D	G	Mag 6	Lemon, J
-7 -5 -3 -3	D	D*ma*	Ps 109	Turle, J
-7 -5 -3 0	D	E	Ps 98	Randall, J
-5 -9 -12 3	D	C*mi*	Ps 81	Willcocks, DV, (after Goodenough, R)
-5 -8 -12 4	D	C	Ps 81	Goodenough, R
-5 -7 -8 -8	D	D	Ps 72	Boyce, W
-5 -7 -8 4	D	AF	TD 2	Attwood, T
-5 -4 -2 -7	Q	BF	BenOm 3	Brown, C
-5 -3 -5 -8	D	C	TD 4	Harris, WH
-5 -3 0 0	D	AF	Ps 119(5)	Thalben-Ball, G
-5 0 2 -1	X	A	Ps 76	Nicholson, SH
-5 4 2 5	S	B	Ps 87	Battishill, J
-4 -9 -7 -7	D	G	TD 4	Elvey, GJ
-4 -9 -7 -5	D	BF*ma*	Ps 6	Carter, AR
-4 -7 -9 -9	D	BF	Ps 50	Thalben-Ball, G
-4 -7 -9 -9	D	AF	Ps 119(14)	Ouseley, FAG
-4 -5 -7 -5	D	D*mi*	Ps 31	Lloyd, CH
-4 -5 -7 -5	D	G	Ps 45	Cooke, R
-4 -5 -7 5	D	D*mi*	Ps 38	Barnby, J
-4 -4 -5 -4	D	A	Ps 94	Woodward, R
-4 -3 -8 -3	D	CS*mi*	Ps 14	Attwood, T

Fingerprint				*Type*	*Key*	*Reference*	*Composer*
-4	-3	-8	-3	D	C*mi*	Ps 53	Attwood, T
-4	-3	5	4	D	E*mi*	Ps 41	Stainer, J
-4	-2	-5	-5	D	GF	Ps 18	Wesley, SS
-4	-2	0	0	D	GF	Ps 119(15)	Oakeley, HS
-4	0	-2	5	D	E	Ps 131	Rogers, JL
-4	0	3	1	X	EF	Ps 148	Willcocks, DV
-4	1	-2	3	S	FS	Ven 4	Champneys, FH
-3	-8	-7	-5	D	BF*mi*	Ps 6	Carter, AR
-3	-7	-2	-3	D	G	TD 3	Smart, H
-3	-7	2	0	D	D	Mag 5	Miller, CE
-3	-5	-8	-3	D	BF*mi*	Ps 37	Howells, HN
-3	-5	-7	-7	Q	G	Ps 78	Mann, AH
-3	-5	-5	-3	S	D	Jub 8	Elgar, E
-3	-3	-5	4	D	G	Ps 78	Cooper, G
-3	-2	-5	-7	S	AF	Ps 134	Turle, J
-3	-2	0	0	D	DF	Ps 34	South, CF
-3	-2	0	2	D	AF	Jub 4	Stewart, HC
-3	-2	0	5	S	D	Ps 60	Stewart, RP
-3	-2	0	5	S	D	Ps 108	Stewart, RP
-3	-1	-4	-8	D	F*mi*	Ps 119(22)	Goss, J (from Clarke, J)
-3	0	2	0	S	C	Ps 150	Stanford, CV
-3	0	5	7	D	C	Ps 96	Gray, A
-3	0	7	0	D	G	Ben 3	Murrill, H
-3	2	0	0	S	F	Ven 9	Rimbault, EF
-2	-5	-4	-8	D	BF	Ps 132	Maunder, JH
-2	-5	-4	1	D	G	TD 8	Bevan, M
-2	-5	-4	3	D	AF	Mag 3	Turle, J
-2	-4	-7	-5	D	A	Ps 25	Turle, J
-2	-4	-5	-9	D	AF	Ps 119(18)	Hopkins, EJ
-2	-4	-5	-5	D	A*mi*	Ps 90	Mann, AH
-2	-4	-5	-4	D	AF	Ps 119(7)	Jones, J
-2	-4	-5	-3	X	G	Ps 101	Nicholson, SH
-2	-4	-5	-2	D	G*ma*	Ps 28	Hopkins, EJ
-2	-4	-5	-2	S	AF	Ven 5	Monk, EG
-2	-4	-5	3	S	A*mi*	Ps 13	Croft, W
-2	-4	-5	3	D	A*mi*	Ps 89	Battishill, J
-2	-4	-2	-4	D	AF	Ps 149	Stanford, CV
-2	-4	1	0	D	G	Ps 42,43	Wesley, S
-2	-4	1	0	Q	F	BenOm 3	Oakeley, HS
-2	-4	3	0	D	G	Ps 124	Garrett, GM
-2	-4	3	1	D	E	Ps 82	Parratt, W
-2	-4	3	1	D	G	Ps 97	Stainer, J
-2	-4	3	1	T	G	Ps 136	Bielby, JL
-2	-3	-5	-7	D	G	Ps 95	Crotch, W
-2	-2	-3	-5	D	DF	Ps 119(16)	Goss, J
-2	0	-9	-9	D	AF	Ps 112	Jacobs, W
-2	0	-5	1	D	GF	Ps 4	Elvey, GJ
-2	0	-4	-4	D	A	Ps 126	Garrett, GM
-2	0	1	0	S	A	Ps 70	Aldrich, H
-2	0	1	0	S	D	Ps 107	Bairstow, EC
-2	0	1	0	S	D	Ps 107	Bairstow, EC
-2	0	1	0	D	DF	Ps 119(12)	Armes, P
-2	0	1	5	D	E	Ps 139	Soaper, J
-2	0	2	4	S	D	Ps 107	Bairstow, EC
-2	0	5	4	D	C	TD 7	Barnard, J
-2	1	0	5	D	E	Ps 18	Smart, H
-2	3	-4	5	D	EF	Ps 16	Havergal, WH
-2	5	3	1	D	EF	Ps 145	Hanforth, T

Fingerprint				Type	Key	Reference	Composer
-1	-5	0	-12	D	D	Ps 47	Davy, J
-1	-3	-5	-8	D	C	TD 3	Ley, HG
-1	-3	-5	2	D	AF	Ps 119(17)	Coward, J
-1	-3	-5	4	D	A*ma*	Ps 89	Anon. (from Battishill, J)
-1	-3	-4	-1	D	G*mi*	Ps 28	Hopkins, EJ
-1	-3	2	0	D	E*mi*	Ps 42,43	Anon. (from Wesley, S)
-1	-3	4	4	D	A	Ps 139	Day, EF
-1	-1	-3	-3	D	D	Ps 30	Lloyd, CH
-1	-1	-3	-3	S	BF	Ps 50	Thalben-Ball, G
-1	-1	-3	2	D	F*mi*	Ps 143	Hervey, FAJ
-1	0	-5	-5	D	BF*mi*	Ps 57	Hopkins, EJ
-1	0	-5	-5	D	BF*ma*	Ps 57	Hopkins, EJ
-1	0	2	3	S	A*mi*	Ps 70	Hine, W
-1	0	2	4	D	A	Ps 69	Attwood, T
-1	0	2	5	D	F	Ps 55	Foster, J
0	-5	-4	-4	S	A	EAnth 3	Sidwell, M
0	-2	-5	-4	D	A	Ps 75	Lloyd, CH
0	-2	-5	0	D	BF	Ps 119(19)	Hemmings, AS
0	-2	-4	1	D	G	TD 3	Cooper, G
0	-2	-3	-5	D	B*mi*	Ps 106	Stewart, C Hylton
0	-2	-3	0	D	EF	Ps 119(21)	Mornington, Lord
0	-2	-3	2	X	E	Ps 117	Dearnley, CH
0	-2	-2	-4	D	AF	Ps 119(11)	Gauntlett, HJ
0	-2	1	-2	S	A	Ps 13	Tomkins, T (arr. from Responses)
0	-1	-8	-8	D	G*mi*	Ps 137	Lang, CS
0	-1	-3	0	D	D*mi*	Ps 78	Goss, J
0	-1	2	0	D	A	TD 5	Gray, A
0	-1	2	5	D	BF	Ps 102	Tranchell, PA
0	0	-5	-1	D	D	Ps 46	Anon. (from Luther, M)
0	0	-2	-2	Q	D*mi*	Ps 103	Tranchell, PA
0	0	-2	2	S	C	Jub 9	Bevan, M
0	0	-2	3	D	D	Ps 71	Bevan, M
0	0	-1	-2	D	D*mi*	Ps 12	Wilton, CH
0	0	-1	0	D	FS*mi*	Ps 22	Wesley, S
0	0	-1	0	D	G*mi*	Ben 8	How, M
0	0	0	0	D	EF	Ps 9,10	Attwood, T
0	0	0	0	D	EF	TD 2	Attwood, T
0	0	0	1	D	F	Ps 49	Walmisley, TA
0	0	2	-2	D	E	Ps 118	Wesley, S
0	0	2	2	D	G	TD 1	Garrett, GM
0	0	2	2	S	C*mi*	Nunc 6	Bexfield, WR
0	0	5	-3	D	EF	Ps 111	Woodward, R
0	0	5	2	T	F	BenOm 1	Naylor, J
0	0	9	5	D	C	TD 4	Parratt, W
0	1	-2	0	D	G	Ps 78	Pring, J
0	1	0	-2	D	E	Mag 1	Camidge, J
0	2	-2	2	X	EF	Ps 133	Mossman, DC
0	2	-1	-2	S	G*mi*	Ps 58	Wesley, SS
0	2	-1	-2	S	F*mi*	Nunc 3	Wesley, SS
0	2	-1	0	D	F	Ps 86	Turle, J
0	2	-1	0	S	G*mi*	Nunc 4	Kelway, T
0	2	-1	3	D	A*mi*	Ps 44	Anon. "Cambridge Chant"
0	2	3	3	D	F*mi*	Ps 35	Stonex, H
0	2	4	4	D	EF	Ps 56	Bayley, W
0	3	2	2	D	G*mi*	Ps 78	Barnby, J
0	4	2	4	D	E	TD 5	Gray, A
0	5	4	2	D	EF	Ps 119(6)	West, H
0	5	4	3	D	D*mi*	Ps 20	Roseingrave, R

Fingerprint				Type	Key	Reference	Composer
0	5	4	4	D	A*mi*	Ps 74	Smart, H
1	-4	0	0	D	C*mi*	Ps 142	Stewart, C Hylton
1	-2	-5	-4	S	A	Ven 11	Nares, J
1	-2	0	3	D	A*mi*	Ben 6	Bridges, MM
1	-2	3	5	S	BF*mi*	Nunc 7	Hesford, B
1	0	-2	-4	S	F*mi*	Ps 114	Anon. "Tonus Peregrinus"
1	0	-2	-4	D	EF	Mag 4	Camidge, M
1	0	-2	-2	D	F	Ps 55	Martin, GC
1	0	-2	0	D	D	Ps 39	Atkins, IA
1	0	-2	5	D	EF	Ps 110	Turle, J
1	0	5	3	D	EF	Ps 11	Elvey, S
1	0	5	3	D	C	TD 6	Joubert, J
1	1	0	-4	S	D*mi*	Ps 60	Goss, J
1	1	1	0	D	D*mi*	Ps 78	Goss, J
1	1	2	-3	D	E	Ps 26	Sinclair, GR
1	3	-4	-4	S	A	Jub 6	Hancock, G
1	3	-4	-2	D	E	Ps 84	Parry, CHH
1	3	-4	0	D	A	Ps 78	Gauntlett, HJ
1	3	0	0	S	F*mi*	Ps 54	Wise, M
1	3	0	5	S	C*mi*	Ps 36	Stewart, C Hylton
1	3	5	3	D	EF*ma*	Ps 52	Scaife, GA
1	3	5	3	D	D	TD 1	Alcock, WG
1	3	5	3	D	G	Ben 4	Cooke, R
1	3	5	7	D	D	Ps 78	Stanford, CV
1	5	-2	3	D	EF	Ps 119(20)	Walmisley, TA
2	-5	4	4	D	AF	Ps 144	Monk, EG
2	-3	-5	0	D	BF	EAnth 1	Smith, PM
2	-2	-5	0	D	G	TD 6	Jackson, F
2	-1	0	-3	D	G*mi*	Ps 119(2)	Nares, J
2	0	-3	-5	S	GF	Ps 1	Elgar, E
2	0	-2	-3	D	D	Ps 122	Martin, GC
2	0	-2	0	D	DF	Ps 3	Hopkins, EJ
2	0	-1	-5	D	A	Ps 73	Ouseley, FAG
2	0	5	5	D	C	Ps 104	Parratt, W
2	0	5	7	D	AF	Ps 80	Atkins, IA
2	2	0	0	D	D	Ps 106	Stewart, C Hylton
2	2	0	5	S	C	Ps 106	Stewart, C Hylton
2	2	3	3	D	F*mi*	Ps 88	Flintoft, L
2	2	3	5	D	E*mi*	Ps 140	Camidge, M
2	2	4	6	D	E*ma*	Ps 140	Elvey, GJ, (after Camidge, M)
2	2	4	7	D	EF	Ps 17	Turle, J
2	2	5	4	D	EF	Ps 56	Thalben-Ball, G
2	3	-4	-4	D	D	Ps 107	Bairstow, EC
2	3	4	4	D	B*mi*	Ps 130	Macpherson, C
2	3	5	0	D	EF*mi*	Ben 7	Archer, M
2	3	5	3	D	D*mi*	Ps 78	Atkins, IA
2	3	5	7	D	E*mi*	Ps 106	Stewart, C Hylton
2	4	-5	0	D	D	Ps 100	Attwood, T
2	4	0	-3	S	BF	Ps 67	Selby, B Luard
2	4	0	-1	D	A	Ps 73	Crotch, W
2	4	2	2	D	D	Ben 1	Bairstow, EC
2	4	5	-3	S	BF	Ven 6	Macfarren, GA
2	4	5	2	D	A	Ps 127	Goss, J
2	4	5	4	D	EF*mi*	Ps 52	Scaife, GA
2	4	5	4	D	G*mi*	Ps 61	Stewart, C Hylton
2	4	5	5	D	D	Ps 27	Hopkins, JL
2	4	5	7	D	EF	TD 2	Attwood, T
2	4	7	5	D	D	TD 6	Archer, M

Fingerprint				Type	Key	Reference	Composer
2	5	0	0	D	BF	BenOm 3	Lloyd, CH
2	5	0	5	D	D	Ps 74	Noble, TT
2	5	4	2	D	EF	Ps 62	Boyce, W
2	5	4	5	S	B	Ven 12	Elvey, GJ
2	5	4	7	S	F*mi*	Nunc 8	Dakers, L
2	5	7	0	S	C	Ps 150	Talbot, GS
2	5	7	9	D	AF	Ps 115	Knight, GH
2	5	9	4	S	C	Ps 93	Macfarren, GA
2	5	12	7	D	AF	Ps 113	Vann, WS
2	7	4	4	D	G	Ps 104	Trent (Bevan, S)
2	7	5	4	T	DF	Ps 2	Ashfield, R
2	7	7	5	D	EF	Ps 63	Atkins, IA
2	7	7	9	D	G	Jub 2	Darlington, S
2	9	7	5	D	GF	Ps 119(13)	Marchant, S
3	-4	-5	-2	S	AF	Ps 15	Gibbons, C
3	-4	0	0	D	E	TD 5	Gray, A
3	-4	1	0	D	D	Ps 21	Goss, J
3	-2	1	3	S	G	Jub 7	Slater, GA
3	0	-4	3	D	EF	Ps 119(1)	Pye, KJ
3	0	-2	-4	S	G	Ps 125	Lloyd, CH
3	0	-2	0	X	E	Ps 23	Stewart, C Hylton
3	0	-1	-1	D	A*mi*	Ps 94	Clark, R
3	1	-2	-2	S	E	Nunc 1	Anon. "Parisian Tone"
3	1	-2	0	D	F	Ps 119(3)	Garrett, GM
3	1	0	-2	D	E	Ps 128	Goss, J
3	1	0	3	D	C	Jub 5	Bertalot, J
3	1	0	4	D	A*mi*	Ps 69	Barnby, J
3	1	0	5	X	B*mi*	Ps 30	Scott, JG
3	1	3	2	D	F	Ben 2	Fitzherbert, W
3	2	-2	0	D	G	Ps 40	Harwood, B
3	2	0	0	D	F*mi*	Ps 79	Stewart, C Hylton
3	2	0	5	S	G	Nunc 5	Slater, GA
3	2	7	7	D	E*mi*	Ps 44	Barnby, J
3	3	-4	-2	D	EF	Ps 132	Edwards, E
3	3	2	0	D	EF	Ps 51	Bairstow, EC
3	3	8	-4	S	EF	Ps 36	Hopkins, EJ
3	3	8	5	D	C	Ps 138	Turle, J (after Purcell, H)
3	5	-2	-4	D	E	Ps 91	Davies, H Walford
3	5	8	0	D	D	Ps 121	Davies, H Walford
3	5	8	7	D	DF	Mag 7	Barnard, J
3	7	8	7	D	EF*mi*	Ps 5	Davies, H Walford
3	7	8	7	Q	D*mi*	BenOm 2	Bevan, M
3	7	12	7	S	D*mi*	Ps 60	Harrison, J
4	0	-3	-1	D	A	Ps 48	Goss, J
4	0	-1	0	D	D*mi*	TD 1	Turle, J
4	0	5	4	D	A	Ps 105	Ouseley, FAG
4	0	7	7	D	D	Ps 68	Smart, H
4	2	-5	-3	T	C	BenOm 1	Armstrong, THW
4	2	-1	-3	D	AF	Ps 64	Bennett, GJ
4	2	0	5	D	A	Ps 31	Lloyd, CH
4	2	5	4	D	FS*mi*	Ps 71	Day, EF
4	2	7	7	T	C	BenOm 1	Stewart, C Hylton
4	4	7	0	D	EF	Ps 119(8)	Attwood, T
4	4	7	7	D	D	Jub 3	Poston, E
4	5	7	-1	D	AF	Ps 119(9)	Mothersole, WJ
4	5	7	4	D	FS*mi*	Ps 85	Parratt, W
4	5	7	7	S	EF	Nunc 2	Keys, I
4	7	0	0	D	A	Ps 89	Norris, T

Fingerprint				Type	Key	Reference	Composer
4	7	5	2	D	D	Ps 105	Ley, HG
4	7	5	4	D	A	Ps 118	Gray, A
4	7	9	7	Q	D	BenOm 2	Bevan, M
4	7	12	7	S	D	Ps 108	Harrison, J
4	7	12	9	D	D	Ps 29	Ley, HG
4	7	12	9	D	D	Ps 105	Ley, HG
4	7	12	9	S	D	Ps 108	Hurford, P
4	7	12	12	D	D	Jub 1	Randall, J
4	9	7	5	D	EF	Ps 119(10)	Skeats, H
4	9	7	7	D	E	Ps 24	Barnby, J
5	-3	-2	2	D	DF	Ps 18	Walmisley, TA
5	-2	-3	2	S	E	Ven 3	Ayrton, E
5	0	2	2	D	BF	Mag 2	Thalben-Ball, G
5	2	-2	-5	S	EF	Ven 8	Ouseley, FAG
5	2	0	-3	D	E	Ps 18	Robinson, J
5	2	0	-3	D	E	Ps 116	Robinson, J
5	2	4	0	D	EF	Ps 147	Stanford, CV
5	3	-4	-4	S	G	Ven 10	Davies, H Walford
5	3	1	0	D	Dmi	Ps 59	Stanford, CV
5	4	2	0	D	E	Ps 89	Russell, W
5	4	2	2	S	DF	Ven 7	Goodson, R
5	4	2	4	D	A	Ps 92	Crotch, W
5	4	5	2	D	EF	Ps 135	Elvey, GJ
5	4	5	2	D	BF	Ps 146	Monk, EG
5	4	9	7	D	AF	Ps 9,10	Stainer, J
5	4	9	7	D	AF	Ps 9,10	Stainer, J
5	4	9	7	D	G	TD 7	Barnard, J
5	5	0	3	D	E	Ps 141	Bertalot, J
5	5	3	8	D	C	Ps 119(4)	Stewart, C Hylton
5	5	4	2	D	DF	Ps 18	Walmisley, TA
5	5	4	5	D	A	Ps 99	Day, EF
5	5	4	5	S	Bmi	Ps 120	Stewart, C Hylton
5	5	4	7	D	EF	Ps 32	Russell, W
5	5	9	5	D	B	Ps 129	Walmisley, TA
5	7	8	7	D	Ami	Ps 77	Stainer, J
5	7	9	9	D	A	Ben 5	Martin, GC
5	7	10	9	D	A	Ps 37	Howells, HN
5	8	5	7	X	GSmi	Ps 83	Willcocks, DV
5	9	2	2	S	C	Ven 1	Russell, W
5	9	7	12	D	A	Ps 22	Smart, H
5	9	9	7	D	A	Ps 27	Wolstenholme, W
7	5	4	5	D	F	Ps 65	Hopkins, EJ
7	9	7	4	D	AF	Ps 33	Turle, J
7	9	12	7	D	C	TD 7	Hewitt-Jones, T
8	7	4	0	S	D	Ps 123	Palmer, CC
8	7	5	1	D	Cmi	Ps 7	Cooke, R
9	5	2	2	S	BF	EAnth 2	Elvey, GJ
9	5	2	2	S	C	Jub 10	Sidwell, M
9	5	10	7	D	BF	Ps 66	Atkins, IA
9	7	5	2	D	DF	Mag 8	Edwards, P
9	7	5	4	D	C	TD 8	Bevan, M
9	7	5	5	D	Cma	Ps 8	Corfe, J (from Lawes, H)
9	12	5	9	D	A	Ps 19	Walmisley, TA
12	10	7	7	D	CSmi	Ps 37	Howells, HN